THE RENAISSANCE DISCOV

TO

ALETHEA VALENTINE MARY WEISS

THE RENAISSANCE
DISCOVERY OF
CLASSICAL ANTIQUITY

ROBERTO WEISS

Second Edition

BASIL BLACKWELL

Copyright © Basil Blackwell 1969, 1988

First published 1969
Reprinted 1973
Second edition 1988

Basil Blackwell Ltd
108 Cowley Road, Oxford, OX4 1JF, UK

Basil Blackwell Inc.
432 Park Avenue South, Suite 1503
New York, NY 10016, USA

British Library Cataloguing in Publication Data
Weiss, Roberto, 1906–1969
  The Renaissance discovery of classical
  antiquity.—2nd ed.
  1. Classical antiquities. Archaeological
  investigation, ca 1300–1527
  I. Title
  938′.0072

  ISBN 0-631-16077-9

Library of Congress Cataloging in Publication Data
Weiss, Roberto
  The Renaissance discovery of classical antiquity/Roberto Weiss.
  —2nd ed.
      p.   cm.
  Bibliography:p.
  Includes index.
  ISBN 0-631-16077-9 (pbk.)
  1. Italy—Antiquities. 2. Renaissance—Italy. 3. Humanists—
Italy. I. Title.
DG431.W4 1988
937′.0072045—dc 19   88–6586
                                                              CIP

Printed in Great Britain by Page Bros (Norwich) Ltd

CONTENTS

PREFACE TO THE SECOND EDITION

Roberto Weiss (1906-69) designed his bookplate, which reads *FABVLA NE FIAT/QVAE FVIT HISTORIA*, and this could have been the motto of his book which concludes that 'modern archaeology really began when the *Mirabilia* ceased to be taken seriously' (p. 204).

As Weiss explains in his Introduction (p. xi), the aim of the book is to 'give an account of the rise and early development of an interest in the tangible remains of classical antiquity and the study that developed from it'. As he says, no full study on the subject had so far appeared, although many of its different aspects had been investigated. What Weiss has given us is a unique synthesis based to a considerable extent on his own discoveries of unpublished material, as his Index of Manuscripts reveals. If one were to look for a context for Weiss's book, it might best be found in the circle of Flavio Biondo or of Bernardo Rucellai – Renaissance scholars who relied on multiple antique sources in their attempts to explain the visible remains of antiquity. It is through an examination of the late mediaeval and Renaissance sources that Weiss has demonstrated and evaluated their contributions to the development of archaeology.

Like the humanists and antiquarians whom he studied, Weiss received much information from his friends and colleagues who indicated 'forgotten sources' (see his Acknowledgements). Most of his material, however was gathered over the years while working on similar or quite different aspects of humanism (listed in the bibliography of his 153 writings published from 1934 to 1972 which Conor Fahy and John D. Moores compiled in his posthumous *Mediaeval and Humanist Greek: Collected Essays*, Padova, 1977 which they edited with Carlo Dionisotti). Whenever he came upon a reference to specific humanist concern with antique monuments, he noted it down. His material ranged from unpublished manuscripts to incunables and rare books containing studies from numismatics to architecture which engaged the attention of humanists, antiquarians, topographers, epigraphers and the like who examined local Roman remains, not only in Rome but throughout Italy and Greece.

When he came to write his book, this accumulation, sorted according to genre, determined the chapter headings and gave substance to the framework. 'Most of its chapters', he writes in his Introduction, 'might easily have been developed into a book.' The virtue of this book is its intended brevity, but its wealth of references to the sources gives it a far larger dimension.

Unlike those antiquarians who tend to ramble, Weiss keeps to his scheme so well that different aspects of the same document are cited under the relevant headings. This enhances the value of his framework where, under clearly defined investigations, the exact illustrative source and the standard study on it can be found. Such thoroughness and Weiss's evaluation of each writer within the development of scientific archaeology give us the measure of his mastery of the history of this tradition.

Weiss's English, of irreducible economy and classical purity, preserves a continental elegance and flow. In its clarity of arrangement, content and style, this book has already become one of the most admired and useful works on the Renaissance.

After nearly 20 years, much has been written along the lines set out by Weiss, but so far no other published book has so profoundly explored the history of archaeology from the Middle Ages to the Sack of Rome in 1527. Many individual points discussed by Weiss have been developed, and discoveries like the Augustan sundial in the Camp Marzio have been made which would have interested him intensely. They may modify or enrich the details, but do not alter Weiss's basic structure.

In the Bibliography, I note recent studies on and new editions of some of Weiss's Renaissance sources which the reader may find useful. They are arranged according to chapter and are repeated where relevant. I should like to thank the scholars who have added valuable titles to the Bibliography, among them Martin C. Davies, Jill Kraye, Paul Oskar Kristeller, and Nigel Wilson. I am particularly grateful for the help of my husband and devoted friend of Roberto Weiss, Nicolai Rubinstein.

Ruth Olitsky Rubinstein

ACKNOWLEDGEMENTS

It is with a deep sense of gratitude that I express here my warm thanks to all those who have helped me in so many ways, by indicating forgotten sources, discussing problems, collating passages in books and manuscripts, securing photographs, etc. It is therefore with pleasure that I recall here the help of Giovanni Aquilecchia, Giuseppe Billanovich, Umberto Bosco, Vittore Branca, Augusto Campana, Maria Corti, Carlo Dionisotti, Denys Hay, Paul Oskar Kristeller, Otto Kurz, Giovanni Mardersteig, Charles Mitchell, John Moores, Franco Panvini Rosati, Elisabeth Pellegrin, the late Augusto Pepponi, Allessandro Perosa, Deoclecio Redig de Campos, Dennis Rhodes, Sergio Rossi, Giovanni Rotondò, Nicolai Rubinstein, Otto Skutsch, J. B. Trapp, the late Berthold Louis Ullman, and Nereo Vianello.

The generous granting of two terms leave of absence by University College London enabled me to give several months exclusively to the task of bringing this book to completion; while the great resources of the libraries of the British School at Rome, University College London, and the Warburg Institute enabled me countless times to read in my own surroundings a great number of books and articles seldom found even in the great national libraries.

Roberto Weiss
University College London
April 1968

INTRODUCTION

One of the difficulties in a work such as this, is that most of its chapters might easily have been developed into a book. There is at any rate no doubt that each of the last nine chapters could have been expanded into a substantial monograph, particularly as the additional information required for such an expansion is not lacking. In fact both published and unpublished materials on the subjects covered here are so plentiful, that in many cases the real problem was not so much what to include, as what to leave out. Much indeed had to be excluded, and amongst it there must inevitably be some significant evidence, which was only omitted because it did not come to my notice.

The absence of some obvious topics from this book calls for some explanation. To the question as to why there are no chapters on the impact of classical antiquity upon Renaissance art or on the study of Roman institutions, one may reply as follows: to include a study on classical antiquity and the Renaissance artist, would have meant to deal with a subject already adequately studied by several outstanding scholars, Müntz and Warburg among them, and at the same time so vast that at least three long chapters would have been required.[1] A chapter on the rise of the study of Roman institutions would certainly have been very desirable, particularly as this subject had commanded the attention of several distinguished humanists since the days of Leonardo Bruni and Flavio Biondo. But if there had been such a chapter, how could there not be also chapters on the study of Roman Law and ancient history? Another matter which had to be decided, was whether to limit this study to Italy or whether to extend it to the main European countries. And the real reason for not extending the survey outside Italy was that, apart from Germany and to a much lesser extent France, the western European contribution to the study of classical antiquities had not been at all impressive during the period covered here.

Some of these excluded subjects are, all the same, touched upon in passing. This was of course inevitable. For how could

---

[1] For the same reasons I have refrained from giving an account of the many sketch books with drawings of Roman antiquities made during the fifteenth and the first quarter of the sixteenth century. A Census of antique works of art known to Renaissance artists is being prepared by the Warburg Institute.

one give a reliable account of numismatic studies during the Renaissance and leave out Budé, or give a survey of Renaissance epigraphy without mentioning Peutinger? Or make no reference whatever to those artists who also happened to be collectors in the chapter on the collections of antiquities, or leave out altogether the impact exerted by the coins of ancient Rome on painters, sculptors, illuminators, and medallists during the Renaissance? The resulting picture would certainly have suffered if they had been omitted.

The aim of this book is to give an account of the rise and early development of an interest in the tangible remains of classical antiquity and the study that developed from it.[1] Apart from an introductory chapter on the approach to these remains during the Middle Ages, the period considered here stretches from the early fourteenth century to 1527, when the sack of Rome by the troops of the Emperor Charles V brought to an end that Renaissance which had seen its best days between the pontificate of Nicholas V (1447–1455) and that of Leo X (1513–1521). Broadly speaking, what is given here is a history of classical archaeology in its early stages, showing how it really started in the time of Petrarch (1304–1374), and how it was developed by the enthusiasm and industry of countless humanists, who saw in the statues, the inscriptions, the coins, the ruined buildings, in short in the concrete legacy of classical antiquity an invaluable commentary to those poetic and prose texts which were revealing to them what ancient civilization really meant.

[1] No full study on this subject had so far appeared. Among recent contributions on the subject one may mention A. Momigliano, 'Ancient History and the Antiquarian', *Journal of the Warburg and Courtauld Institutes*, XIII (1950) 285–315, and reprinted in A. Momigliano, *Contributo alla storia degli studi classici*, (Roma, 1955) 67–106, R. Weiss, 'Lineamenti per una storia degli studi antiquari in Italia', *Rinascimento*, IX (1958) 141–201, R. Weiss, 'Il primo Rinascimento e gli studi archeologici', *Lettere Italiane*, XI (1959) 89–94, M. Pallottino, *Che cos'è l'archeologia?* (Firenze, 1963) 21–28, H. Kaiser, *Kleine Geschichte der Archäologie*, (Gütersloh, 1963), A. Mandowsky and C. Mitchell, *Pirro Ligorio's Roman Antiquities*, (London, 1963) and the review of this work by C. Dionisotti in *Rivista storica italiana*, LXXV (1963) 890–901.

CHAPTER ONE

THE MIDDLE AGES

An interest in classical antiquity never waned altogether during the centuries of the Middle Ages. In the West and particularly in Italy, the great Latin classics never ceased to be studied in the schools and cherished by individuals with a bent for letters. It is true that writers like Tacitus and Lucretius, Propertius and Catullus, just to give a few leading examples, fell quickly into oblivion after the Carolingian age, only to reappear again with the rise of humanism. But Virgil and Cicero, Ovid and Lucan, Persius and Juvenal, Horace and Terence, Seneca and Valerius Maximus, Livy and Statius, and the list is by no means complete, were always read. Virgil became also a prophet of Christianity by the fourth century and a sorcerer in the twelfth century. Some of Ovid's poems were given a Christian interpretation, while Seneca, besides being hailed as the traditional exponent of ancient morality, was also cherished as the correspondent of St. Paul, which he certainly was not. Even after the fall of the Roman Empire, the idea of Rome as 'caput mundi' never faded out in the West. Neither Constantinople nor Aachen ever succeeded in achieving the universal prestige of Rome, just as neither Ravenna nor Antioch, nor Milan, nor Aquileia, nor Treves, had ever come near it during the last centuries of the Empire. The very Barbarians who invaded Italy succumbed to Latin civilization, just as some centuries before the Romans had surrendered to that of conquered Greece. Towns were proud of their Roman origins. At Pavia an inscription, testifying to the existence of the town in Roman times, was preserved as a relic in a church,[1] while the equestrian statue of a Roman Emperor, known as the 'Regisol' and removed from Ravenna, adorned one of its squares and was the visible symbol of the town and its traditions until its destruction at the hands of the French in 1796.[2]

That some interest in the ancient monuments remained alive

[1] R. Sòriga, 'La tradizione Romana in Pavia e la statua del Regisole', *Atti e memorie del primo Congresso Storico Lombardo*, (Milano, 1937) 6 of the offprint.

[2] On this statue see especially G. Bovini, 'Le vicende del "Regisole" statua equestre ravennate', *Felix Ravenna*, ser. 3, fasc. 36 (1963) 138–54.

is not surprising, just as it is not surprising that even smaller
antiquities, such as coins, ivories, or engraved gems, were
continually sought after during the Middle Ages. 'What was
lost, notwithstanding the reminder contained in St. Augustine's
Civitas Dei, was the Varronian idea of 'antiquitates'—the idea of
a civilization recovered by systematic collection of all the relics
of the past.'[1] What led to the collection of antique objects
during the Middle Ages was not their antiquity but their appeal to
the eye or their rare or unusual materials, or simply because
they were different; or even in some cases because they were
thought to be endowed with magical powers. The antiques
preserved in the treasuries of cathedrals were kept there because
their materials or their craftsmanship were considered precious,
not because they were ancient. Even those few who
had a genuine interest in Antiquity were drawn to it by an
attraction tempered by utilitarian considerations. The Latin
classics were considered above all as repositories of unusual
information or moral teachings or as collections of fine phrases,
suitable for quotation or insertion into one's own writings.
They were certainly not seen as the expressions of a great
civilization. Roman remains were employed as building
materials, or as architectural models, as can be seen for instance
in the interior of Autun Cathedral and on the façade of that
of Saint Gilles, or they could influence sculpture, as happened
in France during the early thirteenth century, when art
acquired there a new vitality through the study of ancient
marbles. The inscriptions left wherever Rome had ruled were
sometimes considered useful models, and as such were transcribed and imitated. Statues and sarcophagi were used again,
while smaller antiques were often employed for various purposes.
Roman cinerary urns were frequently turned into small stoups
for holy water, as may be seen in more than one church in Rome,
or could even be provided with a fresh inscription, as was the
case with the urn now in the Lateran Museum, which bears an
inscription in honour of St. Agnes and St. Alexander, placed there
during the thirteenth century by Marco, Abbot of Santa Prassede.[2]
The ivory diptychs of the consuls became covers of gospel books

---

[1] Momigliano, *Contributo alla storia degli studi classici*, 73. Recent information on medieval
antiquarian studies is given *ibid*. 73, n. 13, to which add C. L. Wrenn, *Anglo-Saxon Poetry
and the Amateur Archaeologist*, (London, 1962).
[2] Pl. I, O. Marucchi, *I monumenti del Museo Cristiano Lateranense*, (Milano, 1910) 43, pl.
XLIV.

or were even employed to record the dead of a particular church, as happened for instance to the Boethius diptych of 487, on which were entered the names of the deceased of the church of Brescia. Sometimes the figures of the consuls carved on them were turned into saints or biblical characters, as happened in a diptych now at Monza, where they became King David and St. Gregory, and in one at Prague, where the consul was transformed into none other than St. Peter himself. Engraved gems went to adorn crowns and diadems, crosses, reliquaries, and book covers.[1] Thus the cross given to the Minster at Aachen by the Emperor Otho III has an ancient cameo of the young Augustus; and also at Aachen the eleventh century ambo still displays some antique ivory tablets with decidedly pagan deities.

One thing that must be borne in mind is that the Middle Ages did not envisage classical antiquity as a different civilization or a lost Paradise. Despite the difference in religion, until Petrarch medieval men failed to notice a fracture between the classical age and their own times. To them Frederick Barbarossa was as much a Roman Emperor as Augustus or Trajan and only differed from Constantine by his having been born several centuries after him. The medieval empire and that founded by Augustus were believed to be one and the same, and classical myth was often used for decoration in a religious setting. In fact the frequent warnings that pagan art was dangerous found little response even in ecclesiastical circles. During the early Middle Ages a vigorous classical revival took place under the Carolingians. This was in many ways a real renaissance, and the widest in scope ever witnessed before that which illuminated the fifteenth and sixteenth centuries. It was initiated at the court of Charlemagne, and to it we owe the preservation of most of those Latin classics, which humanism in turn handed on to us. This Carolingian Renaissance, which was able to achieve such classical works as Einhard's Suetonian *Vita Karoli*, looked with unfeigned enthusiasm at the relics of Antiquity. Late imperial Roman art found a reflection in that of the Aachen court. Many monuments of the Carolingian capital were partly built with spoils from Rome and Ravenna; and this was the very age when enthusiasm for the antique led even to the accurate copying of illustrated manuscripts of the late Empire. Some manuscripts of Virgil and

---

[1] See for instance L. Vitali, *Il tesoro del Duomo di Monza*, (Milano 1964) 30–31, pl. 45–48.

Terence,[1] the extant copies of the Calendar of 354 and the *Notitia Dignitatum*, both of which reproduce lost Carolingian books which were in turn faithful copies of late antique exemplars[2], bear witness to this. Furthermore, the style and spirit of ancient books could even be re-captured: the celebrated psalter executed at Rheims about 930 and now at Utrecht, shows what is in fact a successful attempt to imitate, both in the handwriting and in the illustrations, the appearance of manuscripts of late Antiquity.

Carolingian classicism survived in a degenerate form in Othonian Germany. Yet in the early eleventh century this Othonian classicism, which was able to salvage more than one Latin classic for us, could achieve such heights as the column planned by Bernard of Hildesheim on the analogy of that of Trajan, thus supplying a smaller but effective version of one of the greatest monuments of Antiquity. This same Bernard, who had been one of the tutors of Otho III, carried his conformity to Antiquity even as far as having his name stamped on tiles in the Roman manner.[3] But the echoes of this Othonian classicism went well beyond the sphere of art. The imperial dreams of Otho III and his residence in Rome led to a re-awakening of a consciousness of the city's historic mission, thus paving the way for the various attempts to restoring the ancient republic, from that of Crescentius in 998 down to that of Stefano Porcari in 1453.

What still remained of ancient Rome during the Middle Ages was enough to make a deep impression upon pilgrims and other travellers. Nor were the ruins of Rome the only ones to attract notice. In other parts of Italy also the pilgrims who came from across the Alps stopped astonished before the huge arches, the amphitheatres, the walls, and all the more striking relics of Roman power. During the first decade of the twelfth century Archbishop Hildebert of Tours had voiced in two Latin elegies his emotion, mingled with a sense of 'vanitas', on remembering the ruins and the statues which he had been able to admire in Rome.[4] Over a generation later Otto of Freising, the uncle of Frederick Barbarossa, registered in his *Gesta Friderici I Impera-*

---

[1] P. Courcelle, 'La tradition antique dans les miniatures inédites d'un Virgile de Naples', *Mélanges d'archéologie et d'histoire*, LVI (1939) 249–79.

[2] A. W. Byvanck, 'Die antike Buchmalerei III, Der Kalender vom Jahre 354 und die *Notitia dignitatum*', *Mnemosyne*, N.S. VIII (1940) 177–98, H. Stern, *Le Calendrier de 354* (Paris, 1953) 14–41.

[3] W. Oakeshott, *Classical Inspiration in Medieval Art*, (London, 1959) 67.

[4] *The Oxford Book of Mediaeval Latin Verse*, ed. F. J. E. Raby, (Oxford, 1959) 220–22.

toris an accurate description of a triumphal arch, noted by him in north Italy in 1158,[1] during the expedition in which he participated with his formidable nephew. A description of ancient remains was also included by the chancellor of the Emperor Henry VI, Conrad of Querfurt, in a letter to the Provost of Hildesheim, where he described his Italian journey of 1194.[2] But to return to Rome, the fact that it was the capital of western Christianity, soon created a need for itineraries, in order to supply pilgrims with a reliable guide to the main churches and the most famous holy places. Several of these itineraries have come down to us, the best known being the ninth century manuscript at Einsiedeln, which is really an abridged version of an older and more extensive text, now lost.[3] Now in these itineraries the triumphal arches, the amphitheatres, the more prominent ancient buildings, in fact, are included. They are, however, given mainly as points of reference. Just as to-day we would indicate a church, a public house, or a very unusual building, when describing the way to a particular place, so in the itineraries many old monuments were mentioned, not because they were anceint, but merely because they were conspicuous. Thus the Einsiedeln itinerary mentions thermae and circuses, theatres, porticoes, and palaces, along with churches, monasteries, and particularly holy spots. The archetype of this itinerary was certainly accompanied by a plan of the city.[4] These primitive plans were circular in shape and depicted several ancient buildings, such as the Coliseum, the Pantheon, Hadrian's Mausoleum, and many others. They were in fact stylized representations of what was still left of ancient Rome, and what is most prominent in them is not the Christian element but the ancient pagan one. This is also true of the views of Rome on the imperial golden bulls from Frederick Barbarossa down to Frederick III. Here Rome appears as the 'caput mundi' and the proud motto 'Roma caput mundi regit orbis frena rotundi' surrounds the view of the eternal city.[5]

Views of Rome did not depart from this type until the

[1] *Ottonis et Rabewini Gesta Friderici I. Imperatoris*, ed. G. Waitz, 3rd ed., (Hannoverae et Lipsiae, 1912) 216–17.

[2] *Arnoldi Chronica Slavorum*, ed. G. H. Pertz, Hannoverae, 1868) 174–83.

[3] C. Huelsen, *La pianta di Roma dell'Anonimo Einsidlense*, (Roma, 1907) 7–9.

[4] *Ibid.* 7.

[5] W. Erben, *Rombilder auf kaiserlichen und päpstlichen Siegeln des Mittelalters*, (Graz-Wien-Leipzig, 1931) passim and pl. II–III, P. Sella, *Le bolle d'oro dell'Archivio Vaticano*, (Città del Vaticano, 1934) 41 and pl. I.1.

Renaissance. Even in the early fifteenth century the fresco by
Taddeo di Bartolo in the Palazzo Pubblico at Siena, the representation by Leonardo da Besozzo and the illumination in the
Très Riches Heures of the Duke of Berry, present the conventional
medieval panorama.[1] Views of this kind were by no means
restricted to pictures of Rome. The town of Classe figures
already in one of the mosaics of Sant' Apollinare Nuovo at
Ravenna. To the tenth century belongs the view of Verona, in
which ancient buildings, such as the 'Arena' and the palace of
Theodoric, stand out prominently.[2] From itineraries and views
to actual descriptions of towns is but a short step, and in fact
such descriptions are not lacking either. It is true that descriptions such as that of Verona, written during the Carolingian age,[3]
deal mainly with the ecclesiastical aspect of the city, that is to
say churches, monasteries, and the more important relics. The
situation in Rome was, however, different. It is true that here
also handbooks on the sacred places of the city were by no
means scarce; it is sufficient to recall in this connexion the so-
called catalogues of the Lent stations. Some detailed descriptions
of major basilicas have also reached us, such as the *Descriptio
Lateranensis Ecclesiae*,[4] written during the eleventh or twelfth
century, or the description of St. Peter's,[5] drawn up by the
canon Pietro Mallio and dedicated by him to Pope Alexander III
(1159–81). But side by side with these, there were the *Regionarii*[6]
of secular Rome, the most ancient of which belong to the times
of Constantine. And around the remains of the ancient city
there arose a crop of legends, several of which were incorporated
into his chronicle by William of Malmesbury,[7] while others
found their way into the *Mirabilia Romae Urbis*,[8] that tract where
the historical and the legendary enliven what would otherwise
have been a dreary topographical catalogue.

The *Mirabilia* was more than a mere guide to ancient Rome.
Compiled about the middle of the twelfth century, it obviously

[1] A. P. Frutaz, *Le piante di Roma*, (Roma, 1962) I, 123–26, 131–32, II, pl. 148–49, 154.
[2] Reproduced for instance in G. Monticelli, *Raterio vescovo di Verona*, (Milano, 1938) plate facing p. 48.
[3] Published in L. Simeoni, *La descriptio rithmica Veronae*, (Bologna, 1920).
[4] *Codice topografico della città di Roma*, ed. R. Valentini e G. Zucchetti, III, (Roma, 1946), 326–73.
[5] *Ibid*. III, 382–442.
[6] *Ibid*. I, 89–258.
[7] W. Malmesburiensis, *De gestis regum Anglorum libri quinque*, ed. W. Stubbs. I (London, 1887) 202–03, 256–59.
[8] *Codice topografico della città di Roma*, III, 17–65.

breathes the consciousness of the city's imperial destiny, that
had been re-awakened in the days of Otho III; that same consciousness which, in its last expression in Dante's *Monarchia*,
marked also the end of the Middle Ages. As a handbook on what
remained of the old city the *Mirabilia* dominated all subsequent
accounts of Roman topography until the Renaissance, and was
still the most popular guide to Rome during the sixteenth
century, when it was printed several times and translated into
various languages. In it Rome is very much the 'caput mundi'.
Of course the nomenclature of the monuments is often wildly
inaccurate or hopelessly corrupt. But where the author turns to
the foundation of the Aracoeli church or the 'Dioscuri' of the
Quirinal or the so-called 'caballus Constantini', that is to say the
equestrian statue of Marcus Aurelius then at the Lateran, history
surrenders to legend, almost to poetry, notwithstanding the
scholarly pretensions of the author, who even makes an occasional
use of inscriptions.

The same climate of the *Mirabilia* pervades the *De mirabilibus
urbis Romae* compiled by a Magister Gregorius, probably an
Englishman, 'sociorum meorum rogatu' during the late twelfth
or early thirteenth century.[1] If anything, the outlook here is
even more secular than in the *Mirabilia*. Admittedly Hildebert's
lines on Rome[2] made Magister Gregorius feel that the end of the
world was not very far off. Yet this sense of impending doom
did not stop him from admiring a statue of Venus in her usual
attire, or, more accurately, lack of attire. The ninth or tenth
century author of the charming lyric 'O admirabile Veneris
idolum'[3] had here a spiritual follower. What interests Magister
Gregorius is ancient, not Christian, Rome. Unlike the author of
the *Mirabilia*, he obviously did not lack some critical power.
Thus having to choose between the versions of the pilgrims and
of the Romans he chose the latter version. He definitely had an
eye for the antique bronze statues at the Lateran and was in fact
the first to mention the youth with a thorn now in the Capitol, of
which he said: 'Est etiam aliud eneum simulacrum valde ridico-
losum quod Priapum dicunt. Qui demisso capite velud spinam
calcatam educturus de pede, asperam lesionem pacientis speciem

---

[1] G. M. Rushforth, 'Magister Gregorius De Mirabilibus Urbis Romae: A New Description of Rome in the Twelfth Century', *The Journal of Roman Studies*, IX (1919) 14–58, *Codice
topografico della città di Roma*, III, 143–67.
[2] *Supra*, 4.
[3] *The Oxford Book of Mediaeval Latin Verse*, 142.

representat. Cui si demisso capite velut quid agat exploraturus suspexeris, mire magnitudinis virilia videbis'.[1] Alone with Petrarch,[2] he mentions an arch of Pompey erected for his victory against Mithridates. But like most of his contemporaries he was ill at ease with ancient inscriptions, to the point of being unable to make anything out of an antique inscription on a bronze tablet,[3] then in the Lateran and now in the Capitol. To the same tradition of the *Mirabilia* and Magister Gregorius's tract belongs the *Graphia Aurea Urbis Romae*.[4] There is no doubt that its author was also a firm believer in the divine mission of Rome, which is stressed by him in an introduction, where he seeks to prove the sanctity of the city's origins. But its topographical section could really be described as hardly more than a new edition of the *Mirabilia* with additions and recasting to improve its usefulness as a guide book.

The pride and belief in the greatness of Rome, the very prophecy already voiced by the Pseudo-Bede, that 'Quamdiu stat Colisaeus, stat et Roma, quando cadet Colisaeus, cadet et Roma; quando cadet Roma, cadet et mundus',[5] were not powerful enough to stop the continuous and implacable destruction of what remained of ancient Rome. Ever since the last centuries of the Empire Rome had been turned into the largest quarry of marble that the world had ever seen, as well as a huge warehouse of ancient sculpture, from which anyone was free to draw at pleasure. It was marble, marble everywhere. The translation of the bodies of the saints and martyrs into churches had led to a search for suitable marbles with which to adorn their new tombs, while sarcophagi were sought after and employed to receive the remains of the faithful. After the sack of 1084 by Robert Guiscard's Normans, definite excavations were carried out in order to secure materials for the rebuilding of the city's churches, and this quarrying of ancient stones went on and on. In 1139 Pope Innocent II used among other things some Ionic capitals from the Baths of Caracalla when rebuilding the church of Santa Maria in Trastevere.[6] Nor was the demand for such materials confined to Rome. Already

[1] Rushforth, *op. cit.* 49.
[2] Petrarca, *Rerum Familiarium Libri*, VI. 2.
[3] Rushforth, *op. cit.* 58.
[4] *Codice topografico della città di Roma*, III, 77–110.
[5] J. P. Migne, *Patrologia Latina*, XCIV, (Paris, 1862) 543, F. Schneider, *Rom und Romgedanke im Mittelalter*, (München, 1926) 66–67, 251.
[6] R. Lanciani, *Storia degli scavi di Roma*, I, (Roma, 1902) 7.

in the sixth century Theodoric had some pillars from the Domus Pinciana sent to Ravenna, and marbles of Roman origin were also used not only in the building of Italian cathedrals, of which those at Pisa, Lucca, and Amalfi, are leading examples, but even as far as Constantinople, Aachen, and Westminster. The export of marbles from Rome was a regular trade for about ten centuries. Pagan sarcophagi were, as we saw, often employed as Christian tombs, and this still went on during the Renaissance. In one of them was placed the corpse of Charlemagne. A famous sarcophagus with the story of Phaedra and Hippolytus became during the eleventh century the tomb of Beatrice, Countess of Tuscany. In the thirteenth century one formed part of the tomb of Cardinal Guglielmo Fieschi in San Lorenzo at Rome; another harboured the remains of the Senator Luca Savelli and can still be seen in the Aracoeli church, and these are but a few instances.

Also antique statues were often traded. The Roman stone cutters now known as 'Cosmati', besides digging for models and materials valuable to their craft, also sold ancient statuary, and more than one piece of antique sculpture has reached us with the name of one of these craftsmen engraved upon it.[1] Nor did these statues, whether altered into saints or untouched, lack customers. A famous instance in this country is that of Henry of Blois, Bishop of Winchester, who, while in Rome about the middle of the twelfth century, acquired an impressive amount of ancient marbles and statuary, defending such purchases by saying that he was removing these old statues in order to prevent the Romans from worshipping them again and thus renewing the cult of such idols as they already served spiritually because of their innate and accursed avarice.[2] Not for nothing had Henry spent some time at the Curia!

Undeniably the majority of people at all times looked with an indifferent eye on the ruins of Rome. It is, however, equally undeniable that in every century there were people who surrendered to their fascination. One of them was that Nicolaus Crescentii who erected for himself, not far from Santa Maria in Cosmedin and the Velabro quarter, a small palace with fragments of ancient buildings and statuary incorporated into the walls.

[1] P. Fedele, 'Sul commercio delle antichità in Roma nel XII secolo', *Archivio della Società Romana di Storia Patria*, XXXII (1909) 465–70.

[2] J. Saresberiensis, *Historiae Pontificalis quae supersunt*, ed. R. L. Poole, (Oxford, 1927) 81–2.

His aim in doing so was stated in the metrical inscription above the door, where he declared that he had been moved to build by a desire 'Romae veterem renovare decorem', thus anticipating by over three centuries what was done by Lorenzo Manili in 1468,[1] when humanism was in full flower. Some concern for the ancient monuments is also expressed in various efforts to afford them some protection. This was naturally one of the outcomes of the attitude to which we owe the *Mirabilia* and the revolution of Arnold of Brescia. Apart from those ancient buildings which had been turned into baronial strongholds, many outstanding monuments were not publicly owned, but this did not prevent the enacting of some protective legislation. In the tenth century the Antonine Column belonged to the monastery of San Silvestro in Capite, while two centuries later the Abbess of San Ciriaco was the owner of Trajan's Column.[2] The idea of protection was actually voiced by Arnold of Brescia, when he spoke about the necessity of restoring the Capitol.[3] But it was only eight years after his tragic death, in 1162, that the Roman Senate on confirming possession of Trajan's Column to the Abbess of San Ciriaco, threatened at the same time with capital punishment and confiscation of goods anyone who 'eam minuere temptaverit'.[4] Steps also appear to have been taken to forbid the export of ancient marbles without the sanction of the Senate. At any rate this is suggested by the letter written by Charles I of Anjou, King of Sicily, in 1276 to the treasurer of the Capitol, about his wish to purchase the 'conca porfidi' which had contained the body of Pope Innocent IV.[5] It is therefore not surprising that in such an atmosphere the discovery in Rome of a gigantic corpse in 1045 led at once to its being identified with the remains of Pallas the son of Evander.[6] Not for nothing did the *Aeneid* still enjoy some readers in eleventh-century Rome!

The view that pagan art was dangerous had hardly any more devotees during the twelfth and thirteenth centuries than it had had before. The funeral genii with torches reversed came straight from an antique model and they still figure on the twelfth-century front of Modena Cathedral and certainly express the common disregard of such warnings. It has already been shown

---

[1] R. Weiss, *Un umanista veneziano—Papa Paolo II*, (Venezia-Roma, 1958) 44.

[2] A. De Boüard, 'Gli antichi marmi di Roma nel medio evo', *Archivio della Società Romana di Storia Patria*, XXXIV (1911) 240–41.

[3] *Ottonis et Rahevini Gesta Friderici I. Imperatoris*, 134.

[4] De Boüard, *op. cit.* 241, n. 1.

[5] *Ibid.* 243.

[6] Malmesburiensis, *op. cit.* I, 258–59.

that small antiques, such as ivories or engraved gems, had been employed as ornaments. To this may be added that the latter were also often used as charms or as seals, both in Italy and beyond the Alps.[1] Ancient inscriptions also commanded some attention. The earliest manuscript collections of them were naturally restricted to Christian epitaphs and were connected with pilgrimages to Rome. They were originally put together as illustrations or appendices to itineraries or to descriptions of sacred buildings. Furthermore, those in verse furnished useful anthologies of sepulchral poetry. What is obvious is that their collection was certainly prompted neither by archaeological nor historical considerations. Such gatherings of inscriptions were quite common during the Carolingian age, nor were these collections restricted to epigraphic texts from Rome. Inscriptions from Milan, Pavia, Ivrea, Tours and other towns were also sedulously copied, and so were those of important basilicas, such as St. Peter's, Rome. This epigraphic activity started, however, to decline swiftly after the ninth century, so much so that antique inscriptions became eventually quite unintelligible to men with eyes accustomed to Gothic script. All the same there were some medieval scholars who had not overlooked them altogether. Already in the seventh century Nennius had drawn information for his *Historia Britonum* from ancient inscriptions as well as from coins.[2] During the twelfth they were not entirely disregarded by the author of the *Mirabilia*, and a considerable display of them was made by Pietro Mallio in his description of St. Peter's, Rome. The inscription on the Arch of Constantine attracted the attention of John of Salisbury during his Roman sojourn about the middle of the twelfth century,[3] and during this same century the scribe of a copy of Plato's *Timaeus* in the Latin version of Chalcidius transcribed between the translator's preface and the beginning of the text, an inscription of Hadrian of A.D. 119,[4] which perhaps figured already in his

---

[1] G. Demay, *Des pierres gravées dans les sceaux du Moyen Age*, (Paris, 1877), J. Adhémar, *Influences antiques de l'art du Moyen Age Français*, (London, 1939) 106–09, H. Wentzel, 'Portraits "à l'antique" on French Medieval Gems and Seals', *Journal of the Warburg and Courtauld Institutes*, XVI (1953) 342–50, H. Wentzel, 'Italienische Siegelstempel und Siegel all'antico im 13 und 14 Jahrhundert', *Mitteilungen des Kunsthistorischen Instituts in Florenz*, XVII (1955) 73–86.

[2] R. S. Loomis, *Wales and the Arthurian Legend*, (Cardiff, 1956) 3–4.

[3] J. Saresberiensis, *Policraticus*, ed. C. C. J. Webb, I, (Oxonii, 1913) 7.

[4] British Museum, Ms. Royal, 12.B.xxii, f. 2r. One may add the inscription from Lucus Feroniae copied in a twelfth century manuscript from the Abbey of Farfa, cf. Vatican Library, Ms. Vat. lat. 6808, f. 113r, R. Bartoccini, 'L'anfiteatro di Lucus Feroniae e il suo fondatore', *Atti della Pontificia Accademia Romana di Archeologia, Rendiconti*, XXIII (1959–60) 173–74.

archetype. Such cases are certainly not very numerous. In fact the interpretation of inscriptions could lead to ludicrous howlers. For instance in mid-thirteenth century the bronze tablet with Vespasian's *Lex de imperio* was actually identified by the glossator Odofredus (d. 1265) as part of the laws of the Twelve Tables themselves.[1]

As was only to be expected, a man like Frederick II could hardly remain indifferent to the call of Antiquity. His dream of universal power made him regard himself as an emperor of classical times and a direct successor of Augustus. It was therefore natural that what had been handed down from Roman times should fascinate him. Little wonder, then, that in 1240 he licensed Osberto Commenali to excavate near Augusta 'in loca in quibus sperat firmiter inventiones maximas invenire',[2] or that he acquired all the antique objects upon which he could lay hands. Thus we find him removing from Grottaferrata and forwarding to Lucera a bronze group, which had attracted his fancy, representing a man and a cow,[3] and disbursing the very considerable sum of 1230 gold 'unciae' for a large onyx cup and other antiques.[4] These antiquarian tastes were nevertheless not so strong as to interfere with the security of the state. In fact we find Frederick II ordering the pulling down of some ancient remains, in order to erect some urgently needed fortifications.[5]

Frederick II tried to imitate the Roman Caesars in more than one way. Actually he came closer to the rulers of the later Empire than to those of the first two centuries of our era; but that is another question. These attempts to pose as a Roman Emperor led him to encourage the revival of ancient Roman art. Art was for him one of the means to exalting his lay state, and for Frederick the state was what mattered above all. The golden 'augustales', where Frederick is portrayed with the attire and laurels of the Roman Caesars,[6] the triumphal arch of Capua, now represented only by some fragments in the local museum,[7] certainly reflect more than anything else these efforts to revive the art of

---

[1] *C.I.L.* VI. I, 930, K. Burdach, *Vom Mittelalter zur Reformation*, II. 5. (Berlin, 1929) 359.
[2] J. L. A. Huillard-Bréholles, *Historia Diplomatica Friderici Secundi*, V.2, (Parisiis, 1859) 825.
[3] *Ibid.* I, DXLV.   [4] *Ibid.* V. 1, 477.
[5] E. Müntz, *Precursori e propugnatori del Rinascimento*, (Firenze, 1920) 4.
[6] See S. Ricci, 'Gli "Augustali" di Federico II', *Studi Medievali*, ser. 2, I (1928) 59–73.
[7] On this arch see, for instance, C. A. Willemsen, *Kaiser Friedrich II. Triumptor zu Capua*, Wiesbaden, 1953), E. Battisti, *Rinascimento e Barocco*, (Torino, 1960) 16–29.

ancient Rome 'ad majorem imperii gloriam'. The letter and some of the spirit of classicism are certainly there.

The age of Frederick II paved the way towards a new appreciation of classicism, to a new period when the most intelligent interpreters as well as the acutest students of Antiquity are to be sought among the artists rather than among the men of letters. Before the rise of humanism the real antiquarians were the artists, and classicism was an approach to form which found little counterpart in contemporary rhetoric. The letter of Antiquity had been sedulously followed before Frederick II. But the idiom had generally remained Romanesque or Gothic, and such it remained, but for a few exceptions, after the death of the 'stupor mundi'. For instance one could certainly consider as such, that is as translations of classical objects into a Gothic idiom, the drawings of antique statuary in the well known sketch book of Villard de Honnecourt[1] or the drawing of an ancient cameo by Matthew Paris.[2] In a sense they stand to Antiquity in the same way as Brunetto Latini's versions of some of Cicero's orations in his everyday speech, where ancient offices and institutions are turned into what was considered to be their thirteenth century equivalent.[3] But then a sense of historical anachronism is a modern trait. Even during the high Renaissance ancient heroes were often represented in sixteenth century attire; later in the seventeenth century the baroque fashion of representing monarchs, generals or statesmen in Roman costume, a fashion which was to be seen even as late as the nineteenth century, shows the same conception in reverse.

Some decades after Villard de Honnecourt and Matthew Paris, the chapter on ancient Arretine ware in Ristoro d'Arezzo's vast compilation,[4] probably completed in 1282, presented what is perhaps the first account of an aspect of ancient art to be written since classical times. In it Ristoro not only furnished a minute description of the vases which were then being unearthed so plentifully in his own native town, but he also told his readers of the universal admiration with which these objects were

---

[1] *Bibliothèque Nationale—Département des Manuscrits, Album de Villard de Honnecourt architecte du XIIIe siècle*, (Paris, s.a.) passim.

[2] T. Wright, 'On antiquarian excavations and researches in the Middle Ages', *Archaeologia*, XXX (1844) 444–45.

[3] F. Maggini, *I primi volgarizzamenti dei classici latini*, (Firenze, 1952) 22.

[4] *La Prosa del Duecento a cura di Cesare Segre e Mario Marti*, (Milano-Napoli, 1959) 1038–40. Ancient Arretine pottery was later mentioned by Giovanni Villani, cf. A. Fabroni, *Storia degli antichi vasi fittili aretini*, (Arezzo, 1841) 16.

regarded and, furthermore, and this is not without interest, he
considered them as the products of another age, quite different
from his own. It is true that what really prompted him to
dedicate a chapter of his encyclopaedia to this ware was a
desire to proclaim the excellence of his native town by exalting
the perfection of these vases and the consummate artistry of the
ancient Arretine craftsmen. All the same, his account is also
indicative of a sensitivity to classical art, and of an approach to
it which is not so distant from the ideals of the Renaissance. It
was at about the same time, during the second half of the
thirteenth century, that a successful rendering of the antique was
achieved by Nicola Pisano and his immediate followers. With
Nicola the imitation of classical models ceases to be merely
skin deep. What we now have is a thorough assimilation of
ancient models, particularly of those antique vases and sarcophagi
then lying about Pisa and now mostly harboured in the Campo-
santo, which were still being enthusiastically studied by artists in
the days of Cellini.[1] Nicola was particularly struck by the
sarcophagus with the story of Phaedra and Hippolytus, which
was used to harbour the mortal remains of Beatrice, Countess of
Tuscany. Thus the Phaedra of this sarcophagus became the
Virgin of the adoration of the three Kings in Nicola's pulpit in
the Baptistery of Pisa.[2] Nicola's figures show a deep and genuine
feeling for the antique idiom, to the point that even his panels on
the tomb of St. Dominic at Bologna, showing some of the
Saint's miracles, breathe this antique spirit. His is a pure classicism, which is not put out of tune by anachronism, and it is accompanied by a new historical perspective, unmatched after him and
his pupil Fra Guglielmo until the Renaissance. Thus in Nicola's
works the soldiers are attired like Roman legionaries and not
like thirteenth century warriors; Christ and his followers are
garbed like early Christians; and he also conforms with the
conventions of early Christian art by giving no haloes to his
holy characters. His recapture of the 'gravitas' of classical art
could hardly have been carried out more successfully, and to

---

[1] B. Cellini, *Vita*, ed. O. Bacci, (Firenze, 1901) 23.

[2] The strong influence of ancient sculpture is also apparent in the enthroned Madonna
and Child by Arnolfo di Cambio which surmounts the tomb of Cardinal Guillaume de
Braye in the church of San Domenico at Orvieto. It is interesting to note that the Madonna's
tiara, ear-rings, and necklace reproduce antique jewellery, cf. Pl. II, A. Lazzarini, 'Coscienza
Etrusca in Orvieto medievale', in *Sopravvivenze e memorie etrusche nella Tuscia medievale*, (Orvieto,
1964) 59. The relief with the 'resurrection of the flesh' on the front of Orvieto Cathedral
and executed c. 1330, cf. Pl. IV, shows the resurrected emerging from Roman sarcophagi.

find a parallel we must wait for Donatello. This powerful classicism pervades also the work of Nicola's devoted follower Fra Guglielmo, who achieved it at its best in the pulpit of San Giovanni in Fuorcivitas at Pistoia. On the other hand, with Giovanni Pisano this classicism gave way to Gothic values; his pulpit in Pisa Cathedral is in a Gothic idiom despite the inclusion in it of a nude figure, taken straight from an antique statue of the Medici Venus type.[1]

Giovanni Pisano was the contemporary of Giotto, and Giotto's rejection of Gothic led, not to a return to Byzantine models, but to a new classicism which acquired some of the spirit while avoiding the narrow letter of antique art. With Giotto the first morning lights of the Renaissance begin to appear on the medieval sky.

[1] Pl. III. Meanwhile during the late thirteenth and early fourteenth century art in Rome sought inspiration mainly from late antique and early Christian prototypes, cf. C. Mitchell, 'The Lateran fresco of Boniface VIII', *Journal of the Warburg and Courtauld Institutes*, XIV (1951) 6, n. 2. Pope Boniface VIII even went as far as having himself represented in the Lateran fresco as an emperor of the later empire, cf. *ibid.* 6.

CHAPTER TWO

THE FORERUNNERS OF PETRARCH

Dante's deep devotion to Virgil and what he stood for did not carry with it any feeling for ancient remains, such as John of Salisbury shows before or Petrarch after him. His own interests never strayed from philosophy, politics, and the field of letters; antiquities appear very seldom in the *Divine Comedy*. The stone tombs in the Roman cemeteries at Arles and Pola and the gigantic pine cone of St. Peter's, Rome, were, it is true, turned into similes in the *Inferno*.[1] But they are the only similes of this kind in the whole poem. Indeed when he mentions the antique statue of Mars, still visible in his day at one end of the Ponte Vecchio in Florence,[2] he does not conceal his contempt for what appeared to him to be a relic of a superstition, still surviving in the teeth of Christianity. Nor were his attempts at archaeological reconstruction particularly happy. Thus, when he attempted to represent in the *Purgatorio* the so-called Justice of Trajan,[3] what he succeeded in achieving was a medieval scene with a medieval Emperor surrounded by his barons, and with the eagles of the legions turned into the banners of the Holy Roman Empire. The visible relics of the ancient greatness of Rome left Dante indifferent, just as the new humanist rhetoric by-passed him entirely.[4] Similarly unaffected by the new rhetoric was Dante's contemporary, the Florentine chronicler Giovanni Villani. Yet he is worth mentioning, not because he had to deal in the first book of his *Cronica* with the origins of Florence, which meant repeating various legends on the subject then current in the city, but because he occasionally referred to ancient remains still visible in his day. Although he was not really an antiquarian in the modern sense of the word, he thought it advisable to state that some of the original paving of Florence came to light when digging was done in certain quarters of the town,[5] and

---

[1] *Inferno*, IX. 112–17, XXXI. 58–59.

[2] *Ibid.* XIII. 146–47, *Paradiso*, XVI. 145–47.

[3] *Purgatorio*, X. 73–93. On Dante and Roman antiquity see V. Bracco, 'Il ricordo di Roma e del mondo romano nella *Divina Commedia*', *Studi Romani*, XIII (1965) 281–95.

[4] R. Weiss, 'Dante e l'umanesimo del suo tempo', *Lettere Italiane*, XIX (1967) 279–90.

[5] G. Villani, *Cronica*, I. 38.

modern archaeology has confirmed the accuracy of his statement.[1] On the other hand, when he indicated that the Battistero had been originally a temple of Mars,[2] he merely repeated a tradition which had no foundations of fact except in the imagination of medieval Florence. It may, however, be said here in his defence that he neither was nor pretended to be a scholar, a fact also vividly brought home to us by the meagre and disappointing list of the books deposited in his house.[3]

The age of Dante was also the age which witnessed the first dawn of humanism in Italy. It was in fact during the second half of the thirteenth century that a new rhetoric, which carried alongside with it a novel appreciation and a deeper knowledge of the classics, was beginning to conquer a field hitherto dominated by a 'ratio studiorum' unchanged for centuries. The centre of the new movement was Padua, nor is it surprising that it happened there rather than at Bologna. For since the rise of the glossators and the beginning of their new interpretation of Roman Law, no attempts had been made in Bologna to extend this classical revival beyond the boundaries of jurisprudence. At Bologna rhetoric had remained the handmaid of the Jurists, while poetry did not go beyond being a form of relaxation confined to the everyday language. In Padua, on the other hand, the youthful energy of the new university succeeded in achieving what was nothing less than the linear ancestor of Renaissance humanism. The knowledge of ancient Roman poets displayed by the early Paduan humanists was unrivalled in their time, either in Italy or beyond the Alps.[4] Its range may, in fact, be gauged when we realize that works like the poem of Lucretius and the *Silvae* of Statius, which were regarded until very recently as unknown until Poggio's discovery of them during the second decade of the fifteenth century,[5] were probably familiar to some Paduan scholars during the late thirteenth.[6] Admittedly it was a humanism which had not entirely eliminated the Gothic element. It was, moreover, a movement not only stimulated by memories

[1] G. Maetzke, *Florentia*, (Roma, 1941) 27.

[2] Villani, *op. cit.* I. 42; G. Maetzke, 'Ricerche sulla topografia fiorentina nel periodo delle guerre goto-bizantine', *Atti della Accademia Nazionale dei Lincei—classe di scienze morali, storiche e filologiche*, ser. 8, III (1948) 103.

[3] P. Guidi, *Inventari di libri nella serie dell'Archivio Vaticano* (1287–1459), (Città del Vaticano, 1948) 29.

[4] Guido Billanovich, ' "Veterum Vestigia Vatum" nei carmi dei preumanisti padovani', *Italia Medioevale e Umanistica*, I (1958) 155–243.

[5] R. Sabbadini, *Le scoperte dei codici latini e greci ne' secoli XIV e XV*, I, (Firenze, 1905) 80–2.

[6] Billanovich, '*Veterum Vestigia Vatum*', 182–90, 238–43.

of Roman Padua, but also nourished by the exceptional resources of the Abbey Library of Pomposa,[1] that is to say one of the wealthiest repositories of the Carolingian legacy.

The real founder of humanism in Padua, Lovato Lovati (1241-1309), was a jurist with a passion for classical literature. A judge by profession, he even aroused the admiration of so exacting a critic as Petrarch, who openly declared about forty years after Lovato's death, that he would have been the greatest Latin poet of his age and the preceding one, had he given poetry precedence over the study of the law.[2] Lovato's brilliant decoding of Seneca's tragic metres,[3] his rôle in the rediscovery of forgotten traditions of Livy's *Decades*,[4] and his poetic remains do not really concern us here. What instead is definitely of interest to us are his antiquarian tastes, which drew inspiration from the ancient traditions of Padua. Now in Lovato's time, when each commune looked for a Roman founder, and if one was not available invented one, a legend had been current in the city, attributing its foundation to the Trojan Antenor.[5] Little wonder then, that when about 1283 a skeleton of impressive proportions came to light during some building excavations, Lovato had no hesitation in identifying it at once with the mortal remains of the city's legendary forefather.[6] What had taken place in eleventh century Rome,[7] now happened in Padua. Lovato convinced Padua and Padua in turn resolved to erect a tomb to its alleged founder. This cenotaph, still standing in one of the squares of the town, could hardly have been conceived on less classical lines, while its inscription, contributed by Lovato,[8] indicates plainly that the formulae of classical epigraphy were still unfamiliar to him. Ignorance in this field is, however, hardly surprising at a time when the study and imitation of ancient inscriptions had been slumbering since the setting of the Carolingian sun. All the same, such an episode in late thirteenth century Padua is not unimpressive, particularly when viewed as an attempt to give a new lease of life to an ancient tradition in an idiom still stiffly Gothic. In more than one way the tomb of

[1] *Ibid.* 161-64.

[2] Petrarca, *Rerum Memorandarum Libri*, II, 61.

[3] R. Weiss, 'Lovato Lovati', *Italian Studies*, VI (1951) 21-22.

[4] G. Billanovich, 'Petrarch and the Textual Tradition of Livy', *Journal of the Warburg and Courtauld Institutes*, XIV (1951) 208.

[5] Weiss, *Lovato Lovati*, 7-8.

[6] *Ibid.* 8.   [7] *Supra*, 10.

[8] Weiss, *Lovato Lovati*, 20.

Antenor typifies both the enthusiasm and the weakness of Paduan humanism in its earliest stage.

The Antenor episode is the only known one in which Lovato the humanist turns up in an antiquarian garb. But the humanist re-awakening promoted by him was also bound to produce a climate favourable to antiquarianism. It is therefore no surprise to find Rolando da Piazzola, a humanist and judge, and, further-more, Lovato's own nephew, sedulously transcribing while on embassy to Pope Boniface VIII in January 1303 (that is to say not long before the outrage at Anagni sealed the fate of this Pope and of the medieval Papacy) an inscription which had particu-larly struck him[1] not far from St. Paul's at Rome. That the inscription[2] was apocryphal does not really matter. What instead does matter is that Rolando read and transcribed it accurately, in fact that he bothered to read it at all, in an age when classical epitaphs were not easily intelligible and had not been so for a long time. The difficulties met by Odofredus with the *Lex de imperio*[3] were, as we saw, typical of his age. And this situation was also brought home quite vividly some decades before the days of Rolando by an unknown rhetorician, who is not excluded from being Boncompagno da Signa, that is to say one of the brightest lights of late medieval rhetoric. Whoever was the author of the *Formula litterarum scholasticarum*, the state-ment in it that 'olim fiebant sculpture mirabiles in marmoribus electissimis cum litteris punctatis, quas hodie plenarie legere vel intelligere non valemus',[4] speaks quite clearly. Moreover, if we are to believe what we are told in a very late, but not therefore necessarily untrustworthy source, only about three years before Rolando's visit to Rome, a pilgrim returning from that town caused a great impression in Perugia, merely because he put forward an utterly fantastic interpretation of a perfectly straight-forward, but then unreadable, Roman inscription under the high altar of a local church.[5] To return, however, to Rolando, his antiquarian leanings were certainly well expressed on his tomb, still to be seen near the church of the Santo in Padua. For several odds and ends of ancient statuary were incorporated into it,

[1] C. Girardi, *Rolando da Piazzola*, (Padova, 1909) 21–2.
[2] *C.I.L.* VI. 5, 6*.
[3] *Supra*, 12.
[4] Quoted in G. B. De Rossi, *Le prime raccolte d'antiche iscrizioni compilate in Roma tra il finire del secolo XIV e il cominciare del XV*, (Roma, 1852), 4.
[5] See the unsigned note 'Un antiquario del sec. XIV', *Giornale di erudizione artistica*, I (1872) 184.

while its inscriptions repeated words and formulas lifted straight out of Roman epigraphy.[1]

The antiquarian activity of the Paduans did not stop here. Thanks at any rate partly to Rolando da Piazzola, Padua witnessed also the revival of an ancient ceremony unheard of since classical times. The coronation of Albertino Mussato,[2] the leading star in the humanist firmament of the town since Lovato's demise, with the poetic laurels, was partly Rolando's doing.[3] It was the city's reward to Mussato for his poetic activity, for his *Ecerinis*,[4] and not merely because this was the first secular tragedy written since the fall of the Roman Empire. It was also in a way a recognition of political services. Even nearly sixty years after the liquidation of him and his clan, people in Padua still shuddered at the memory of the unspeakable tyranny of Ezzelino III da Romano. And now the sinister shadow of Cangrande della Scala, Dante's hero and the Paduans' most formidable enemy, was drawing too close for safety, and in Cangrande it certainly looked as if Ezzelino was treading the earth again. In the *Ecerinis* Ezzelino was meant as a warning against the Lord of Verona, and the play was intended above all to drive home the dangers which were looming so uncomfortably near. The revival of tragedy was thus accompanied by the resurrection of the poetic laurel. But very little that was classical survived in the actual ceremony, which was instead turned into a medieval academic function, a kind of honorary degree ceremony. The Italian word for degree, laurea, still commemorates this academic travesty of a classical institution.

In 1315 such an antiquarian revival could have occurred only in Padua, where humanism was well rooted in the University. Just when the first wave of this humanism was approaching its end, the accidental discovery of an ancient sepulchral inscription at a date between 1318 and 1324'[5] made the Paduans once more conscious of their classical heritage. For on it figured the name T. Livius,[6] which made it at once accepted as a relic from the tomb of the great Roman historian. The fact that humanist

[1] A. Prosdocimi 'L'arca di Rolando da Piazzola sul sagrato del Santo', *Bollettino del Museo Civico di Padova*, ser. 3, I–II (1939–41) 19–31.
[2] E. H. Wilkins, *The Making of the Canzoniere and other Petrarchan Essays*, (Roma, 1951) 21–3.
[3] Girardi, *op. cit.* 18, n. 2.
[4] A. Mussato, *Ecerinide*, ed. L. Padrin, (Bologna, 1900).
[5] B. L. Ullman, *Studies in the Italian Renaissance*, (Roma, 1955) 55–6.
[6] *C.I.L.* V. 2865.

Padua failed to note that the epitaph bore also the surname Halys and indicated that this Livius was a freedman, naturally shows the still primitive stage of antiquarian studies. None the less, it is also indicative of a warm if indiscriminate enthusiasm, thanks to which the inscription was solemnly housed on one of the walls of Santa Giustina. In a way the turning up of the pseudo-Livy epitaph marked also the end of early Paduan humanism. The impact of the Carraresi and the collapse of the free Commune soon scattered what had been a flourishing group, while Mussato, the laureate whose honour had stimulated a desire for a similar coronation in Dante,[1] was left to die an exile in Chioggia in 1329. The inheritor of the Paduan traditions was not a native of the city but the Tuscan Petrarch, who in turn bequeathed them to Europe.

During the second half of the thirteenth and the first of the fourteenth century, cultural exchanges between Padua and Verona were not infrequent. Yet at Verona, the dawn of humanism displays a different light.[2] Drawing its inspiration and strength from the fabulous wealth of the chapter library, it also found encouragement at the court of Cangrande della Scala. It was therefore characteristic that at any rate from about 1325–33 the chancery of the Scaligeri, where perhaps Dante himself had worked, was ruled by Benzo d'Alessandria,[3] that is to say a leading figure in north Italian humanism, who was not without a flair for antiquarian investigation.

The chapter library was a collection already flourishing as early as the ninth century, when it was enriched by the Arch-deacon Pacificus, and it could boast ancient riches unmatched anywhere else, either in Italy or abroad. Side by side with the legacy of the Veronese 'scriptoria' of the sixth and seventh centuries, one could handle in it some of the choicest treasures of the Carolingian summer. There were also to be seen the fruits of the humanism of Ratherius of Liège, whose failure as a bishop of tenth-century Verona was tempered by his exceptional scholarly activity in an age when the lamps lit by the Renaissance of the preceding century were flickering out.[4]

---

[1] *Paradiso*, XXV, 1–9.
[2] See R. Weiss, 'La cultura preumanistica Veronese e Vicentina del tempo di Dante', *Dante e la cultura veneta*, ed. V. Branca e G. Padoan, (Firenze, 1966) 263–72.
[3] Sabbadini, *Le scoperte dei codici latini e greci*, II, 129.
[4] G. Billanovich, 'Dal Livio di Raterio (Laur. 63. 19) al Livio del Petrarca (B.M., Harl. 2493)', *Italia Medioevale e Umanistica*, II (1959) 117, n. 2.

If there was a place where all the materials indispensable to a humanist revival were available, it was the Verona chapter library. It is therefore scarcely surprising that it was the cradle of that Veronese humanism whose first movements coincided with the reappearance about 1300 of the poems of Catullus in Verona. The arrival of a volume of his lyrics from France proved an important event, to be duly commemorated in a Latin epigram, hailing the return home of the poet, by a versifier from Vicenza called Benvenuto Campesani.[1] During the fourteenth century the impact of the Verona chapter library could be felt even as far away as Papal Avignon, which of course means Petrarch.[2]

It was actually within the shadow of the Verona chapter library that the humanist passion of Giovanni de Matociis, commonly known as Giovanni Mansionario (d. 1337) from his office in the cathedral, was nurtured. This was a passion which soared to its highest in his tract,[3] where he triumphantly established the existence of two and not only one Pliny, as had hitherto been commonly believed. But even before his careful reading of Suetonius' biography, prefixed to the text of the Natural History of the Elder Pliny, and of the Epistles of the Younger had revealed the truth to him, he had not been idle in the humanist field. From about 1310[4] he had actually been busy on the *Historia Imperialis*, a vast historical compilation ranging from Augustus onwards, where he gave full scope to his humanist and antiquarian leanings. During the early Trecento such a work as the *Historia Imperialis* could have been produced only in Verona. But what really interests us is Giovanni the antiquarian rather than the historian. The former is shown vividly in his autograph copy of the *Historia*. Here for instance, when he talked about games celebrated by the Emperor Balbinus, he felt that something should also have been said about the places where such performances were held. This led him to a digression, where with the assistance of the indispensable Isidore,[5] he

[1] R. Weiss, 'Benvenuto Campesani (1250–55?—1323)', *Bollettino del Museo Civico di Padova*, XLIV (1955) 141–43.

[2] Billanovich, *Dal Livio di Raterio*, 145.

[3] E. Truesdell Merrill, 'On the Eight Book Tradition of Pliny's *Letters* in Verona', *Classical Philology*, V (1910) 186–88.

[4] Sabbadini, *Le scoperte dei codici latini e greci*, I, 2. The autograph copy of the *Historia Imperialis* is in the Vatican Library, Ms. Chig. I. VII. 259. Giovanni was still working on the *Historia Imperialis* in 1320, cf. *ibid.* f. 223 v.

[5] *Isidori Hispalensis Episcopi Etymologiarum sive Originum Libri XX*, ed. W. M. Lindsay, (Oxonii, 1911) XVIII, xxviii–xxxi.

gave an elaborate description of a Roman circus.[1] But this was
not enough in his view; he also drew on the margins of his own
copy a neat diagram of a circus,[2] according to the information in
Isidore's encyclopaedia. A little later, in his account of the
Emperor Philip,[3] he mentioned the 'ludi theatrales et circenses',
which were held under him to celebrate the millenary of the
foundation of Rome. So again here Isidore came to Giovanni's
rescue,[4] and enabled him to give an account of a Roman theatre,[5]
which this time he accompanied not by one, but by two diagrams,
translating into visual terms the facts at his disposal.[6] Even if
these drawings were not his own idea but figured already in his
Isidore, the reproduction of them would in itself have been
quite remarkable. There is, however, no real evidence against
his paternity of them, and in view of his tastes their attribution
to him seems quite safe. These drawings also bring home to us
the primitive character of Giovanni's erudition. Two or three
generations later, the information from Isidore would have been
supplemented by an examination of what could be gathered from
the extant remains of the Arena of Verona.

The antiquarian activity of Giovanni Mansionario did not
stop at his drawings of Roman circuses. His *Historia* is really a
string of biographies of Emperors, several of whose coins also
appear to have been available to him. Before him, therefore, were
the features of several of the monarchs he was writing about, so
that it is not surprising, in view of what we know, to find him
reproducing some of these coins, with a hand still stiffened by
the practice of Gothic handwriting, on the margins of his
volume.[7] Although his aim was to produce an accurate rendering
of these pieces, the lettering of the inscriptions was naturally
conditioned by his own scribal habits. As for the portraits on
them, these assumed a somewhat medieval air, not unlike that
which is so obvious in the golden augustales of Frederick II.[8]
Nevertheless the significance of these drawings leaps to the eye.
Here for the first time in Italy we find a scholar giving visual
expression to his antiquarian interests. Admittedly already during

---

[1] Pl. V., Vatican Library, Ms. Chig. I. VII. 259, f. 13r.
[2] *Ibid*. loc. cit.   [3] *Ibid*. f. 15v.
[4] *Isidori . . . Etymologiarum . . . Libri XX, XVIII*, xlii–li.
[5] Vatican Library, Ms. Chig. I. VII. 259, ff. 15v–16r.
[6] *Ibid*. f. 15v.
[7] *Ibid*. ff. 2r, 3v–5r, 6v, 11r–13r, 14r etc. They range from Pertinax, f.2r, to Lewis the Pious, f. 236r.
[8] *Supra*, 12.

the thirteenth century Villard de Honnecourt,[1] and doubtless other artists, had made sketches of ancient statuary. But their aim had been different. They drew classical figures not because they were ancient, but because they were models worth imitating. Giovanni, on the other hand, reproduced Roman coins in his volume because of their age and the history behind them. In the next stage of Veronese humanism Giovanni Mansionario's real heir was Guglielmo da Pastrengo. But with him one reaches not only the generation of Petrarch but also the circle of that great humanist. In fact he belongs to the second wave of Italian humanism.

Both the Paduans and Giovanni Mansionario can hardly be considered as professional antiquarians. Undeniably an interest in antiquities was alive in them. Their references to antiquities were, on the other hand, almost accidental, and there are no signs on their part of any systematic studies in the field. In them antiquarianism was more an attitude of mind than a really conscious activity. An inscription might be copied occasionally, ancient coins reproduced, a skeleton identified with the remains of an illustrious ancient. But from these to the activities of a Giovanni Dondi[2] half a century later, there is still a long way to go. Nor is this surprising, for Petrarch stands between them and Dondi.

This distance is also brought home to us by the pursuits of Benzo d'Alessandria, who settled in Verona only towards the end of his life. His employment as head of the chancery of Cangrande and his successors lasted only from about 1325–33,[3] that is to say practically until his death. But Verona had also been inspected by him at an earlier stage, probably during the early years of the century and certainly before 1310.[4] During this visit he had the opportunity of handling the treasures of the chapter library, in the same way that a journey to Ravenna enabled him to examine other volumes almost as venerable.[5] Verona revealed to him Catullus and the *Historia Augusta*,[6] and it has been suggested that he was able to take away from the chapter library a manuscript of Ausonius.[7] Yet he hardly

[1] *Ibid.* 13.
[2] *Infra*, 49–53.
[3] *Dante e Verona per il vii centenario della nascita*, (Verona, 1965) 36–37, 146–47.
[4] Sabbadini, *Le scoperte dei codici latini e greci*, II, 146.
[5] *Ibid.* II, 132, n. 23.
[6] *Ibid.* II, 144–5.
[7] *Ibid.* II, 146–9.

belongs to the Veronese group. Rather he should be viewed as an independent scholar, whose intellectual appetite did not need to be whetted by continuous contact with an ancient tradition. His tastes and interests were certainly catholic, and during his travels his eyes were alert for the unusual, which in his case ranged from the newly completed tomb of the Emperor Henry VII at Pisa[1] to the salmon trout of Lake Garda.[2] This and other information gathered in his travels in north and central Italy was poured by him into his encyclopaedia. The execution of this huge compilation was started while he was employed as a notary in Como by Bishop Leone Lambertenghi, whom he served about 1312-20,[3] but it was completed in Verona during his headship of the local chancery. Unfortunately only part of it survives now; but this is amply sufficient to reveal to us his scholarly curiosity and his exceptional critical powers, especially in the discussion of historical sources and legends.[4] Whenever he was on the move he was generally careful to note a description of the seals of the towns which he saw, naturally for future reference in his 'magnum opus'. Thus he mentioned that in his day the seal of Florence bore a Hercules holding a club and the inscription HERCVLEA CLAVA DOMAT FLORENCIA PRAVA.[5] This of course suggests an antique model, if not actually an ancient engraved gem with a medieval inscription. More than once he appears impressed by ancient remains. At Pavia he naturally did not fail to note the 'Regisol'.[6] At Borgo San Donnino he even decided to copy an ancient inscription seen on the front of the main church.[7] Nor, needless to say, did he omit to mention the 'Laberinthum' of Verona, 'quod nunc Harena dicitur', or to point out that its outside walls had been damaged by earthquakes, and that the fallen blocks of stone had been used to build part of the city walls.[8] Roman topography was available to Benzo through the *Graphia aurea Urbis Romae*.[9] But of Rome he left no description, unless one was included in the now lost parts of his encyclopaedia.

[1] *Ibid.* II, 132, n. 19.   [2] *Ibid.* II, 133, n. 29.
[3] *Ibid.* II, 131.
[4] *Ibid.* II, 134.
[5] *Ibid.* II, 132, n. 21. On this seal see N. Rubinstein, 'Vasari's painting of the *Foundation of Florence* in the Palazzo Vecchio', *Essays in the History of Architecture presented to Rudolf Wittkower*, (London, 1967) 67, n. 47.
[6] Sabbadini, *Le scoperte dei codici latini e greci*, II, 133, n. 33.
[7] *Ibid.* II, 132, n. 26.
[8] *Ibid.* II, 133, n. 30.
[9] *Ibid.* II, 136, n. 48.

Benzo undoubtedly had antiquarian tastes. It must, however, be borne in mind that he was above all a humanist, nor must we be surprised if antiquarian details in his encyclopaedia never go very deep. This of course makes him really not so dissimilar on one side from the scholars of Padua and Verona, and on the other from his contemporary Opicino de Canistris, who was, however, much less of a humanist, if perhaps more of an antiquarian. In 1330 Opicino completed in the Avignon of Pope John XXII his *Liber de laudibus civitatis Ticinensis*, a work only recently identified as his.[1] The scope of this treatise was quite different from Benzo's whose aims were purely the advancement of learning. Opicino's aims were much more immediate; his book was in fact a defence of his native Pavia, against the papal interdict for siding with the excommunicate Emperor Lewis IV of Bavaria, whose coronation in Rome by the syndics of the Roman people was supposed to have followed the pattern of the Romans' alleged gift of the Empire to Charlemagne. Accordingly, Opicino conjured up the vision of Pavia sanctified by its numerous churches and monasteries. As a description of a town it therefore belongs to the same category as the Carolingian description of Verona,[2] to which should also be assigned perhaps the *De magnalibus urbis Mediolani*[3] written a little before Benzo by Bonvesin da Riva, and in which antiquarian interest is conspicuous by its absence. What Opicino really gives is a 'Papia sacra'. It would nevertheless be inaccurate to assert that he turned a completely blind eye to the remains of Antiquity. In fact his tract included a by no means uninteresting account of the 'Regisol', which he says had been removed from Ravenna by the people of Pavia.[4] He also had a shot at explaining its strange name, but his interpretation remains unconvincing despite its ingenuity. The figure of the 'Regisol', standing on the top of a pillar, was also included by Opicino in his large drawing of Pavia Cathedral and its square,[5] an achievement which should make us forgive him for not having been more communicative about the Roman remains of the town. Still he actually men-

---

[1] In F. Gianani, *Opicino de Canistris l' Anonimo Ticinese*, (Pavia, 1927).
[2] *Supra*, 6.
[3] 'Bonvicini de Rippa de Magnalibus Urbis Mediolani', ed. F. Novati, *Bullettino dell' Istituto Storico Italiano*, No. 20 (1888). On such descriptions of towns see J. K. Hyde, 'Medieval Descriptions of Cities', *Bulletin of the John Rylands Library*, XLVIII (1966) 308–40.
[4] *Anonymi Ticinensis Liber de laudibus Civitatis Ticinensis*, ed. R. Maiocchi and F. Quintavalle, (Città di Castello, 1903) 18.
[5] R. Salomon, *Opicinus de Canistris*, (London, 1936) pl. II.

tioned some old statuary then to be seen about Pavia,[1] and when he dealt with the ancient basilica of S. Pietro in Ciel d'Oro, he did not forget to stress the tombs of St. Augustine and Boethius inside it, going even as far as to give the epitaph on the tomb of the latter placed there by the Emperor Otho III and his tutor Gerbert, later Pope Sylvester II, in 998 and using the information supplied by this inscription.[2]

To find a parallel to such a use of an inscription before Petrarch, it is necessary to move southward and enter the secluded field of Greek studies. It may perhaps be opportune to recall here that before Petrarch this was a field entirely foreign to humanism. To start with, in Italy it was restricted to the Greek-speaking zones in the south and in Sicily, that is to say territories controlled by Angevins and Aragonese. At the court of Naples translators from the Greek hailing from the south were active at least from the time of Charles II (1285–1309).[3] During the reign of his successor Robert I (1309–43), a king who won the contempt of Dante and the panegyrics of Petrarch, both humanists and translators admittedly enjoyed his patronage. But their activities lay in separate fields. The translators moved among the physicians and the theologians, while the humanists were mainly concerned with rhetoric and looked to the law for a living. Antiquities do not figure in their writings, and it was left to one of the translators in Robert's pay, the physician Niccolò di Deoprepio of Reggio, to apply his own learning to turn into Latin the Greek inscription on the front of the temple of the Dioscuri at Naples. The now nameless writer of the earliest section of the *Cronacha di Partenope*, who was probably writing in the days of King Robert, moved rather by civic pride than humanist and antiquarian considerations, had deemed it essential to mention the 'mirabile templo de marmore', which was still standing so conspicuously in the city.[4] What baffled him naturally was the Greek inscription on the front. He accordingly turned for help to Niccolò, who promptly obliged with a Latin rendering of it, and straight away inserted it in vernacular attire into the *Cronacha*, not without an acknowledgement of Niccolò's help.[5] Notwithstanding the inclusion of this

---

[1] *Anonymi Ticinensis Liber de laudibus Civitatis Ticinensis*, 18–20.

[2] *Ibid.* 12–13.

[3] R. Weiss, 'The Translators from the Greek of the Angevin Court at Naples', *Rinascimento*, I (1950) 195–226.

[4] A. Altamura, *Testi napoletani dei secoli XIII e XIV*, (Napoli, 1949) 153.

[5] F. Lo Parco, *Niccolò da Reggio grecista italiota del sec. XIV e l'interpretazione dell' epigrafe greca del tempio dei Dioscuri di Napoli ricordata nella 'Cronaca di Partenope'*, (Napoli, 1909).

inscription, the *Cronacha* remains a late medieval document, offering the most ludicrous legends as truth. Yet this translation really constitutes a landmark. It is very probably the first version ever made of a Greek classical inscription, and to find such translations again we must wait until the fifteenth century.[1]

As will be seen,[2] it was King Robert who promoted the poetic coronation of Petrarch in a Rome forsaken by Pope and Emperor. Despite its desolation, so vividly brought home by Petrarch in one of his most famous 'canzoni',[3] antiquarianism was not altogether extinct in the city. The traditions codified by the *Mirabilia* and the *Graphia Aurea* were still alive and a source of inspiration, to which the first Roman humanists seemed to have preferred Livy and the *Liber Pontificalis*.[4] Yet it was in these days that one hears for the first time of a collection of antiques on almost Renaissance lines. Collectors had of course existed before. But the activity of Oliviero Forzetta is really the earliest known instance of a systematic chase after ancient objects, not because their shapes were unusual or their materials were uncommon, but simply because they were old. What must strike us at once is that Forzetta did not hail from Rome or Ravenna, that is to say from a city dominated by ancient memories and still basking in the sunshine of ancient glory, but from Treviso, a town until three generations earlier the centre of a tradition of chivalry and courtliness, still recalled with nostalgia by Dante. There was not, however, much courtliness about Forzetta, who was not even a scholar, but a moneylender and the son and grandson of usurers. Throughout a long life (he died in extreme wealth in 1373, that is to say just before Petrarch) Forzetta collected every antique on which he could lay his hands. He was already indulging in his pastime as early as 1335, when he was busy gathering marbles, bronzes, coins, engraved gems,[5] and even trying to secure 'quattuor pueris de Ravenna lapideis qui sunt taglati Ravenne in Sancto Vitale'.[6] His death

---

[1] *Infra*, 142, n.9.   [2] *Ibid.* 32.

[3] Petrarca, *Rerum vulgarium fragmenta*, 53.

[4] G. Billanovich, 'Gli umanisti e le cronache medioevali', *Italia Medioevale e Umanistica*, I (1958) 103–37.

[5] A. Serena, *La cultura umanistica a Treviso nel secolo decimoquinto*, (Venezia, 1912) 321–22. Another collection of curiosities and antiques, including ancient coins, three Roman inscriptions found at Treviso, and two swords was assembled by Marin Falier, who was Doge of Venice from 1354–55. Cf. G. M. de Gheltof, *La collezione del doge Marino Falier e i tesori di Marco Polo*, (Venezia, 1881), C. A. Levi, *Le collezioni veneziane d'arte e d'antichità dal secolo XIV ai nostri giorni*, I, (Venezia, 1900) XXXVI–XXXVII.

[6] Serena, *op. cit.* 322.

led to the dispersal of his collections, which could doubtless have compared not unfavourably with those assembled during the next century. In fact his preoccupations as a collector disclose a discrimination which was unknown in his time except among bibliophiles and lovers of jewels.

One may agree that the frame of mind behind Forzetta's collecting was not that of Petrarch, whose antiquarianism was the corollary of his classical scholarship, and one may well ask whether it carried with it Petrarch's almost religious veneration for even the crumbs of Antiquity. To expect this is, however, to expect too much. Such a veneration really belongs to a later age, and even during the high Renaissance it was restricted to comparatively few individuals. In the fourteenth century the spirit which had led earlier to the transformation of ancient statues into Christian saints, had not quite disappeared. When in 1335 the 'Regisol' was returned to Pavia after its Milanese exile, it was regilded and restored. But medieval restorers were not swayed by antiquarian niceties. It was clear to them that the statue represented a Roman Emperor. They would therefore see to it that it was given the trappings of an Emperor, even if these were rather up-to-date.[1] This anachronistic approach also vanished during the Renaissance.

[1] G. de La Flamma, *Opusculum de rebus gestis ab Azone, Luchino et Johanne Vicecomitum*, ed. C. Castiglioni, (Bologna, 1938) 14, M. Cagiano de Azevedo, *Il gusto nel restauro delle opere antiche*, (Roma, 1948) 11–12.

CHAPTER THREE

THE AGE OF PETRARCH

Petrarch was not only the restorer of classical scholarship. He was also the initiator of a new approach in antiquarian studies: if Biondo was the father of Roman archaeology, Petrarch was certainly its grandfather. This should not be taken to imply that as an archaeologist he achieved the same heights he reached as a textual critic, for this was certainly not so. But then as a critic of ancient texts Petrarch had no rivals until the second quarter of the fifteenth century and the appearance of Lorenzo Valla; moreover, Valla had Petrarch's achievement behind him. Little wonder then, that even to-day editors of Livy, Cicero, the Latin geographers, and other texts, can overlook Petrarch's work on these authors only at their own risk. Here was an achievement unique in the chronicles of scholarship; for no scholar of his time, or for that matter of any other, did so much with so little to help him. Apart from anything else, it is to him that we owe the merging and rescuing of the slender streams of textual traditions, dating back to the Symmachi and Nicomachi in fifth century Rome and to the Ravenna of Theodoric the Goth.[1] But as an archaeologist his critical powers, though certainly not dormant, were not as sharp.[2] For his evidence he relied mainly on literary sources and was often ready to believe what he was told by such dubious guides as the *Mirabilia* and the *Graphia Aurea*. Such a weakness, so striking when viewed against his achievement as a textual critic, is, however, understandable. Despite his veneration for the relics of Antiquity, Petrarch did not feel for them that boundless enthusiasm with which he approached ancient literature, and even here his attitude towards Greek remained rather lukewarm,[3] compared to his passionate love for

[1] Billanovich, *Petrarch and the Textual Tradition of Livy*, passim, G. Billanovich, 'Dalla antica Ravenna alle biblioteche umanistiche', *Aevum*, XXX (1956) 343–50, G. Billanovich, 'Petrarca e i classici', *Petrarca e il Petrarchismo—Atti del III Congresso dell' Associazione Internazionale per gli studi di lingua e letteratura italiana*, (Bologna, 1961) 21–33.

[2] On this see also R. Weiss, 'Petrarch the Antiquarian', *Classical, Mediaeval and Renaissance Studies in Honour of Berthold Louis Ullman*, II, (Roma, 1964) 199–209.

[3] R. Weiss, 'Petrarca e il mondo greco', *Atti e memorie della Accademia Petrarca di lettere, arti e scienze*, N.S. XXXVI (1952–57) 65–96, A. Pertusi, *Leonzio Pilato tra Petrarca e Boccaccio*, (Venezia-Roma. 1964) passim.

the great Roman writers. His devotion to Virgil, Livy, and Cicero, was never dimmed by his liaison with Homer, though we must remember here that Homer was intelligible to him only in a third-rate Latin version. Had Petrarch's interest in ancient art been as overwhelming as his interest in bibliophily, he would probably have left behind the greatest archaeological collection ever seen before the Renaissance, side by side with that magnificent library of his, where some of even the rarest texts could be found in duplicate and in triplicate.

As an antiquarian, Petrarch was not above accepting some puerile traditions. Nor was it natural for him, as it is to us, to perceive an obvious anachronism, such as, for instance, the representation of Roman soldiers in the garb of medieval warriors. Still, an attraction towards what was left of classical antiquity, was certainly exceptionally developed in him. Thus his notes on the margins of his sumptuous Livy, now in Paris, indicate an interest in the topography of ancient Italy.[1] Those written on his copy of Eusebius's chronicle in the Latin attire supplied by Saint Jerome, show a similar feeling for the more famous buildings of ancient Rome.[2] Furthermore this same text often proved of great help to him in the solution of some archaeological problems. He may have preferred texts to buildings and literature to art.[3] There is, however, no doubt that the ancient ruins spoke to him very deeply. To him they were nothing less than the skeleton of the past rising before his eyes, like the proverbial skeleton at the Roman feast, to admonish and remind the present, as well as a tangible commentary on what was being confided to him by his reading of the great ancients. His love for them was enhanced in 1337, when at last Rome was revealed to him, so that he was able to see what till then had been familiar to him only from literature.

The remains of ancient Rome aroused Petrarch's enthusiasm because they were ancient ruins, and because they were the ruins of Rome. The walls, the arches, the baths, the amphitheatres, in fact all the visible relics of Roman power, moved him deeply. To him they proved also a source of inspiration, and in fact gave

---

[1] P. De Nolhac, *Pétrarque et l'humanisme*, 2nd ed., II (Paris, 1907) 29.

[2] G. Billanovich, *Un nuovo esempio delle scoperte e delle letture del Petrarca. L'Eusebio— Girolamo—Pseudo Prospero*', (Krefeld, 1954) 48–50.

[3] It is interesting to note that Petrarch made a careful study of Vitruvius, cf. L. Ciapponi, 'Il "De Architectura" di Vitruvio nel primo umanesimo', *Italia Medioevale e Umanistica*, III (1960) 59–99.

strength to his resolve to compete with the great Roman writers, with Virgil in the *Africa* and with Livy in the *De viris illustribus*, as well as sharpening his desire for the poetic laurels. The coronation of Albertino Mussato[1] had revived an ancient institution and created a precedent. Although only a municipal occasion, it had aroused interest throughout Italy, to the point that after it poets, from Dante downwards, began to crave a similar honour for themselves. Naturally such a desire did not pass Petrarch by. And in him the longing for the poetic laurels was increased by the connexion between Apollo's tree and Laura's name and the desire to be honoured like a poet of Antiquity. If the ceremony had been revived for Mussato, it could also be revived for him; his influential friends would see to it. They did, and in 1341 the great event took place. King Robert of Naples consented to sponsor the ceremony and publicly examined Petrarch before his court. But the actual crowning took place in Rome, in the audience hall of the senatorial palace on the Capitol on April 8th.[2] As in Mussato's, so in this coronation the classical element was somewhat thin. Even more than before, it had dwindled into a kind of university graduation, the university element being particularly emphasized now by King Robert's preliminary examination and by the award of a diploma as well as his laurel crown to the new laureate.

During his first visit to Rome in the spring of 1337, Petrarch had the opportunity to wander to his heart's content among the ruins. His companion and guide in these sentimental journeys was the Dominican Giovanni Colonna, who shared Petrarch's tastes for Antiquity and interest in Livy, thus proving a most congenial companion to him. Shortly after leaving Rome Petrarch wrote to Colonna, and in his letter to him[3] he recalled their wanderings of a few weeks before. Like more than one great writer after him (the names of Goethe and Stendhal leap naturally at once to one's mind) he delighted in setting down in writing his 'promenades dans Rome', nor did he omit to remind his correspondent of their stops and conversations in the Baths of Diocletian, after they had walked themselves out. What we

---

[1] *Supra*, 20.
[2] Wilkins, *The Making of the Canzoniere and other Petrarchan Studies*, 9–69.
[3] Petrarca, *Rerum Familiarium Libri*, VI. 2. For the date of this letter and this visit to Rome see Billanovich, *Gli umanisti e le cronache medioevali*, 129. A different dating is assigned to the letter in E. H. Wilkins, 'On Petrarch's Ep. Fam. VI. 2', *Speculum*, XXXVIII (1963) 620–22.

have here is a diary rather than a letter, in which Petrarch re-lived the wonder and awe that he had felt in the presence of ancient Rome. We can see Petrarch moving among the antique remains, his imagination stirred by the pages of Virgil and Livy, seeking to identify the very spots where the greatest events in Roman history had occurred. Often these identifications were quite off the mark, but this does not really matter; for to him they were the truth.

Petrarch's letter is not a guide to old Rome, nor does it set out to be one. He does not try to describe the monuments; instead he just mentions them, and with them he also recalls memories of the early Christian city. Quite obviously he had the *Mirabilia* handy, or at any rate he had read it very carefully. Thus when he mentions the legend of Augustus and the Sibyl, or states that the ashes of imperial Caesar were inside the sphere on the top of the Vatican obelisk, one sees projected the mendacious shadow of the *Mirabilia*. His reliance on so tainted a source is, however, justifiable. Where, apart from the *Mirabilia* and the *Graphia Aurea* could Petrarch have turned for guidance on Roman topography? It is quite true that Giovanni Colonna had been his devoted guide in Rome. But, characteristically, he trusted his texts much more than he trusted Colonna. And if he had consented to rely upon him, this was not because Colonna was a Roman and member of one of the most powerful baronial families in the city, but rather because he was aware that he too from his youth had felt the appeal of the antiquities.[1] As a matter of fact Petrarch had no illusions about the ignorance and lack of interest of the Romans in their own city, and had told Colonna so in his letter to him.[2] So when Colonna indicated to him as a temple of the sun an old and impressive ruin incorporated into the monastery of San Gregorio al Celio, he refused to accept such an identification and, thanks to St. Jerome's text of the chronicle of Eusebius, he was able to write to him triumphantly: 'Hoc Severi Afri Septizonium, quam tu sedem Solis vocas, sed meum nomen in historiis scriptum lego'.[3]

Giovanni Colonna did not take Petrarch's strictures to heart. Instead in his *Mare historiarum*, a vast and incredibly dull historical

---

[1] Petrarca, *Rerum Familiarium Libri*, VI. 2.

[2] A similar complaint was uttered by Petrarch to another Roman noble, Paolo Annibaldi, cf. Petrarca, *Epistole Metrice*, III, 13.

[3] Petrarca, *Rerum Familiarium Libri*, VI. 2, Billanovich, *Un nuovo esempio delle scoperte e delle letture del Petrarca*, 19, 68.

compilation, on which he was still busy in 1340 and which is, not surprisingly, still unpublished, he accepted Petrarch's corrections. 'Edificavit preterea', he said here of the Emperor Septimius Severus, 'Rome Septizolium ut ex Africa venientes suum opus viderent'.[1] As for the temple of the Sun, he now attributed it to the Emperor Aurelian,[2] without, however, committing himself as to its precise location. Other Roman buildings were also mentioned in the *Mare historiarum* and were accompanied by topographical details,[3] derived from what was then current knowledge in Rome. Of course Colonna was not always accurate. But then Petrarch also had his limitations. Apart from failing to distinguish between imperial and republican walls, he accepted the traditional identification of the pyramid in the Borgo Nuovo as the tomb of Romulus,[4] a tradition which did not save it from demolition in the days of Pope Alexander VI. If Poggio is to be believed,[5] and there are no strong reasons why he should not be, Petrarch also accepted the current view that the pyramid of Cestius was the tomb of Remus. A much more serious mistake was the attribution of Ponte Sant' Angelo to Trajan,[6] in view of the fact that Hadrian's name was clearly inscribed on both sides of it in very large letters. He also believed Trajan's column to have been the tomb of this Emperor,[7] an error which can be ultimately traced to the Chronicle of Eusebius, where he had read that Trajan was the only Emperor buried in Rome.[8] But one could go on for some time noting Petrarch's archaeological slips, which range from his following the traditional identification of the Pantheon with the temple of Cybele,[9] to a belief that the Vatican obelisk was dedicated 'divis imperatoribus'.[10] Some of these inaccuracies were, however, realized and rectified by him later. Thanks to Suetonius, he corrected in the *De remediis* his error about the Pantheon,[11] while in the

[1] S. L. Forte, 'John Colonna O. P.—Life and Writings (1298—c. 1340)' *Archivum Historicum Fratrum Praedicatorum*, XX (1950) 409–10.

[2] *Ibid.* 410.

[3] *Ibid.* 409–10.

[4] Petrarca, *Rerum Familiarium Libri*, VI, 2.

[5] P. P. Trompeo and G. Martellotti, 'Cartaginesi a Roma', *Nuova Antologia*, (1943) 262, n. 1.

[6] Weiss, *Petrarch the Antiquarian*, 204.

[7] *Ibid.* loc. cit.

[8] *Eusebius Werke, Siebenter Band-Die Chronik des Hieronymus*, ed. R. Helm, (Berlin, 1956) 197.

[9] Petrarca, *Rerum Familiarium Libri*, VI, 2.

[10] *Ibid.* loc. cit.

[11] Petrarca, *De remediis utriusque fortunae*, I, 118.

marginal notes of his Eusebius he recorded 'Nam et Capitolium regium opus est et Pantheon Agrippe'.[1] Similarly in the *De remediis* the 'Palatium Antonini' of the letter to Giovanni Colonna now became, more correctly, the 'Balneum Antonini'.[2]

A few years after writing his letter to Colonna, Petrarch returned to the topography of ancient Rome. He had decided to represent in the eighth book of his *Africa* an imaginary tour of Rome made by the Carthaginian envoys to the Senate, which meant of course a reconstruction of the Rome of the Scipios. This naturally implied a marshalling of all his archaeological knowledge. Yet, archaeologically, the outcome was hardly a success. Petrarch's republican city is not only too magnificent for the Rome of the Punic Wars, but, moreover, it is also made to include buildings and monuments that were certainly not there at the time. For example, he placed in it the two *Dioscuri* of the Quirinal, whom he believed to be by Pheidias and Praxiteles, thus showing at any rate an improvement on the *Mirabilia*, where the statues were given as representing two young philosophers so named: and he slipped badly by introducing into it the Pantheon, which he still believed then to have been the Temple of Cybele. On the other hand, one can say to his credit that neither the Septizonium nor the Antonine and Trajanic columns figure in his panorama of the city in republican times.[3]

The archaeological interests of Petrarch naturally extended also to classical art. Thus the 'Regisol' of Pavia was described by him to Boccaccio in admiring terms in a letter, where he also showed himself fully aware of its origin in Ravenna.[4] Also much admired by him were the bronze horses of St. Mark's, Venice.[5] It is therefore strange that he made no mention, either in his letter to Colonna or elsewhere, of the equestrian statue of Marcus Aurelius and the other classical statuary, then placed on the top of pillars outside St. John the Lateran and now in the Capitol. He seems to have studied some of the portrait busts of the Roman Emperors; hence when reading in the *Historia Augusta* that Gordian the Younger had been 'forma conspicuus',[6] he felt compelled to intervene on the margins of his own copy and

[1] Billanovich, *Un nuovo esempio delle scoperte e delle letture del Petrarca*, 48.
[2] Petrarca, *De remediis utriusque fortunae*, I, 118.
[3] Trompeo e Martellotti, *op. cit.* 254–64.
[4] Petrarca, *Rerum Senilium Libri*, V, 1.
[5] *Ibid.* IV, 2.
[6] *Scriptores Historiae Augustae, Gordianus*, 17.

note 'Si hoc verum fuit malum habuit sculptorem.'[1] Statues were not forgotten by him even in the *De remediis*,[2] although here his appreciation of them was naturally distorted by the ascetic climate of the treatise. Nor was his taste for art restricted to that of the classical period. Early Christian monuments also met with his praise, and the most prominent Christian relics had not been overlooked by him during his visits to Rome,[3] where he is also known to have admired the Cemetery of Callixtus.[4]

Ancient inscriptions were not neglected by Petrarch. Yet epigraphy was a field where, one feels, he did not do himself full justice. Not that he was uninterested in it, on the contrary and indeed in his old age he still recalled that in his youth he had been shown in Rimini the old inscribed stone, marking the spot where Caesar was alleged to have addressed his army after crossing the Rubicon.[5] Inscriptions were actually often noted and remembered by him: to the point that when it came to writing a Latin epitaph for Tommaso Caloiro,[6] the Sicilian friend of his Bologna student days, he included in it a pentameter borrowed from an early Christian inscription in the Roman church of Santa Maria in Trastevere.[7] Some lines from an epigraphic elogium,[8] which he believed to be of the elder Drusus, may be seen in the *De remediis*.[9] It is therefore surprising to find him accepting unquestioningly as Livy's tombstone the epitaph preserved in Padua; so much so that he even dated his fictitious letter to the great Roman historian 'in Vestibulo Iustine Virginis et ante ipsam sepulcri tui lapidem, VIII Kal. Martias MCCCLI'.[10] Together with his friend Gabrio dei Zamorei he accepted an inscription on the front of Parma Cathedral as the epitaph of the Roman writer Macrobius,[11] which is not so surprising in Gabrio, but is perhaps surprising in Petrarch. Far less surprising is his conformity to the traditional types and his avoidance of any classical formulae in those Latin inscriptions which he himself

---

[1] De Nolhac, *op. cit.*, II, 59.
[2] Petrarca, *De remediis utriusque fortunae*, I, 41.
[3] Petrarca, *Rerum Familiarium Libri*, VI, 2.
[4] *Ibid.* loc. cit. Petrarca, *Epistole Metrice*, II. 5, 97–100.
[5] A. Campana, *Il cippo riminese di Giulio Cesare*, (Rimini, 1933) 10–13.
[6] *Poesie minori del Petrarca*, ed. D. de' Rossetti, III, (Milano, 1834) Appendix, 4.
[7] *Inscriptiones Christianae Urbis Romae septimo saeculo anteriores*, ed. I. B. De Rossi, II. 1, (Roma, 1888) 316.
[8] *C.I.L.* VI. 1, 1207.
[9] Petrarca, *De remediis utriusque fortunae*, I, 114.
[10] Petrarca, *Rerum Familiarium Libri*, XXIV, 8.
[11] Weiss, *Petrarch the Antiquarian*, 206–07.

dictated,[1] as can be seen, for instance, in the epitaph he wrote for his little grandson, Francesco da Brossano, the original stone of which, still to be seen at Pavia, was furthermore engraved in Gothic characters.[2]

While the study of ancient inscriptions did not take much of a step forward with Petrarch, his study of ancient coins shows a definite advance on Giovanni Mansionario. As we saw,[3] Giovanni had not gone beyond drawing some of the ancient imperial coins available to him. Petrarch went further than that; he used them as historical sources and became known as something of an authority on the subject. The digger in Rome who unearthed an antique gem and some gold and silver coins, knew what he was doing when he brought them to Petrarch for identification and possibly purchase.[4] Not surprisingly, Petrarch actually assembled a small collection of Roman coins, of which he sedulously studied the iconography and the inscriptions. To him they really were a small portrait gallery of Roman Emperors, placing before his eyes the departed glory of Rome. It was because of this, because of the message they conveyed, that he presented a selection of them to the Emperor Charles IV when he met him in Mantua in 1354, saying at the same time 'ecce, inquam, Caesar, quibus successisti, ecce quos imitari studeas,'[5] which makes us hope that the most disreputable Roman Emperors were not represented in this gift. Incidentally the golden bull of Charles IV with its view of ancient Rome aroused the admiration of Petrarch,[6] whose delight was increased by seeing 'Aurea Roma' written on it, because, as he gravely explained to the Bishop of Olmütz, he had employed those very words in his *Africa*.[7]

There is ample testimony to Petrarch's use of coins as historical evidence. In the *Rerum Memorandarum Libri* we find him appealing to the golden and silver coins of Vespasian in connexion with that Emperor's features,[8] showing at the same time the knowledge that such pieces were very common. A coin of Faustina led to his writing in the margin of the passage 'Uxo-

---

[1] See for example *Poesie minori del Petrarca*, III, Appendix, 4, 6, 8, 10.

[2] V. Rossi, *Scritti di critica letteraria—Studi sul Petrarca e sul Rinascimento*, (Firenze, 1930) 70–81.

[3] *Supra*, 23.

[4] Petrarca, *Rerum Familiarium Libri*, XVIII, 8. On Petrarch as a numismatist see A. Magnaguti, 'Il Petrarca numismatico', *Rivista Italiana di Numismatica*, XX (1907) 155–57.

[5] Petrarca, *Rerum Familiarium Libri*, XIX, 3.

[6] *Ibid.* XXI, 2. On the bull see Erben, *op. cit.* 83, 111–12.

[7] Petrarca, *Le Familiari*, ed. V. Rossi, IV, (Firenze, 1942) 53, n., Petrarca, *Africa*, VI, 883.

[8] Petrarca, *Rerum Memorandarum Libri*, II, 73.

rem Faustinam Augustam appellari a senatu permisit' in his copy
of the *Historia Augusta* now in Paris, the observation 'Hac
appellatione est Faustina major me penes, in auro, similiter et
minor, sed eo amplius Pii Aug. fil.'[1] Another time, for example,
a gold piece of Agrippina, presented to him by the Augustinian
Luigi Marsigli, enabled him to elucidate a passage in Suetonius,
which had baffled him.[2]

Much more than Roman inscriptions, Roman coins show
Petrarch as a true antiquarian. His study of them shows him able
to make full use of the evidence available in them, just as it
discloses too his deep interest in ancient iconography. It is
therefore not surprising, in view of this, to find Petrarch's
shadow lurking behind the decoration of the 'Sala Virorum
Illustrium' ordered by Francesco da Carrara the Elder, the Lord
of Padua. For the frescoes in it seem to have been inspired by
Petrarch's *De Viris Illustribus*, the very work in which he had
seen himself as a new Livy; while the *Compendium* of this treatise
may well have been meant as a guide to these decorations, in
which the Roman monuments that figure in more than one scene
were also derived in all probability from information supplied by
the great humanist.[3]

The Paduan hall of great men was a pictorial glorification of
ancient Rome in a medieval idiom. Despite Petrarch's part in it,
the various figures were attired not in classical but in fourteenth-
century garb. In fact, apart from their subject matter, the
decorations of this hall were as distant from the spirit of Antiquity
as the revolution of Cola di Rienzo, whose two tribunates were
never more than a pathetic caricature of the classical original.
Yet at the beginning of Cola's rule even Petrarch had hailed it as
the genuine article, though not for long. Still Antiquity undeniably had a tremendous appeal for Cola di Rienzo, the ill-fated
tribune of Rome, whose dramatic career inspired an opera by
Wagner and a novel by Lord Lytton, if not one of Petrarch's
'canzoni'.[4] Cicero, Seneca, and Valerius Maximus, and above
all Livy were Cola's inspirers. But, as sources of his enthusiasm
for Antiquity, they were outdistanced by the ruins of Rome,

---

[1] De Nolhac, *op. cit.* II, 64.
[2] G. Billanovich, 'Nella biblioteca del Petrarca', *Italia Medioevale e Umanistica*, III (1960)
49–50.
[3] T. E. Mommsen, 'Petrarch and the Decoration of the Sala Virorum Illustrium in
Padua', *The Art Bulletin*, XXXIV (1952) 95–116.
[4] It is no longer believed that Cola was the recipient of Petrarca, *Rerum vulgarium fragmenta*, 53.

which he saw daily, rising everywhere among the churches, the fortresses, the mean hovels, and the grazing plots, which formed the medieval city. It was above all these ruins which made him see the past as a lost paradise, and a return to the ancient institutions the only way to save Rome from its anarchy and desolation and perhaps even make it once more the 'caput mundi'. None of Cola's contemporaries, not even Petrarch, felt so powerfully the impact of these remains or studied them more enthusiastically: 'tutta die se speculava nelli intagli de marmo, che iaccio intorno a Roma'[1] wrote his contemporary biographer. In an age when very few could make anything of an ancient inscription, his epigraphic competence was bound to impress his fellow citizens. The unknown contemporary who wrote his life was therefore repeating what must have been common talk, when he stated: 'Non c'era aitri che esso che sapessi leijere li antichi pitaffij. Tutte scritture antiche vulgarizzava; queste fegure de marmo iustamente interpretava.'[2]

Strangely enough, Cola's living in such an antiquarian make-believe had little influence on his literary style. His Latin never achieved a classical flavour, remaining to the end a faithful echo of the flamboyant phraseology of the 'dictatores'. This was of course the inevitable legacy of the notarial art, which gave him a training and supplied him with a living. It was a contradiction, but one which was not in contrast with his antiquarianism. For his vision was not that of a Petrarch; it was not a desire to revive classical learning, but to lead Rome back to its ancient glory. Hence his was really a humanism which by-passed literature and concentrated instead upon politics, with the result that his two short-lived tribunates show, besides the corrupting influence of absolute power and a good deal of charlatanry, a desperate attempt to make ancient Rome a present reality. Not surprisingly, his pathetic efforts to rule in fourteenth-century Rome according to the precepts of Livy and the visionary dreams of the latter-day saints of Joachim of Flora, tempered by despotism and corruption, proved too weak for the realities of the day. His formula to sway the masses was to appeal to the example of the ancients. But the example of the ancients worked in Rome only as long as things went well, and with Cola things did not go well for long. Yet it was an appeal that was still powerful in Italy. Only

[1] Anonimo Romano, *La vita di Cola di Rienzo*, ed. A. Frugoni, (Firenze, 1957) 33.
[2] *Ibid*. loc. cit.

a few years after Cola's death, Iacopo Bussolari, the Austin Friar who made himself the 'Savonarola' of Pavia a century before the appearance of the great reformer of Florence, was able to encourage the inhabitants of besieged Pavia to resistance, by recalling to them the example of the ancient Romans.[1]

Cola's antiquarian passion remained unabated to the end, and even when in prison in Avignon after the collapse of his first tribunate, he sought consolation from the pages of Livy.[2] It was a passion that found its supreme expression in politics, led him to absolute power, and yet was sincere. Although the collection of inscriptions ascribed to him is no longer believed to be his work,[3] his epigraphic pursuits made, as we have already seen, a deep impression in Rome, where he was unanimously considered the leading authority in the field. To Roman imperial coins he owed his knowledge of the ancient cult of Rome, and on them he noticed how the personified city was often represented as enthroned.[4] But the climax of his antiquarian activity occurred in 1346 or thereabouts, when he found in St. John Lateran the bronze tablet with Vespasian's *Lex de imperio*. Here was the very tablet which Odofredus a century before had been unable to read, a detail which had not stopped him from identifying it as part of the law of the Twelve Tables.[5] Cola, however, was able to read it and he was quick to see in it a most effective propaganda weapon. Here was, he thought, the proof that supreme power had belonged to the Roman people, who had merely delegated it to the Emperors. There could then be no better way to make the Romans conscious of their wonderful power. Cola certainly took this view, and acted on his belief. As a mass agitator he had already employed allegorical paintings. This time he saw that the tablet 'la quale nullo sapeva leijere nè 'nterpretare, se non solo esso',[6] was fixed on a wall inside St. John Lateran and, furthermore, he instructed a compliant painter to fresco around it the Roman senate conferring the 'imperium' upon Vespasian. His next step was to summon the Romans to come and listen to his interpretation of the discovery. This took place in St. John Lateran where, on 20 May 1347,

---

[1] P. Azarius, *Liber gestorum in Lombardia*, ed. F. Cognasso, (Bologna, 1926–39) 120.
[2] Anonimo Romano, *op. cit.* 168.
[3] A. Silvagni, 'Se la silloge signoriliana possa attribuirsi a Cola di Rienzo', *Archivum Latinitatis Medii Aevi*, I (1924) 175–83.
[4] K. Burdach, *Riforma-Rinascimento-Umanesimo*, (Firenze, 1935) 66.
[5] *Supra*, 12.
[6] Anonimo Romano, *op. cit.* 42.

before an audience of friends and foes and merely curious onlookers, he opened the proceedings with a speech in which, as could be expected, he made the usual contrast between the glorious past and the miserable present of the city. After this Cola had the text of the 'lex' read aloud. Then he spoke again. He outlined the immediate prospects of the city, reminding his audience that the jubilee of 1350 was drawing near. Huge masses of pilgrims would then descend upon Rome. Yet no plans were being made, and unless something was done there would not be only dangers to the city, but also a considerable loss.[1]

Cola's effort went down well. It was the first time that a classical inscription had furnished a text for a political sermon, and its success may be ascribed not only to the extraordinary eloquence of the speaker, but also to the fact that, despite the Romans' indifference to their past that Petrarch had been quick to notice,[2] the memory of ancient power was still in their minds. From the times of Pope Boniface VIII until Cola's discovery of it, the bronze tablet with the 'Lex de imperio' had been resting with the written side against an altar. This had been due to the action of a builder. But in this Cola saw a political motive, and in 1350, while a prisoner in Prague, he said in his long-winded apologia to Archbishop Ernst von Pardubitz that the tablet had been purposely hidden by Pope Boniface VIII from hatred of the Empire and that he, Cola, had brought it to light again and placed it where it could be seen by everyone.[3]

With Cola di Rienzo's short-lived rise to power in 1347 a new antiquarian climate permeated the city's government. It found expression in Cola's assumption of the title 'Tribunus Augustus'; it was present in his theatrical assumption of knighthood, which included his presenting himself as a 'candidatus' wearing the classical 'vestis triumphalis' and his bathing in the font, where it was commonly believed that Constantine had been cleansed from leprosy by Pope Sylvester. This was a performance in which the influence of the teaching of Joachim of Flora's extremist disciples was also evident, and to which relief was brought by a banquet. More ceremonies took place on August 15th, 1347, when Cola was given the 'laurea tribunicia'. These resulted in a mixture of ill-digested memories of ancient

---

[1] *Ibid.* 41–6.
[2] *Supra*, 33.
[3] Burdach, *Vom Mittelalter zur Reformation*, II. 3, 258.

triumphal customs contaminated by medieval ceremonial, during which Cola received not one but six crowns. Five of them were of foliage and symbolized his various achievements. The sixth, which was of silver, and had been zealously watched by the Archbishop of Naples, lest someone make away with it, symbolized the seven gifts of the Holy Ghost,[1] the very gifts which Cola so markedly lacked!

No doubt Cola's antiquarian behaviour made a deep impression in Rome. Even if his career had a miserable end, his example was not forgotten. A century later Stefano Porcari, himself a humanist and antiquarian, tried to make himself a new Cola and ended even more miserably. In fact during the Renaissance an enthusiasm for Antiquity proved a stimulating force behind political conspiracies. But such humanist conspiracies invariably failed, both in the Rome of Pope Nicholas V and in the Milan of the Sforzas.

Cola di Rienzo was not the only Roman of his time who drew inspiration from the ruins of Rome. Another Roman who felt their impact was Giovanni Cavallini dei Cerroni, Canon of Santa Maria Rotonda, i.e. the Pantheon, and 'Scriptor Apostolicus' at the Avignon Curia. Giovanni was enough of a humanist to collate his Valerius Maximus with other manuscripts[2] and to gather information about copies of the Latin classics at Montecassino. His belief that Cicero's *De Republica* and the second Decade of Livy were to be found there, was of course the result of faulty information.[3] With the topography of ancient Rome he was obviously on safer ground; but only up to a point, for his topographical directory was nothing better than a copy of the *Graphia Aurea*, 'que est apud ecclesiam sancte Marie nove de Urbe, quam vidi et legi pluries'.[4]

The archaeological interests of Giovanni Cavallini are mainly to be sought in his *Polistoria*, a work aiming at the exaltation of Roman traditions, written or at any rate completed between 1343 and 1352, and where he supplied details about the gates, hills and regions, of ancient Rome,[5] not so long after the main classical buildings of the city had been represented on the golden

---

[1] P. Piur, *Cola di Rienzo*, (Milano, 1934) 97–113.
[2] Sabbadini, *Le scoperte dei codici latini e greci*, II, 47, n. 19.
[3] *Ibid.* II, 49, n. 29. Billanovich, *Petrarch and the Textual Tradition of Livy*, 169.
[4] Sabbadini, *Le scoperte dei codici latini e greci*, II, 50, n. 43, *Codice topografico della città di Roma*, IV, 27.
[5] *Ibid.* IV, 20–54.

bull of the Emperor Lewis of Bavaria.[1] One would, however, look in vain, despite his use of Livy and medieval sources and records, for any serious step forward from the puerilities of the *Graphia Aurea*. In fact his only significance is that he shows that Petrarch was not the only one in his time to employ literary sources in order to identify ancient remains. As a matter of fact such sources also appear to have been used by Boccaccio, whom Cavallini never met and Petrarch befriended. To a man with Boccaccio's wide humanist interests, it was natural that Antiquity should have exerted its appeal upon him. Yet as a humanist he lagged behind Petrarch. The reason for this was not so much a question of lesser intelligence as of a different temperament and approach. There was also the fact that their upbringings had not been the same. Whereas Petrarch had been brought up in cosmopolitan Avignon, when this town was the acknowledged centre of the Christian and humanist worlds, Boccaccio had been educated in the narrow circle of the Florentine colony in Angevin Naples. Little wonder then, that when Petrarch was busy resurrecting some long forgotten books of Livy, Boccaccio was still flirting with Ovid and the tarnished charms of the *ars dictaminis*. The 'Zibaldone Laurenziano' of Boccaccio, that substantial commonplace book into which he copied anything of particular interest to him, betrays a predilection for just the kind of writings which the new humanism was putting rapidly out of fashion,[2] and is indicative of a wide variety of interests as well as of a self-made culture, with a definite bent for encyclopaedism and a taste for genealogies, both divine and human, in fact the very features which are so conspicuously behind his massive Latin treatises. Boccaccio's great achievement as the rescuer of much of Tacitus and Apuleius must now be handed over to the infinitely less gifted, but steadier Zanobi da Strada.[3] On the other hand, the rôle of Boccaccio in the early humanist study of Greek is just beginning now to appear far greater than had been hitherto suspected.[4]

The appeal of Antiquity was already felt very powerfully by Boccaccio during his Neapolitan youth. Even if Filippo Villani's story about his decision to dedicate himself entirely to poetry

[1] Erben, *op. cit.* pl. III.
[2] See V. Branca, *Tradizione delle opere latine di Giovanni Boccaccio*, I, (Roma, 1958) 201–03.
[3] G. Billanovich, *I primi umanisti e le tradizioni dei classici latini*, (Friburgo, 1953), 30–33.
[4] Pertusi, *Leonzio Pilato fra Petrarca e Boccaccio*, passim, G. Billanovich, 'Il Petrarca e i retori latini minori', *Italia Medioevale e Umanistica*, V (1962) 119–22.

after a visit to the alleged tomb of Virgil at Mergellina,[1] is to be discarded as a fairy tale, his intellectual interests during this period are clear, and are obviously advertised by the subscription 'sub monte Falerno apud busta Maronis Virgilii'[2] in his earliest letters which have reached us. Already by then he had developed an interest in ancient inscriptions. That this was actually so, is testified by his earliest known Latin poem, the so-called elegy for Costanza,[3] which was modelled on the first century A.D. inscription of Claudia Homonoea,[4] fifteen lines of which actually figure in it. There are no details of how Boccaccio came to know this epigraphic text, which later proved so popular with Renaissance humanists. Still, whether he had access to the original stone, or merely to a transcript of it, his use of this inscription is remarkable and certainly explains his later interest in the alleged sepulchral inscription of Livy at Padua.[5] The text of this epitaph was already included by Boccaccio in the lines on Livy, which he wrote in his 'Zibaldone' now at Florence in the Laurentian Library.[6] These very lines were later incorporated by Boccaccio into his abridgement of the Lives of Suetonius. But this time instead of giving the inscription he merely wrote 'ETC.' in its place.[7] Eventually the passage on Livy was re-elaborated by Boccaccio into a short biography of the great historian. By then the authenticity of the epitaph, which Petrarch had never doubted,[8] seemed no longer so certain to him. Hence in the biography the text of the inscription was now followed by the cautionary 'quas [i.e. literas] in suum epytaphium sculptas credunt'.[9]

The epigraphic interests of Boccaccio did not stop at inscriptions in Latin. One in Greek, then at San Felice ad Ema, just outside Florence, also attracted the mind of the man who had done more for Greek studies than any of his Italian contempor-

---

[1] *Philippi Villani Liber de civitatis Florentiae famosis civibus*, ed. G. C. Galletti, (Florentiae, 1847) 17. For Boccaccio as an antiquarian see C. C. Coulter, 'Boccaccio's archaeological knowledge', *American Journal of Archaeology*, XLI (1937) 397–405.

[2] G. Boccaccio, *Opere latine minori*, ed. A. F. Massèra, (Bari, 1928) 110, 114, 124. Throughout his life Boccaccio never lost his interest in Virgil's birthplace, cf. *Ioannis Boccatii ΠΕΡΙ ΓΕΝΕΑΛΟΓΙΑΣ Deorum . . . eiusdem de montium sylvarum . . . et marium nominibus*, (Basileae, 1532) 466, or in Virgil's tomb, cf. *Tutte le opere di Giovanni Boccaccio a cura di Vittore Branca*, I, (Milano, 1967) 377, VI, (Milano, 1965) 44–45, E. Cocchia, 'L'elemento osco nella Campania e la tomba di Virgilio', *Atti della R. Accademia di archeologia, letteratura e belle arti di Napoli*, N.S. IV. 1 (1916) 259–64.

[3] Branca, *Tradizione delle opere latine di Giovanni Boccaccio*, I, 201–29.

[4] *C.I.L.* VI. 2, 12652. [5] *Supra*, 20–21.

[6] Boccaccio, *Opere latine minori*, 369. [7] *Ibid.* 370.

[8] *Supra*, 36. [9] Boccaccio, *Opere latine minori*, 258.

aries. To find that he actually took a copy of it in his Laurentian 'Zibaldone', in a hand trying hard to reproduce the Greek lapidary lettering,[1] does not therefore surprise us. Also of some interest here is his superscription 'Lictere infrascripte reperte sunt apud sanctum Felicem ad emam in quadam marmorea tabula'. A fifteenth century humanist would not have been more careful in furnishing the whereabouts of the original! Perhaps it would be too much if we said that this copy by Boccaccio inaugurates a new era in epigraphical studies. All the same, it is the earliest known copy of a Greek inscription made by a western scholar. To find the next example we must go on to the fifteenth century and the full development of humanism.

The influence of the lettering of inscriptions may be detected in more than one autograph of Boccaccio. His note on Petrarch's coronation in the Laurentian 'Zibaldone',[2] is actually set out as an inscription and written in large capital uncials, while the colophon of his transcript of a Latin version of Aristotle[3] displays a definite attempt to write in the lapidary characters of ancient Roman epitaphs, in a script betraying different writing habits. On the other hand, as in Petrarch so in Boccaccio the study of ancient epitaphs is not apparent in the inscriptions that he himself dictated,[4] which certainly show none of the formulas used in classical epigraphy. This is not surprising, as it was only during the next century that these formulas started to be employed again. What is instead rather strange is Boccaccio's seldom more than lukewarm interest in Rome and its antiquities. It is quite clear that Rome held no great attractions for him. He certainly did not see it in the romantic light in which Petrarch viewed it, and he stated in one of his short stories 'In Roma, la quale come è oggi coda, cosí già fu capo del mondo'.[5] Admittedly in 1372 he confessed in his letter to the logothete of the King of Sicily his sorrow for the decay of the city.[6] But the distance between these sighs, which were of

---

[1] O. Hecker, *Boccaccio-Funde*, (Braunschweig, 1902), pl. XV.

[2] H. Hauvette, 'Note sur les manuscrits autographes de Boccace à la Bibliothèque Laurentienne', *Mélanges d'archéologie et d'histoire*, XIV (1894) pl. II, E. H. Wilkins, 'Boccaccio's Early Tributes to Petrarch', *Speculum*, XXXVIII (1963) pl. I.

[3] Hecker, *op. cit.* pl. VII.

[4] Boccaccio, *Opere latine minori*, 105, Branca, *Tradizione delle opere latine di Giovanni Boccaccio*, I, 231–39.

[5] Boccaccio, *Decameron*, V. 3.

[6] Boccaccio, *Opere latine minori*, 197. Similar laments were uttered by Boccaccio in the *Filocolo*, cf. *Tutte le opere di Giovanni Boccaccio a cura di Vittore Branca*, I, 70–71, and in *De casibus virorum illustrium*, VIII. 17.

course 'de rigueur' at the time, and the lamentations and hopes of Petrarch or Cola di Rienzo, is very considerable. The only relic of a real interest in the monuments of Rome on his part is a list 'De hedifitiis memorandis Urbis Rome secundum fratrem Martinum',[1] which he drew from the chronicle of the unreliable Martinus Polonus and copied into one of his 'Zibaldoni', and admittedly this is not much. One may suppose that during his visits to Rome he looked at the main monuments, but one may equally suppose that the impression they made upon him did not go very deep. Needless to say, he was quite happy to follow the common tradition and regard the pyramid of Cestius as the tomb of Remus.[2] Yet he was not indifferent to classical art and perhaps, like Petrarch, he also assembled a small collection of ancient Roman coins. Certainly their value as historical sources was not lost upon him, as is shown by his *De claris mulieribus*, where the gold, silver and copper coins of Faustina are appealed to as pieces of evidence in his section on that Empress.[3] References to ancient statues and buildings occur in the *Genologia Deorum*. Unfortunately they were drawn from literary sources and either no longer existed in his day, or had never really existed at all. For instance, his description of the temple of Juno at Samos[4] is pure fiction, while it was on Varro that he relied for his mention of a bronze statue of Europa, set up at Tarentum by Pythagoras.[5] Boccaccio certainly had his limitations. Yet if Petrarch, who never taught, proved the greatest of all humanist teachers, in fact the humanist teacher of Europe, Boccaccio was certainly his greatest disciple.

Beside the antiquarian pursuits of Boccaccio, those of his contemporary Fazio degli Uberti pale into utter insignificance. Yet one should not omit to mention this second rate poet here. For in his dreary *Dittamondo*, a poem now known to few and entertaining to none, he not only introduced a personified Rome, whom he makes tell her history from the coming of Noah to Italy right down to the coronation of the Emperor Charles IV in 1355, but he also gave a description of the ancient city,[6] really

---

[1] Biblioteca Nazionale Centrale, Florence, Ms. II, II. 327, f. 88ʳ. One should not, however, forget his descriptions of Rome in the *Filocolo*, cf. *Tutte le opere di Giovanni Boccaccio a cura di Vittore Branca*, I, 615–17, 652–63, and his reference to the Coliseum in his own note on his *Teseida*, II. 20, cf. *ibid*. II. 303, n.

[2] Boccaccio, *Genologia Deorum*, IX, 40.

[3] Boccaccio, *De claris mulieribus*, ch. 96.

[4] Boccaccio, *Genologia Deorum*, IX, Preface.

[5] *Ibid*. II, 62, Varro, De lingua latina, V, 32.

[6] F. degli Uberti, *Dittamondo*, II, xxxi.

hardly more than a versified catalogue of the principal monuments, drawn from Solinus, the *Mirabilia*, and Martinus Polonus.
Naturally it adds nothing to what was already known.

With the generation which followed Petrarch and Boccaccio
new methods started to creep into the study of Antiquity.
Compared to the generations which preceded and followed
them, it was an age of keen and hard-working mediocrities, of
dwarves standing on the shoulders of the giants who had come
before them. Yet they accepted the great inheritance which fell
upon them and, what is more important, were able to transmit
it to their children.

CHAPTER FOUR

THE HEIRS OF PETRARCH

The death of Petrarch in 1374 did not bring humanism to a halt. What instead took place during the two decades which followed was a slowing down in pace, almost a recoil before the swift leap forward that was to come in the early fifteenth century. It was above all at Padua and at Florence that the traditions of Petrarch were carried on by enthusiastic disciples, who had either known or been in touch with him. These traditions also included antiquarian activity, and here during the late fourteenth century Padua was well ahead of Florence. An interest in the tangible relics of the classical world had not been shared by all Petrarch's friends. The insertion of the pseudo-epitaph of Livy in his biographical repertory[1] is for instance the sole archaeological feature which we can associate with Guglielmo da Pastrengo, despite his having been for several decades the leading exponent of humanism in Verona. Similarly with Barbato da Sulmona, the friend to whom Petrarch dedicated his collected epistles in Latin verse, antiquarian interest cannot have been particularly strong. Admittedly, the rise to power of Cola di Rienzo in 1347 brought him to the point of envisaging a return of the ancient Republic with Cola and Petrarch at the head of it.[2] Yet the tract in which he sketched the outlines of his scheme also proves that archaeology had no place among his enthusiasms. But such a lukewarm approach to antiquarian studies was not universal among Petrarch's friends. Boccaccio, as we saw, was far from uninterested in this field, and archaeology was certainly no stranger to some of Petrarch's most gifted admirers of the younger generation.

In the field of antiquarian studies Petrarch's bequest showed itself in more than one way. With Niccolò Beccari of Ferrara it found expression in an interest in ancient numismatics.[3] With Lombardo della Seta, the devoted friend and counsellor of

---

[1] G. Pastregicus, *De originibus rerum libellus*, (Venetiis, 1547) f. 70v.

[2] R. Weiss, 'Barbato da Sulmona, il Petrarca e la rivoluzione di Cola di Rienzo', *Studi Petrarcheschi*, III (1950) 13–22.

[3] H. Helbling, 'Le Lettere di Nicolaus de Beccariis (Niccolò da Ferrara)', *Bullettino dello Istituto Storico Italiano per il Medio Evo e Archivio Muratoriano*, n. 76 (1964) 244–46, 281–83.

Petrarch's old age, as well as literary executor and continuator of the *De viris illustribus*, it manifested itself mainly in a taste for antique art. It was such a taste which prompted him to import into Padua from Florence an ancient statue, unearthed during some digging underneath one of the houses of the Brunelleschi family, a transaction which did not pass unobserved. So much so, that it was still remembered by Ghiberti after Lombardo had been dead for a long time and the statue had been ceded by his son and heir to the ruler of Ferrara.[1] In Padua the interests of Lombardo della Seta were shared by another friend of Petrarch's old age, the physician Giovanni Dondi dell' Orologio, though in him such interests went still further. The dislike of Petrarch for the medical profession is well known and was loudly voiced by him in the *Invective in Medicum*. Yet his fondness for Dondi was as great as his distaste for Dondi's profession. He even went as far as to proclaim him 'princeps medicorum',[2] nor is this really surprising, for Dondi happened to be a humanist as well as a doctor and astronomer. In fact, together with his contemporary Domenico Bandini, he may be said to have inaugurated that very long line of humanist physicians, which culminated in and closed with Giovio and Fracastoro in the sixteenth century. Dondi's humanist activity was somewhat remarkable for his time. His Latin style may have been undistinguished, just as his Italian poetry remained flat and uninspired, but on the other hand, the classics were represented in his library,[3] and it is to him that we owe the rescue of a substantial amount of Latin poetry by the early Paduan humanists and of Boccaccio's biography of Petrarch.[4] Some of Dondi's Latin letters have reached us and naturally throw a light upon his humanist preoccupations. For instance his letter to the friar Guglielmo da Cremona[5] is particularly interesting, for here Dondi made a spirited apologia for the ancients against the moderns. Such a 'querelle des anciens et des modernes' was no novelty in Padua. A century before Dondi wrote, it had been debated in one of Lovato's metrical epistles[6] and, needless to say, it went on being

[1] *Lorenzo Ghibertis Denkwürdigkeiten*, ed. J. von Schlosser, (Berlin, 1912) I, 62, II, 188, n. 2.

[2] V. Bellemo, *Jacopo e Giovanni de' Dondi dell' Orologio*, (Chioggia, 1894) 128.

[3] V. Lazzarini, 'I libri, gli argenti, le vesti di Giovanni Dondi dell' Orologio', *Bollettino del Museo Civico di Padova*, N.S. I (1925) 27–30.

[4] Thanks to his transcript of them, now part of Ms. Lat. XIV. 223 (4340) of the Biblioteca Marciana, Venice.

[5] *Ibid.* ff. 56r–9r.   [6] Weiss, *Lovato Lovati*, 16.

discussed for centuries, long after Dondi was dead and forgotten. Dondi's contribution to the dispute is of interest to us, since, unlike Lovato, he extended it to the sphere of art. Thus we find him pointing out to his correspondent that contemporary artists looked with wonder at antique buildings and sculpture, even going so far as to quote a sculptor he knew, apparently one of the best known at the time, who had declared that the statues and other sculptures which he had seen in Rome were nothing short of a miracle, and that but for their not being animated they would have been far better than living beings.[1]

Such an enthusiasm for antique sculpture was typical of the climate of the time. In Florence, for instance, ancient statuary was by no means rare. Benvenuto da Imola, the commentator on Dante who was active during the second half of the Trecento, noted in a Florentine house one of a type not dissimilar from the Medici Venus.[2] In Siena a statue recently unearthed aroused so much admiration, that it was solemnly placed on the Fonte Gaia in the 'Campo'. It was an admiration from which superstition had not been altogether weeded out. That the statue must have been an ancient idol, was firmly believed. Therefore, it is not surprising in an age when Petrarch himself believed that all the ancient gods were demons[3], that a defeat suffered by the Sienese was promptly seen as a punishment for their idolatry and swiftly followed by a decree of November 7th, 1357, providing for the immediate removal of so dangerous a devil.[4] Much more fortunate was the headless statue of a female, probably a second century A.D. copy of an original of the fourth century B.C., which, after being provided with a new head, was placed in 1368 by order of the lord of the town, the objectionable Cansignorio della Scala, on the top of the fountain then erected in Piazza delle Erbe at Verona,[5] where it can still be seen to-day. The prejudice against ancient statues went on, however, for some time, though humanists might occasionally rise up in their defence. Humanist protests,[6] and

---

[1] Biblioteca Marciana, Venice, Ms. Lat. XIV. 223 (4340) f. 58ᵛ, Prince d'Essling & E. Müntz, *Pétrarque, sés études d'art, son influence sur les artistes*, (Paris, 1902) 45, n. 3.

[2] *Benevenuti de Rambaldis de Imola Comentum super Dantis Aldigherij Comoediam*, III, (Florentiae, 1887) 280.

[3] De Nolhac, *op. cit.* II, 178.

[4] *Lorenzo Ghibertis Denkwürdigkeiten*, I, 62, II, 189, n. 3.

[5] L. Simeoni, *Verona*, (Verona, 1909) 3–4.

[6] *Epistolario di Coluccio Salutati*, ed. F. Novati, III, (Roma, 1896) 285–95, *Epistolario di Pier Paolo Vergerio*, ed. L. Smith, (Roma, 1934) 189–202, V. Zabughin, *Vergilio nel Rinascimento italiano*, I, (Bologna, 1921) 112–13, R. Weiss, *Il primo secolo dell' umanesimo*, (Roma, 1949) 69–70.

loud ones at that, were thus heard in 1397, when Carlo Malatesta
ordered the removal of an ancient statue of Virgil in Mantua,
which he considered the object of a superstitious cult. But then
statues never seem to have been really safe. The destructions by
Reformers and Puritans are too familiar to be recalled here. And
even the so-called age of enlightenment witnessed the destruction
of the 'Regisol' of Pavia and of the statues of Niccolò III and
Borso d' Este at Ferrara, as symbols of tyranny.

The craving of Dondi for Antiquity was to find its greatest
satisfaction during his pilgrimage to Rome in the spring of 1375.
Already on the journey out he had not failed to note the more
striking Roman remains on his way. At Rimini he was impressed
by the bridge built by Tiberius over the Marecchia and took
good care to jot down the first and last words of one of its
inscriptions.[1] The arch of Augustus in the same town also met
with his approval.[2] At Cagli he did not fail to notice the remains
of a Roman bridge,[3] while near Spello he observed the 'Ruine
duarum arenarum parvarum in modum Colixei'.[4] The enthusiasm
of Dondi was, however, bound to reach its highest peaks in
Rome. Here he took copious archaeological notes, which he later
shaped together and copied into the volume where he had
assembled pieces by other humanists, as well as writings of his
own.[5] The result was not, as one might have hoped, an antiquarian itinerary of the town, but rather an account of those
monuments which had caught his eye. Yet if we compare his
with the account in Petrarch's letter to Giovanni Colonna,[6] it is
impossible not to discern a step forward. It is obvious that in
Dondi the pilgrim made way entirely for the antiquarian, so
that one may well wonder how much time he dedicated while in
Rome to the visiting of churches and to pious practices, and how
much to investigating what was left of the pagan city.

While in Rome Dondi did not limit himself to the taking of
notes on the most prominent ancient remains. He also took
measurements of ancient buildings, which was not so surprising
in a man whose library included one of the very few copies of
Vitruvius then in private hands.[7] It is true that these measure-

[1] Biblioteca Marciana, Venice, Ms. Lat. XIV. 223 (4340) f. 45ʳ.
[2] *Ibid.* loc. cit.
[3] *Ibid.* loc. cit.
[4] *Ibid.* loc. cit.
[5] Dondi's account of Rome may be read in *Codice topografico della città di Roma*, IV, 65–73.
[6] *Supra*, 32–33.
[7] Lazzarini, *op. cit.* 27, Ciapponi, *Vitruvio nel primo umanesimo*, 88–93.

ments, taken with very primitive methods, are not conspicuous
for their accuracy. The very fact that he bothered to take them
is, none the less, remarkable and really marks the beginnings of a
new stage in archaeological investigation, just as Petrarch had
marked the earlier stage. As was only befitting to a student of
Vitruvius, he also examined the structure of ancient buildings,
nor did he overlook inscriptions, but actually copied several of
them, trying hard to imitate their lapidary letters in his transcript.[1] Here his keenness proved, however, greater than his
competence, with the inevitable result that his copies proved far
from accurate. He seems to have had qualms about his measurements, to the point that we find him comparing some of them
with those taken by others. For instance for the obelisk of Saint
Peter's he gave not only his own data, but also those secured by
someone else with a very rudimentary instrument and obtained
by Dondi from a priest living near the monument in question,[2]
as well as those available in the chronicle of Martinus Polonus,[3]
of which he doubtless thought more highly than we do to-day.
Needless to say, Dondi also copied the inscriptions on the obelisk,
quoted Suetonius à propos of it, and also gave in his account a
Latin couplet certainly not taken from it, but drawn from a
literary source.[4] The Pantheon was also measured by him;
furthermore he counted its pillars, and naturally copied the
inscription on its front.[5] Measurements of Trajan's column were
also noted down by Dondi, but here he slipped by attributing
this monument to Hadrian despite having copied its inscription.[6]
But then, as was already noted, epigraphy was not one of his
strong points. So that when it came to copying what was written
on the arch of Constantine, he lamented that there were on it
'multe litere sculpte, sed difficiliter leguntur',[7] and mentioned in
connexion with it the *Policraticus* of John of Salisbury.[8] Several
other epigraphic texts were also copied by Dondi.[9] And it is
interesting to note that he saw a moral and political meaning in
the inscription on the Arch of Septimius Severus, to the point

---

[1] Biblioteca Marciana, Venice, Ms. Lat. XIV. 223 (4340) ff. 45r–6v.
[2] *Codice topografico della città di Roma*, IV, 62.
[3] *Ibid.* loc. cit.
[4] *Ibid.* loc. cit.
[5] *Ibid.* IV, 69.
[6] *Ibid.* IV, 70.
[7] *Ibid.* loc. cit.
[8] *Ibid.* loc. cit.
[9] *Ibid.* IV, 71–73. To the late fourteenth century probably belongs the collection of ten
Roman inscriptions in British Museum, Ms. Add. 34, 758, f. 311r–v.

that in one of his letters he exclaimed about it: 'Ecce res publica restituta consiliis propagationi prefertur imperii et insignes viri domi viris foris insignibus, quanquam procul dubio utrumque sit insigne'.[1] Instead in the Coliseum he noted the number of the orders and pillars, observing at the same time that it was 'ad modum arene veronensis cum gradibus'.[2]

With his measurements and notes of architectural detail, Dondi already anticipated the great antiquarians of the fifteenth century. That he was not alone in his time in taking such measurements is, however, known and we also know that instruments, probably astrolabes, were used then for such purpose. As we saw, Dondi himself told us this[3]; but whereas his notes have reached us, those of others, which would have proved just as interesting, if not more so, failed to survive. But let us turn to another aspect of Petrarch's legacy in Padua. In this town his predilection for Roman imperial coins was not lost on those people with whom he was in touch: in fact it ultimately led to a revival of ancient medallions in Padua, just sixteen years after his death. That such a revival took place there and not elsewhere is quite symptomatic, for this was the very place where Petrarch's antiquarian traditions had found a most receptive ground.

A particular event caused the production of the first Renaissance medals. In 1390 Francesco Novello da Carrara, Lord of Padua, had succeeded in expelling the usurping Visconti and re-entering his capital. Here was clearly an occasion not to be forgotten. Hence in order to perpetuate the memory of it, Francesco ordered the striking of some medals on the pattern of the imperial bronze sesterces, showing his bust in the garb of a Roman Emperor. Other pieces represented his father, Francesco the Elder, in similar attire; all these medals show the Carrara badge on the reverse.[4] By the beginning of the fifteenth century at the latest, specimens had even reached France and the collections of the Duke of Berry,[5] while painters and illuminators also seem to have used them as models.[6] In view of their circulation,

[1] J. Morelli, Operette, II, (Venezia, 1820) 302.
[2] Codice topografico della città di Roma, IV, 72.
[3] Supra, 52.
[4] G. F. Hill, A Corpus of Italian Renaissance Medals before Cellini, (London, 1930) nos. 2–4.
[5] J. Guiffrey, Inventaires de Jean Duc de Berry (1401–1416), I, (Paris, 1894) 153.
[6] Bibliothèque Nationale, Paris, Ms. Lat. 14360, f. 207r, L. Rizzoli, 'Ritratti di Francesco il vecchio e Francesco Novello da Carrara', Bollettino del Museo Civico di Padova, N.S. VIII (1932) figs. 30–32.

it is hardly surprising that imitations of them followed. These were made in Venice, where Lorenzo and Marco Sesto, two engravers already working for the Venetian mint in 1394, produced two medals of the Emperor Galba with a personified Venice on the reverse,[1] while later, in 1417, their kinsman Alessandro Sesto, made another with an obverse taken from some regal portrait on a Greek coin and on the reverse a scene which could be either the rape of Proserpine or Perseus rescuing Andromeda.[2] It is unlikely that the Carrara medals or those by the Sesto stimulated the making of the medallions of Constantine and Heraclius, probably executed in Paris in the early fifteenth century.[3] Classical influence is in fact distinctly absent from them, Gothic models appearing instead to be the actual source of their inspiration. All these efforts to resurrect the antique medallions remained without followers for some decades, indeed until Pisanello, whose earliest piece, the medallion of the Greek Emperor John VIII Palaeologus, was made in 1438.[4] On the other hand, the development of antiquarian pursuits continued unbroken. The study of ancient inscriptions as an aid to classical activities found, for instance, a keen adherent in Coluccio Salutati, that is to say the humanist who, more than any other, may be considered the continuer of the traditions of Petrarch.

The spiritual heir of the great master who never taught, Coluccio Salutati, never taught either; yet more than anyone else he was the teacher of fifteenth century Florentine humanism. Next to Petrarch, he was undoubtedly the greatest scholar of his century as well as its most influential humanist figure. Behind Poggio and Leonardo Bruni, Palla Strozzi and Vergerio, behind the coming of Emanuel Chrysoloras to Florence to teach Greek to Italy, there stands Coluccio Salutati, who was also the very link between Petrarch and the new humanism. Far superior to Boccaccio as a scholar, he was just as much inferior to him in natural ability: Coluccio's *De laboribus Herculis* has everything that may be found in the *Genologia Deorum* except Boccaccio's genius. Antique art does not seem to have ranked among Coluccio's interests, although classical statuary was certainly

---

[1] Hill, *A Corpus of Italian Renaissance Medals before Cellini*, nos. 10–11.
[2] *Ibid.* no. 12.
[3] R. Weiss, 'The Medieval Medallions of Constantine and Heraclius', *Numismatic Chronicle*, ser. 7, III (1963) 129–44.
[4] On which see R. Weiss, *Pisanello's Medallion of the Emperor John VIII Palaeologus*, (London, 1966).

THE HEIRS OF PETRARCH

available in Florence in his time. Instead his tastes were definitely literary and philological, ranging from a warm interest in Greek, which he never quite mastered himself (though he saw to it that others did),[1] to an overwhelming passion for Latin orthography, at a time when very few, if any, gave a thought to correct spelling. It was this passion which drove him to study ancient inscriptions, in order to make certain how to write accurately some Latin words. A letter to Domenico Bandini written probably on 21 July 1403, shows Salutati at work in this field. Bandini had asked him about the ancient name of Città di Castello, the ancient Tifernum, whereupon Salutati started at once to do research on the correct spelling of the town's Latin name. The consultation of twenty manuscripts of St. Gregory's *Moralia*, where the town happened to be mentioned, provided no positive answer.[2] In the end, however, Salutati told his correspondent that he had succeeded in obtaining the copy of an ancient inscription, then preserved in the house of the cathedral canons at Città di Castello, showing that 'Tifernum' should be spelled with an *i* and not with a *y*.[3] Considering the importance he attached to epigraphy, it causes no surprise to find upon Poggio's departure for Rome in 1403, Salutati beseeching him to send copies of ancient inscriptions. Such a desire did not remain unsatisfied, since soon Poggio forwarded to him a small collection of epigraphic texts, which he himself had copied from the originals.[4]

Among the humanists of Salutati's circle, the physician Domenico Bandini of Arezzo may have found some attraction in ancient remains. Yet if this was so, it was not shown in his massive encyclopaedia except for a very few hints. It is true that he says in it when mentioning Luni, the ancient Luna, then already a sad ruin, that 'huius situm vidi cum ad Urbanum sextum ratione curie christiane que fidei summum pontificem Ianuam professus, ubi erat, adii',[5] that he also hints at archaeological visits elsewhere[6] and that he said of Tarquinia 'hactenus

[1] R. Weiss, 'Gli studi greci di Coluccio Salutati', *Miscellanea in onore di Roberto Cessi*, I, (Roma, 1958) 349–56, B. L. Ullman, *The Humanism of Coluccio Salutati*, (Padova, 1963) 118–23.

[2] *Epistolario di Coluccio Salutati*, III, 625, Ullman, *The Humanism of Coluccio Salutati*, 102–03.

[3] *Epistolario di Coluccio Salutati*, III, 627, Ullman, *The Humanism of Coluccio Salutati*, 103.

[4] *Epistolario di Coluccio Salutati*, III, 655.

[5] Lambeth Palace Library, Ms. 35, f. 301r.

[6] *Ibid.* ff. 215v, 287v, T. Hankey, 'Domenico di Bandino of Arezzo', *Italian Studies*, XII (1957) 121, n. 50.

fuerat magna civitas et potens et gloriosa, nunc vero nil preter simplex nomen ac ruinas ostenditur'.[1] Whether he actually visited Tarquinia is by no means certain, and the fact that his section on Rome makes no mention of its monuments[2] shows that his real interests lay elsewhere. Very different here was the attitude of another member of Salutati's circle, Pier Paolo Vergerio, who from the Padua of the Carraresi had moved to Florence to study Greek at the feet of Emanuel Chrysoloras. It was perhaps under the stimulus of the writings of Petrarch, whose *Africa* he edited and whose biography he wrote, that Vergerio turned his attention to the ruins of classical Rome with enthusiasm. The description of Rome, which he incorporated in a letter to a friend written probably early in 1398,[3] is really a diary of the impressions of his first visit to the city. But what perhaps struck him most here was the sacred side, the Christian capital in short, with its relics and churches and the Papal Curia, so that the earlier part of the epistle is hardly more than a description of the 'Stationes Urbis'. His account of the monuments seems, from what he says, to have been made in fulfilment of a promise. All the same, his interest in them is undeniable. It was because of this interest that he sought while in Rome to establish contacts with people who could enlighten him about the ruins. Such people, he regretfully found, turned out to be extremely few and, if this was not enough, his difficulties were increased by the current dialectal nomenclature of so many monuments, as well as the obviously unreliable legends connected with them. Eventually, however, he was able to contact those men and thanks to this he was able for instance to disprove the traditional identification of the pyramid of Cestius with the tomb of Remus and say 'sed qui litteras marmoribus inscriptas legerunt, id negant, quas nunc difficillimum est legere propter arbusta que inter marmorum commissuras oborta sunt'.[4] Unfortunately he does not tell us who were those who had read the inscription, though one may suspect here Francesco da Fiano or someone from his circle. It is true that to Vergerio the Pantheon was still the temple of Cybele, which after all was the traditional view. On the whole, however, he is not too inaccurate and doubtless he was genuinely impressed by what he saw. What also struck him in

[1] Lambeth Palace Library, Ms. 35, f. 312ʳ.
[2] *Ibid.* ff. 307ᵛ–08ᵛ.
[3] *Epistolario di Pier Paolo Vergerio*, 211–20.
[4] *Ibid.* 218.

ancient Rome was the sea of ruins extending everywhere which, more than anything else, brought home to him the ancient greatness of the city. The destruction of ancient marbles and other remains was then in full swing, a sight which made him regret deeply such vandalism, as well as wonder at so much being still left in spite of it.

In expressing such regret Vergerio's voice was by no means the proverbial voice in the wilderness. That of Francesco da Fiano sounded even more loudly, as only was to be expected from the greatest exponent of Roman humanism in the age of the Great Schism. Chancellor of the City of Rome (nowadays we would call him town clerk), Francesco had a deep love for the ancient ruins, only matched by his devotion to classical Latin poetry. At a time when this poetry was being attacked as pagan, he had risen fiercely in its defence in an outspoken invective.[1] Francesco's poetic remains need not detain us here, except for noting that his 'tituli' in Latin hexameters, placed under the frescoes of famous men at Foligno in the Trinci Palace, were long believed to be antique.[2] What matters to us here is his approach to the Roman ruins. For these his feeling went far deeper than those of Dondi and Vergerio. His was a really deep love, which drove him among other things to act as an enthusiastic guide to younger scholars visiting them,[3] and behind which stood his almost religious attitude to any remains of the old Roman world, whether in stone or in writing. Naturally his feelings for the daily destructions could not have been stronger. His pupil Cencio Rustici knew therefore to whom to appeal, when he wrote to him in 1416 from the Council of Constance, asking him to compose an invective against the destroyers of ancient remains.[4] Whether Francesco acceded to such a request, is not known; certainly such an invective is not among his extant writings. The letter of Cencio is, however, also illuminating as showing the feelings of the ordinary layman on the subject, as it informs us that the destroyers of ancient statues justified themselves by holding that they were putting out of the way the idols of false

---

[1] I. Taù, 'Il "Contra oblocutores et detractores Poetarum" di Francesco da Fiano', *Archivio Italiano per la storia della pietà*, IV (1964) 255–350.

[2] A. Messini, 'Documenti per la storia del Palazzo Trinci di Foligno', *Rivista d'arte*, XXIV (1942) 84–98, L. Bertalot, 'Humanistisches in der Anthologia Latina', *Rheinisches Museum*, LXVI (1911) 64–77.

[3] H. Baron, *The Crisis of the Early Renaissance*, II, (Princeton, 1955) 403–04.

[4] L. Bertalot, 'Cincius Romanus und seine Briefe', *Quellen und Forschungen aus italienischen Archiven und Bibliotheken*, XXI (1929–30) 222–25.

gods. Their action was that of bigoted persons who saw in them a danger to religion. The actual truth was, however, more materialistic than Cencio envisaged. Admittedly there were then, as there have always been in every time, fanatics to whom art and beauty meant nothing. But, on the whole, one can say that behind those destructions was the profit motive. It was clearly a case where piety paid dividends. The invective of Cencio does not even spare the Popes, who had been entrusted with these ruins. His voice was the voice of humanism crying against bigotry and greed. It grew louder and louder in defence of what remained of old Rome as the Renaissance advanced, but remained powerless to the end.

CHAPTER FIVE

THE RUINS OF ROME AND THE HUMANISTS

During the fifteenth century the ruins of Rome began to be noticed with new eyes, the eyes of humanism. The swift development of classical studies, so much like that of science to-day, brought about new methods and aroused fresh enthusiasms. A new critical approach, which found in Valla its greatest exponent, led to the waning of the *Mirabilia* and their legends, which were eventually relegated to the limbo of popular literature, as reading fit for semi-literate pilgrims, but hardly worthy of serious attention. The ancient monuments started to appear in a different light and were now studied in a novel way, while new problems were formulated and new answers sought. What was behind all this was the new humanism, which manifested itself more or less simultaneously in philological and archaeological science, in the *Elegantiae* of Valla and the *Roma instaurata* of Biondo. No wonder then, that in fifteenth century Italy the greatest names in archaeology, Poggio, Alberti, Biondo, Leto, were also among the greatest of humanism.

During the first half of the fifteenth century humanism became a leading force in Italian intellectual life—a leading force but not the only one, as former influences were far from extinct. In Italy, scholasticism was by no means liquidated, and at the universities the new ideas did not condition every academic activity. Admittedly at Florence and Ferrara the local universities had shown no resistance to the impact of humanism. But elsewhere, at Padua, Bologna, Pavia, as well as at other places, it was a different story, leading often to some kind of peaceful co-existence. In fact, until the end of the sixteenth century the general outlook of Italian, indeed of European universities, remained quite medieval. Though separated in religion by the Reformation, the academic world from Naples to Cambridge and from Salamanca to Erfurt stood firmly united by Aristotle. But the study of Antiquity in the Quattrocento had changed quite unrecognizably from the preceding century. With humanism's coming of age the number of those who felt the lure of antiquarian activity became considerably larger than hitherto, though not perhaps as large as one might be led at first to think. Hence the copying of an ancient inscription, the relying upon an old coin for historical evidence, the description of some old remains, all these and other similar activities have no longer in themselves the exceptional significance which they would have had in earlier times. For instance descriptions of Rome such as those by Giovanni Rucellai or Nikolaus Muffel, are practically valueless when regarded as expressions of Renaissance anti-quarianism. They may have some significance as instances of lay interest in the antique, but that is about all. Keenness and enthusiasm alone were no longer enough to leave a mark in an age when even genius was not extremely scarce. Needless to say, not every fifteenth and early sixteenth century antiquarian of any note was a genius; for this was certainly not so. Biondo and Alberti undoubtedly were geniuses; Albertini and Fulvio were certainly not: and yet any account of archaeological studies during the Renaissance would be incomplete without any mention of them.

A survey of such studies during this period could not be possibly drawn on the lines followed in the preceding chapters of this book. To lump together every kind of antiquarian pursuit would be no longer convenient in view of the swift expansion of so many aspects of archaeology. The best line to adopt seems instead to consider these various aspects separately. As a result the same individual may occasionally appear in more than one section. Poggio, for instance, figures prominently in this chapter; but he reappears in that on epigraphy and is also mentioned among the early collectors of ancient statuary. Flavio Biondo comes also in this chapter; he also appears later as the author of the *Italia illustrata*.

The return of the Papacy to Rome did not put an end to its desolation. Throughout the long years of the Great Schism urban conditions did not rise from the level to which they had sunk during the absence of the Curia at Avignon, and only under Eugenius IV (1431–1447) the first signs of the Renaissance began to be really noticeable in the town. Yet already in the latter days of the Schism the study of the Roman ruins had started to undergo some change, though it is much too early to speak at this stage of definite innovations in this field. Medieval tradition was too ingrained to vanish overnight. Some progress is never-theless already noticeable in the *Tractatus de rebus antiquis et situ*

Urbis Romae,[1] this being the text usually referred to as the 'Anonymus Maliabechianus' from the present location of one of its manuscript copies. The *Tractatus* still relies very much on the old *Mirabilia*. Its scheme remains that of the old handbook; it is in fact little more than a topographical catalogue, in which the remains of ancient Rome are grouped together according to their nature. Yet the author betrays also a preoccupation to show the reader how to find the various remains, which he does by indicating their current names or the church near to which they stood. For those monuments which were no longer extant he also relied, whenever possible, on knowledge not necessarily drawn from literary sources. Thus about the arch once standing under the bell-tower of the church of Saints Celsus and Julianus, he informs us that it can no longer be seen 'quia cecidit tempore Urbani Quinti'[2], while in connexion with the arch of Theodosius and Valentinian, he notes that 'de quo epitaphium diruptum est: tamen archus est sanus sed non marmoreus'.[3] The inscriptions on the arches and the columns appear to have interested him in particular, though he had a flair for only half understanding them, and he particularly relied on inscriptions for purposes of identification. He was doubtless an enthusiast, quite aware that some of the Roman clergy disapproved of his pursuits: 'Ad Sanctam Crucem in Iherusalem fuit templum Veneris et Cupidinis, de quibus templis non licet me aliter dicere nec largius extendere, quia non esset dominis presbyteris grata ostensio' he wrote, adding, however, 'sed legentes Ovidium de Fastis possent me habere excusatum, in suo volumine tractantem ad plenum',[4] a useful tip no doubt for the humanistic reader.

Needless to say, mistakes of fact are not uncommon in the *Tractatus*, while critical sense is unfortunately only conspicuous by its absence. Not only are many of the errors of the *Mirabilia* repeated in it but, furthermore, whenever the anonymous author reaches an independent interpretation, the odds are that he is wrong. To him—and this is not really surprising—the Pantheon is still the temple of Cybele[5]; as for the Septizonium, he has a brief discussion on it in view of conflicting opinions on the

---

[1] *Codice topografico della città di Roma*, IV, 110–50.
[2] *Ibid.* IV, 117.
[3] *Ibid.* loc. cit.
[4] *Ibid.* IV, 146.
[5] *Ibid.* IV, 139.

subject: 'Ad septem solia fuit sedes omnium septem scientiarum, posito quod aliqui velint dicere templum Solis fuisse, vel domum Severi Afri: sed derivatio sua est septem viarum, idest septem omnium scientiarum domus: et sic creditur et affirmatur per diaconum Aquilegiensem'.[1] He and this deacon, whoever he was,[2] could scarcely have been wider off the mark.

What do we know about this anonymous author? He was certainly writing in the days of the Antipope John XXIII and very probably in 1411.[3] Quite clearly he was a man of some learning, in fact enough of a humanist not to bother with churches and relics and only too ready to jettison the less plausible, if more picturesque, legends of the *Mirabilia*, yet not so fastidious a scholar as to scorn the popular nomenclature of many of the monuments. This was fortunate; for many of these popular names would not have reached us but for his record of them. To a few years after the *Tractatus*, which was incidentally only part of a larger historical compilation starting with the creation of the world and extending as far as Pope Martin V (1417–1431), belongs the account of Rome prefixed by Nicola Signorili, a Roman municipal official, to his collection of inscriptions.[4] This account is, however, still entirely dependent on medieval sources, namely the *Mirabilia* and the chronicle of Martinus Polonus, and is really devoid of any real significance. What is important is Signorili's rôle as an epigraphist, but this will be considered later.[5]

Neither the author of the *Tractatus* nor Signorili reached the new approach to Antiquity which started in their lifetimes. Who actually initiated it, who really began to scrutinize and examine the old remains in a new way, in order to discover their nature, their building techniques, the rules followed by their makers, their meaning, is difficult to say now. If we were to believe what we are told by Antonio Manetti in his life of Brunelleschi, one might link this new approach not with a literary-minded humanist, but with the activities of Brunelleschi and Donatello in Rome

[1] *Ibid*. IV, 146.

[2] Was this 'deacon' the Milanese Giovanni Crivelli, Archdeacon of Aquileia, who died in 1433 and was buried in the Aracoeli, where his marble slab by Donatello is still visible?

[3] *Codice topografico della città di Roma*, IV, 101. It is interesting to note that during his stay in Rome in 1411 Emanuel Chrysoloras was particularly impressed by the reliefs on the arches and pillars, since he thought that these enabled one to visualize life and historical events in ancient times, cf. J. P. Migne, *Patrologia Graeca*, CLVI, (Lutetiae Parisiorum, 1866) 24–29.

[4] *Codice topografico della città di Roma*. IV, 166–69.

[5] *Infra*, 146.

during the earliest years of the century. According to Manetti,[1] here these two artists spent their time among the ancient ruins, busy investigating the architectural and structural problems presented by them. Unfortunately this joint Roman sojourn does not seem to have taken place. Yet Brunelleschi's command of ancient Roman architecture and Donatello's mastery of the antique presuppose a painstaking study of what was left of ancient Rome; so though Manetti's details may be inaccurate, what he says may yet be substantially true, thus leaving open the question whether they were really responsible for launching the new approach. What one can, on the other hand, say with certainty, is that such an approach was already to be found in the Roman Curia under Pope Martin V.

It was in such circles that the antiquarian tastes of Poggio Bracciolini developed. He was a humanist by disposition and a papal secretary by necessity, who having first joined the papal chancery as early as 1403, had shared to the full the squalors of the Curia in the later years of the Great Schism and had fully tasted the 'miseria curialium'. And with the Curia he had moved to the Council of Constance (1414–1417), where his duties were easy enough to permit him to discover many classical Latin texts that had been out of circulation since Carolingian times. To Rome Poggio returned only in 1423, after four unhappy years in an England which had no use for his humanism,[2] and once there he swiftly made up for the time wasted on our side of the Channel. Poggio's first antiquarian steps were apparently in the field of epigraphy.[3] But he had also very much of a taste for ancient ruins and was clearly a devotee of what still remained of ancient Rome. Some of his extant letters to Niccolò Niccoli record in fact visits to old ruins at Ferentino, Alatri, and Grottaferrata.[4] What, however, attracted him most were the visible remains of Rome itself. It is not surprising then, that in Rome he visited the ruins thoroughly and methodically together with his friend and colleague, the humanist Antonio Loschi; the outcome of such excursions was a description of what still remained from the ancient days in the first book of his De varietate fortunae,[5] a

[1] A. Manetti, *Vita di Filippo di ser Brunellesco*, ed. E. Toesca, (Firenze, 1927) 20; G. Vasari, *Le vite de' più eccellenti pittori, scultori ed architettori*, ed. G. Milanesi, II, (Firenze, 1878) 337–39.
[2] R. Weiss, *Humanism in England during the Fifteenth Century*, 3rd ed. (Oxford, 1967) 13–21.
[3] *Infra*, 147.
[4] *Poggii Epistolae*, ed. T. de Tonellis, I, (Florentiae, 1832) 219, 221, 324–25.
[5] Poggius Bracciolinus, *De varietate fortunae*, ed. D. Georgius, (Lutetiae Parisiorum, 1723) 5–25; *Codice topografico della città di Roma*, IV, 230–45.

Latin treatise supplying a humanist version of a typically medieval theme.

Begun shortly after the death of Pope Martin in 1431, the *De varietate fortunae* was released by Poggio only in 1448, when he dedicated it to Pope Nicholas V.[1]   Now the ruins of Rome were a leading example of the instability of fortune, and as such they were assigned pride of place in the treatise.   Just as Gibbon some three centuries later started his main work under the inspiration of Rome's ruins, so Poggio launched his own book with a long description of them.   As an account of what was still left it is important because it is by Poggio and because it definitely breaks upon new ground.   With Poggio archaeology assumed a new complexion; for he was not satisfied with merely giving a description of what he saw.   Instead he chose to question and seek answers from the old remains, scrutinise their structures and secure as much guidance as possible from written sources.   Among them he found particularly rewarding some of those texts which had re-appeared only lately thanks to his own efforts.   We see him turning more than once to the history of Ammianus Marcellinus, that is to say one of his 'trouvailles' at Fulda during his Constance days,[2] while for the Roman aqueducts he naturally found invaluable the handbook by Frontinus, rescued by him at Montecassino.[3]   Moreover he extended the range of his authorities by including among them also some Greek writers, such as Dionysius of Halicarnassus and Aelius Aristides, whom he seems to have confused with Libanius.[4]

The ancient gates of Rome seem to have had an especial interest for Poggio, so that his account of them is particularly illuminating to us.   For here we find him distinguishing between building materials of different ages and relying also on the epigraphic evidence, in order to reach conclusions about dating the gates.   This interest also extended to the so-called Servian walls; yet despite his keenness he failed to trace their original circuit.   The walls of Aurelian were particularly studied by him,[5] and he noticed in them various building techniques, and con-

---

[1] *Ibid.* IV, 224.
[2] N. Rubinstein, 'An unknown letter by Iacopo di Poggio Bracciolini on discoveries of classical texts', *Italia Medioevale e Umanistica*, I (1958) 389, n. 1.
[3] Sabbadini, *Le scoperte dei codici latini e greci*, I, 85, 88.
[4] *Codice topografico della città di Roma*, IV, 231.
[5] *Ibid.* IV, 245.

cluded that more than one architect had worked on them. When facing the pyramid of Cestius he wondered how Petrarch could have believed it to be the tomb of Remus, when the inscription on it clearly indicated otherwise, charitably, adding, however, that perhaps it was hidden by vegetation when Petrarch saw it.[1] Coins were not used by Poggio as an aid to archaeology. For this we must turn to his contemporary Biondo. Despite his humanist prejudice against 'media et infima latinitas', Poggio did not hesitate to rely on the *Liber Pontificalis* in order to locate the Baths of Domitian,[2] just as he sought the guidance of the *Acta Martyrum* to Diocletian's.[3] He was also well aware that hieroglyphs were the form of writing employed by the ancient Egyptians and said so[4] when he spoke of Rome's obelisks.

As an antiquarian Poggio could not be infallible nor was he. But his frequent inaccuracies are no longer the absurdities of former writers. Thus on the one hand we find him identifying the Basilica of Constantine with the Templum Pacis,[5] an error in which he was followed by many other Renaissance antiquarians; on the other, it is refreshing to see him no longer believing that the equestrian statue of Marcus Aurelius, then still at the Lateran, represented Constantine, though he was still wide of the mark in suggesting Septimius Severus.[6] Similarly we can quite forgive him for calling the little round temple by the Tiber not far from Santa Maria in Cosmedin, the temple of Vesta,[7] when picture postcards still tell us so nowadays! Quite naturally he also deplored the relentless destruction of ancient ruins which was proceeding, and à propos of this he recorded sadly how 'Capitolio contigua, forum versus, superest porticus aedis Concordiae, quam, cum primum ad urbem accessi, vidi ferme integram, opere marmoreo admodum specioso; Romani postmodum, ad calcem, aedem totam et porticus partem, disiectis columnis, sunt demoliti'.[8] He cannot have hoped that his laments would make any difference. Still he felt that a protest should be made. To remain silent would have been a betrayal

[1] *Ibid.* IV, 233.
[2] *Ibid.* IV, 236. Poggio himself was the author of some lives of Popes, cf. C. Da Capodimonte, 'Poggio Bracciolini autore delle anonime 'Vitae Quorumdam Pontificum', *Rivista di storia della Chiesa in Italia*, XIV (1960) 27–47.
[3] *Codice topografico della città di Roma*, IV, 237.
[4] *Ibid.* IV, 240.
[5] *Ibid.* IV, 234.
[6] *Ibid.* IV, 241.
[7] *Ibid.* IV, 234.
[8] *Ibid.* IV, 235.

of his beliefs, and of this he would not be guilty.

The enthusiasm behind Poggio's account of ancient Rome is typical of the new humanism. It was a new attitude and appreciation and, above all, a new understanding of Antiquity, which led both to the liquidation of the *Mirabilia* and to the readiness to make use of all the sources available. At the same time we cannot say that Poggio's investigations were methodical and systematic, for it is abundantly clear that they were not so, though it is only fair to remember that his aim was not a scientific description of the old town, but rather a bird's-eye view of its remains, drawn to illustrate a moral.[1] To find a more methodical account we must turn to the *Roma instaurata* of Flavio Biondo.

Biondo too was a curial official as well as a humanist. It is no exaggeration to say that as a scholar he revolutionised every field he touched. As a historian he was the first to devise a general history of Italy, showing a continuity since the fifth century, and to conceive a 'media aetas' standing between Antiquity and his own times.[2] Already in papal employment by 1433, he became an apostolic secretary in 1434, and at the Curia he spent most of his life. The exceptional powers of Biondo are already evident in his *De verbis Romanae locutionis*[3] written in 1435, where he put forward his ideas on the everyday speech of ancient Rome. What actually fascinated him most in the Roman past were the old ruins of the town, and on these he quickly made himself a leading authority. So much so, that even before completing his archaeological handbook he was often consulted on problems about the Roman remains.[4] They were irresistibly attractive to him, not only because he found their appearance pleasing, but also as he saw in them a tangible proof, the still living part of the city's ancient glory. With this there was, moreover, a conviction that to abandon these relics now would have been tantamount to forsaking, indeed losing for ever, what had been Roman civilization. Devotion to ancient Rome and its remains was second only to religion, and to this he also felt

[1] When Poggio finally released his *De varietate fortunae* in 1448, Biondo's *Roma instaurata* had been available for more than one year. It is therefore not surprising that Poggio drew from it before submitting his work to Pope Nicholas V, cf. M. Fubini, *Biondo Flavio*, (Roma, 1966, offprint from his forthcoming article in *Dizionario Biografico degli Italiani*) 14–15.

[2] On Biondo as a medieval historian see now D. Hay, 'Flavio Biondo and the Middle Ages', *Proceedings of the British Academy*, XLV (1958) 97–108. For his antiquarian studies see R. Weiss, 'Biondo Flavio archeologo', *Studi Romagnoli*, XIV (1963) 335–41.

[3] B. Nogara, *Scritti inediti e rari di Biondo Flavio*, (Roma, 1927) 115–30.

[4] F. Blondus, *Romae instauratae libri I–III*, III, 72, 74, 76.

grateful since he believed that Christianity had prevented the old glory from fading altogether. To see, but above all to show to others, what classical Rome had been, was in his view imperative. And what could achieve this better than an account of its site and origins together with an explanation of the functions of many of its monuments and buildings? A reconstruction of the ancient city was in short what Biondo had in mind. Now in order to fulfil such a programme the most essential thing was to gather as much information as possible from the ruins themselves. This Biondo did, but it was clearly not enough. Accordingly he sought evidence from every quarter and source available to him. He consulted the Latin classics, he studied Plutarch and examined carefully the catalogues of the regions of Rome compiled in the age of Constantine. He was too sharp to overlook the fact that Christian and medieval writers had also something to contribute. So Bede too and the dialogues of Saint Gregory, St. Damasus's life of Saint Peter, the *Acta Martyrum* and the *Liber Pontificalis* were studied by Biondo, who did not even disdain the *Graphia aurea* or the chronicle of Martinus Polonus. He did not fail to gauge the significance of ancient building materials. For instance the examination of some large bricks from the ruins around the monastery of San Silvestro in Capite bearing Domitian's name, led him to conjecture that those remains must have belonged either to the baths or to the 'naumachia' of this Emperor.[1] His use of inscriptions proved equally rewarding. For instance one on the actual site and another in the Lateran hospital led him to discover the names of the Emperors responsible for the building of an aqueduct.[2] Nor did he ignore the evidence offered by an old coin or by the carved marble figure on a monument. He perceived the historical potentialities of the popular nomenclature of buildings still in use, and he did not even neglect the archives of churches in his quest for information. Thus we find him establishing on the information supplied by a medieval document found by him in the church of the Santi Apostoli, that a 'hortus Veneris' stood near the Capitol and quite close to the parish boundaries of this church.[3]

To say that Biondo grieved at the daily annihilation of ancient monuments is to state the obvious. But one feels that with him the sense of loss thus brought about went deeper than

---

[1] *Ibid.* II, 12.   [2] *Ibid.* I, 78–79.   [3] *Ibid.* II, 79.

with others; it is no exaggeration to say that one can still feel his
wrath when he relates how he saw some old marbles on the
Aventine being pulled down and swiftly turned into quicklime.[1]
Such destructions certainly embittered Biondo's sojourn in
Rome, just as he could not avoid being shocked by the almost
universal ignorance around him concerning what remained of
the republican and imperial ages. With the names of so many
of the monuments camouflaged by popular usage, it was the
more surprising that a few of them could still be recognized for
what they were. What should be done in view of such a danger
was therefore quite clear, just as it was quite clear that some
action should be taken before even the memory of the monuments vanished altogether.

Biondo's description of ancient Rome conformed to a set
plan. Here his main guide was the catalogue of the urban
regions then attributed to Sextus Rufus, which enjoyed such a
success with fifteenth century archaeologists, and which to him
proved quite invaluable. Love for the past did not, however,
blind him to the new Rome which was rising around him. His
feeling, or perhaps we had better say his love for the city, was
wide enough to include also the Christian side and even some of
the modern monuments, such as Filarete's bronze door of Saint
Peter's,[2] and found its culmination later in the final pages of his
Romae triumphantis libri, where he established a parallel between
the ancient and modern constitutions of the city, and revealed his
warm admiration for the Renaissance town under his eyes.

To offer a vision of ancient Rome was the aim of the Roma
instaurata. Started shortly after Biondo's return to Rome
together with the Curia after nearly ten years of absence, it was
actually composed during the period 1444-46. Poggio may have
begun humanist archaeology, but with Biondo archaeology
took a great step forward, and it was only with the second
edition of Marliani's handbook on Roman topography in 1544,
that Biondo's work was finally superseded. What one may well
ask, made Biondo's work so supreme in its field not only
during his time but also for those next hundred years, which
witnessed the full development of humanism? There was of
course Biondo's deep learning and his burning enthusiasm for
his subject. These were things which naturally counted; but
what made his survey unique in fifteenth century archaeological

[1] *Ibid.* I, 20.   [2] *Ibid.* I, 58.

literature was the quality of the mind behind it, which united to a quickness in grasping what was essential, an uncanny ability to perceive new avenues and unforeseen potentialities in whatever subject he happened to tackle. Admittedly even Biondo was not infallible and mistakes of fact occur in his work. For instance he still accepted the traditional attribution to Pheidias and Praxiteles of the Quirinal Dioscuri[1], a thing perhaps not surprising in someone who had probably never seen an original piece of Greek statuary. But the number of his inaccuracies is certainly small when compared to those of his contemporaries and successors in the field, and the really surprising thing is that he did not make more. In a way he was in archaeology what Valla was in philology, but with the difference that while by 1480 Valla's philology was already outdated, it took a century to make Biondo's archaeology obsolete.

The first book of the *Roma instaurata* starts by dealing with the various gates of the town, whence Biondo proceeds to examine the Vatican region and its pagan and Christian monuments. Needless to say he did not fail to mention here the Vatican obelisk, then still standing on the south side of the basilica, from which it was only removed to the centre of the square by Sixtus V. This obelisk led to a discourse about the other obelisks lying about Rome, and book one ends with an account of the Esquiline and Diocletian's baths. Book two starts with a dissertation on ancient baths. Next he deals with monuments on the Esquiline and the Viminal; there follows an excursus on four localities generally grouped together by the ancients, namely the Carinae, Subura, Tabernola and Via Sacra, to conclude with an account of religious and administrative monuments and the theatres. Amphitheatres and circuses open book three, the rest of which is occupied by descriptions of miscellaneous remains.

As was said before, the *Roma instaurata* launched a new archaeology. No one before Biondo had attempted so comprehensive and thorough a survey of ancient Rome nor tried to explain so much nor did it so acutely. Digressions are by no means rare in Biondo's treatise and some of them are really short dissertations on some antiquarian point. His section on the 'Velabrum',[2] for instance, strives to explain this rather

[1] *Ibid.* I, 99.
[2] *Ibid.* II, 52–55.

obscure name. This he starts to do by rejecting the medieval corruption 'velum aureum', whence he passes on to examine and discuss the evidence offered by Varro, Ovid, Livy, Tacitus, and the inscriptions still left in the locality. The whereabouts of the 'Aerarium' gave him an excuse for a historical dissertation on Roman coinage, mainly drawn from the Elder Pliny.[1] Naturally enough Biondo relied constantly upon the ancient writers, but this did not mean that he accepted them invariably as infallible witnesses. Thus when faced with a statement of Cassiodorus that Pompey had been the first builder of theatres in Rome, he set against it one of Pliny, saying that the first had been Marcus Scaurus,[2] while against another remark of Cassiodorus, attributing to the Emperor Titus the building of the first amphitheatre in Rome, he set a passage of Tacitus, showing that this was not so.[3]

Altogether, with the *Roma instaurata* it was now possible to have a reasonable idea of ancient Rome, not only from a topographical standpoint, but also as far as its growth and the functions of its buildings were concerned. Here, in this work, the historian reveals himself side by side with the archaeologist, the student of ancient institutions with the humanist who has the classics at his fingertips, though without the help of the Teubner series and Pauly-Wissowa's encyclopaedia. No wonder then, that after the *Roma instaurata*, the description of Rome by Giovanni Tortelli does not show any real progress. But, even apart from the fact that Tortelli did not mean to present a systematic description of what remained as Biondo had done, what really distinguishes them is Biondo's genius.

Giovanni Tortelli was also a curial official, who eventually became the chief adviser of Pope Nicholas V (1447-1455) in the building up of the Vatican Library. A couple of years in the Greek East (1435-37) had consolidated his Greek, an asset which proved invaluable to him when composing his huge *De orthographia*. But already in 1438, while at Ferrara for the Council, it had enabled him to translate into Latin the *Vita Romuli* of Plutarch,[4] a text which turned out to be very useful to him when dealing with Roman antiquities. Tortelli's account of

---

[1] *Ibid.* II, 83-87.
[2] *Ibid.* II, 103.
[3] *Ibid.* III, 2.
[4] G. Mancini, 'Giovanni Tortelli co-operatore di Niccolò V nel fondare la Biblioteca Vaticana', *Archivio storico italiano*, ser. 6, XVI (1920) 180.

ancient Rome was not, nor was it intended to be a separate handbook on the subject. It was merely a small section of his book on Latin orthography completed in 1449,[1] where he sought to codify the spelling and discuss the meaning of a large number of Latin words. The work did not, however, stop at this. For it also contains much miscellaneous information as well as countless disgressions about people and places mentioned, these being also meant as a relief from the very dry orthographic discussions. Altogether it may be described as a compilation on philology, ancient history, mythology, and geography, a kind of Politian's *Miscellanea* without the unique sparkle of Politian's genius, just the kind of work Coluccio Salutati might have written, had he lived two generations later.

Among the words which came under scrutiny in the *De orthographia* was 'Roma'; the controversial point here was whether or not it should be spelt 'Rhoma'. Tortelli of course favoured the spelling 'Roma'; 'Romam scribendam puto. Idemque ab antiquis nostris in numismatibus et marmorum inscriptionibus observatum conspeximus'[2] and this was good enough for him, just as it is for us. But Tortelli did not stop here. Instead he went on to consider other aspects of Rome, such as the area of the city in ancient times, etc. The nomenclature of the old gates clearly gave him some trouble; yet he did not shrink from going into the meanings of their names with the help of ancient texts, ranging from Varro to Cassiodorus, as well as Biondo's *Roma instaurata*.[3]

Rather than an antiquarian's methodical account, Tortelli's description is in the nature of a 'catalogue raisonné'. Not that he by-passed archaeological evidence, for he certainly did not, relying in fact on ancient remains and squeezing out all the information he could from inscriptions and coins, and not hesitating, whenever the evidence was contradictory, to attempt a critical assessment of its relative value. At the same time he had certainly at his elbow the *Roma instaurata* of Flavio Biondo, from which at least once he copied almost literally,[4] and to which he

[1] R. Sabbadini, Review of G. Mercati, *Per la cronologia della vita e delle opere di Niccolò Perotti, Giornale storico della letteratura italiana*, LXXXVII (1926) 374–76. For the *De orthographia* cf. Mancini, *op. cit.* 228–39. The section on Rome is in J. Tortellius, *De orthographia*, (Venetiis, 1484) ff. p2v–q4r.

[2] *Ibid.* f. p2v.

[3] *Infra*, n. 4.

[4] For the ancient gates of Rome Tortelli, cf. Tortellius, *op. cit.* ff. p3r–p4r, followed Biondo, whose views on the subject have been disproved by modern archaeology, cf. C. Huelsen, 'Der Umfang der Stadt Rom zur Zeit des Plinius', *Mittheilungen des Kaiserlich deutschen archaeologischen Instituts Römische Abteilung*, XII (1897) 148–60.

was also very much indebted for his own antiquarian methods, so much so that one is led to conclude that without Biondo's Tortelli's account would have been quite different.

Items considered by Tortelli included the Seven Hills, the gates, the forums, triumphal arches, obelisks, thermae, aqueducts, bridges, etc., in short the principal remains of ancient Rome. On the whole, inscriptions and classical writers formed his main sources. But he also kept his own eyes open and relied upon a lively critical sense. Thus on observing the huge bronze head then at the Lateran, he identified it as that of Commodus, 'quod Comodi fuisse ex numismatum imagine deprehendimus'.[1] Occasionally, he also slipped an inscription into his text.[2] Yet, altogether he shows no advance on the methods of Biondo, who praised the De orthographia in his Italia illustrata.[3] Rather one might call him Biondo's first follower. His account of Rome certainly did not pass unnoticed in humanist circles. In fact Agostino Maffei, that is to say one of the leading antiquarians of the Roman Academy, had the section on Rome actually transcribed for him separately by the copyist Leonardo Job.[4]

With Tortelli ends, one might say, the first wave of topographical study of ancient Rome conducted on humanist lines. What followed during the second half of the century and the first quarter of the Cinquecento was more a consolidation of these methods than any startling innovation. The Roman topographical tradition until the sack of Rome remained the tradition of Biondo.[5]

---

[1] Tortellius, op. cit., f. q4r.

[2] See for instance ibid. f. q3r-v.

[3] F. Blondus, Opera, (Basileae, 1559), Italia illustrata, 309.

[4] Vatican Library, Ms. Ottob. lat. 1208, ff. 49r–100v, cf. J. Ruysschaert, 'Récherche de deux bibliothèques romaines Maffei des XVe et XVIe siècles', La Bibliofilia, LX (1958) 337. Another copy of the description of Rome is in Vatican Library, Ms. Vat. Barber. lat. 139, ff. 59r–87v.

[5] Parallel to the rise of a humanist study of the ruins of Rome was the beginning of a humanist interest in early Christian antiquity inaugurated by Maffeo Vegio's De rebus antiquis memorabilibus Basilicae Sancti Petri Romae, completed after 1455 and printed in Acta Sanctorum, Junii, VII. 2, 61–85 and partly in Codice topografico della città di Roma, IV, 377–98. There are two recensions of it, represented by Vatican Library, Ms. Ottob. lat. 1863 and Ms. Vat. lat. 3750. On this work see B. Vignati, 'Alcune note ed osservazioni sul De rebus memorabilibus Basilicae Sancti Petri Romae', Studi su Maffeo Vegio a cura di S. Corvi, (Lodi, 1959) 58–69.

CHAPTER SIX

THE INHERITANCE OF FLAVIO BIONDO

The accounts of ancient Rome by Biondo and Tortelli were not merely followed by other works on similar lines. Descriptions of the city on the lines of the old *Mirabilia* also continued to be composed; such events as the Jubilee of 1450 and the Roman coronation of the Emperor Frederick III in 1452 offered a suitable occasion for the writing of some of them. These treatises were naturally not due to humanists, and their authors hailed from places wide apart, from Florence and even from King's Lynn and Nuremberg. After Poggio and Biondo works such as these do certainly strike an anachronistic note, appearing as out of place as a Victorian painting placed among a group of abstract pictures. It was from Florence that Giovanni Rucellai, the wealthy Florentine merchant whose name is still visible on the façade of Santa Maria Novella, came to Rome in 1450 in order to secure the spiritual advantages of the Jubilee. How much his soul profited from such a visit must be left to conjecture. A series of notes on Rome[1] was, however, among the tangible results of his sojourn in the town, notes not intended for publication, but merely to be inserted into his *Zibaldone Quaresimale*, where he assembled all kinds of miscellaneous information 'per dare notitia et amaestramento a Pandolfo et a Bernardo miei figliuoli di piu chose'.[2] As a deeply religious man Rucellai's main interest was focussed upon the churches and their most spectacular relics. His eye for what was beautiful— not for nothing was he one of Alberti's patrons—is, however, obvious here and there, when he notices a painting by Giotto,[3] or sees the bronze tomb of Pope Martin V in the Lateran.[4] Many of the ancient remains were also noted by him, his guide here being, as was only fitting to a pilgrim, the old *Mirabilia*. He also jotted down some rough measurements of the obelisk of Saint Peter's and of the Pantheon,[5] and he even tried to compile a list of the triumphal arches.[6]

[1] *Giovanni Rucellai e il suo Zibaldone* I. '*Il Zibaldone Quaresimale*', ed. A. Perosa, (London, 1960) 67–78.
[2] *Ibid.* 2.   [3] *Ibid.* 69.   [4] *Ibid.* 70.
[5] *Ibid.* 72.   [6] *Ibid.* 75.

During his two weeks in Rome Rucellai made it a rule to visit the principal churches in the morning and the antiquities in the afternoon, while in the evening he took notes on what he had seen during the day.[1] Thus his description of Rome does not attempt to be and is not a guide to the town. It is rather a series of notes, or more precisely a list of those things which attracted his attention during his visit. As such it is not without interest, also because it discloses a mind in which the old traditions were tempered by some appreciation of the new humanist values. Thus side by side with remarks such as that on the 'Templum Pacis', 'che si dice era uno tempio d'idoli, et che i Romani dicevano ch'egli aveva a durare insino che una vergine partorisse, et che apunto cascò et rovinò la notte che naque N. S. Giesù Cristo',[2] which is just nonsense, we find him giving vent to a typically humanist enthusiasm for the late antique mosaics of Santa Costanza: 'Appresso alla sopra scripta chiesa di Sancta Agnesa è una cappella di Sancta Chostanza, tonda, con colonne doppie a coppie, con begli archi, e nella volta bellissimi musaichi con figure piccole in perfectione et con fogliami et alberi et molti spiritegli che navicano in diverse maniere, il quale è il più vacho, gratioso et gentile musaicho non che di Roma, ma di tutto il mondo; et da torno uno andito in volta, con musaicho nella volta molto piacevole con animali, uccegli et fogliami et altre gentileze'.[3] A professional humanist could not have achieved a more sensitive appreciation of one of the master-pieces of late antique art!

Rucellai had written his notes for private consumption. John Capgrave, an Augustinian and one of the least entertaining writers in the whole of English literature, had, however, wider aims. For his *Solace of Pilgrims*[4] meant to be nothing less than a guide for English visitors to Rome, where he himself was in 1450. A guide, but chiefly one to Christian Rome, supplying descriptions of the main churches and their lenten stations, the so-called 'stationes quadragesimales',[5] not to mention relics and indulgences. But besides this, his text included also what was

---

[1] *Ibid.* 68.
[2] *Ibid.* 76.
[3] *Ibid.* 74.
[4] J. Capgrave, *The Solace of Pilgrims*, ed. C. A. Mills, (Oxford 1911), *Codice topografico della città di Roma*, IV, 330–49.
[5] It was usual during the fifteenth century to have the *Mirabilia* as an introduction to the accounts of Roman churches and their lenten stations, see for instance Hain, nn.11189–11219.

really an English paraphrase of the *Mirabilia*, supplemented by information secured elsewhere, from some classical and medieval writings and even from the massive encyclopaedia by Domenico Bandini.[1] The presence of Bandini's work among Capgrave's sources is certainly surprising, but this surprise vanishes when we learn that a copy of it was owned by his patron William Gray,[2] who became Bishop of Ely in 1454.

Needless to say Capgrave's standards are those of the age of the *Mirabilia* rather than those of Biondo's times. Yet this was only natural; for despite the efforts of Humfrey, Duke of Gloucester, and his many exchanges with humanist Italy, humanism had made very little headway indeed in England by the time of the Duke's death in 1447. What can be said of Capgrave's description of Rome, applies also to that by the Nuremberg senator Nikolaus Muffel,[3] whose visit to Rome in 1452 was prompted by the coronation of the Emperor Frederick III by Pope Nicholas V. Muffel's special interest was also in churches and other religious places. He did not, however, overlook antique remains, and although Biondo's *Roma instaurata* remained beyond his reach, Poggio's *De varietate fortunae* did not, and from it he must have derived the name 'Septimosephero', which he gave to the bronze statue of Marcus Aurelius at the Lateran.[4]

It is not surprising that Muffel's approach to Antiquity remained uncritical or that he swallowed without blinking what he was told by the *Mirabilia*. For between him and the world of Biondo there was nothing less than an abyss, the huge chasm which then separated Italian humanism from the learning of a country still virtually untouched by it. Hence notwithstanding his typically German thoroughness in recording measurements and other data, his account of Rome marked no progress whatever in antiquarian studies. Here in a way he was a German counterpart of Rucellai, with Gothic Nuremberg instead of Alberti's Florence as a background. Other accounts of Rome were also written during the fifteenth century in several languages for the benefit of pilgrims. As such they dealt solely with those aspects of interest to their readers, which means that they had no

[1] Capgrave, *op. cit.* 13, 43, 45, 49.
[2] Weiss, *Humanism in England*, 90, n. 15.
[3] *Codice topografico della città di Roma*, IV, 354–73.
[4] *Ibid.* IV, 354. For other derivations from Poggio see *ibid*. IV, 363, n. 2, 365, nn. 1–4 and passim.

room for the classical side of the town.[1] Hence they could
hardly prove a substitute for and certainly did not displace the
new archaeology, which Poggio and Biondo had so powerfully
launched. Roman humanism was much too vigorous for this to
be possible, and during the second half of the fifteenth century
the Roman Academy of Platina and Pomponio Leto proved a
source of real strength to antiquarian studies.[2] Pomponio Leto
was not, it is true, the author of a full description of ancient
Rome like Biondo's. Yet if Biondo and Poggio were pioneers in
the antiquarian study of the city, Leto was certainly its main force
during the next generation. Leto's studies of ancient Roman
topography are scattered here and there among his writings.
These 'disjecta membra' are none the less quite sufficient to give
us a good idea of the range of his knowledge. He also relied on
epigraphy as well as historical and literary sources. Yet the
distance between him and Biondo remained considerable. Leto
certainly did not lack Biondo's enthusiasm and industry. What
he lacked was a mind of Biondo's calibre. His scholarship,
though diligent and painstaking, was neither imaginative nor
immune from errors, nor was he much of a philologist and he
had practically no Greek. Still, despite his weaknesses, Leto was
undoubtedly the most influential figure in the antiquarian world
of his time, and his hold upon archaeology was still powerfully
felt during the Cinquecento.

Pomponio Leto's work on the topography of ancient Rome
included a revision of the so-called *Notitia regionum Urbis*,[3] that
is to say one of the early catalogues of the urban regions. It was
a revision, however, which went well beyond a mere emendation of
faulty readings. For Leto did not hesitate to interpolate the text
with data noticed by him in the Latin classics or in inscriptions,
and to carry on with this revision for many years.[4] But his most
significant work in this field which has reached us is his *Excerpta*,
these being notes taken down from his mouth by one of his

---

[1] See for example *The Stacions of Rome* (*In verse from the Vernon Ms., ab.* 1370 *a.d., and in
Prose from the Parkington Ms. No.* 10, *ab.* 1460–70 *a.d.*) *and the Pilgrims Sea Voyage*, ed. J.
Furnivall, (London, 1867); *A XV century Guide-Book to the Principal Churches of Rome
compiled c.* 1470 *by William Brewyn, Translated from the Latin with Introduction and Notes by*
C. E. *Woodruff*, (London, 1933). Needless to say these texts were meant for English pilgrims.

[2] The fullest account of the Roman Academy is in V. Zabughin, *Giulio Pomponio Leto*, I,
(Roma, 1909) 38–189.

[3] *Codice topografico della città di Roma*, I, 89–188.

[4] G. B. De Rossi, 'Note di topografia romana raccolte dalla bocca di Pomponio Leto e
testo pomponiano della Notitia Regionum Urbis Romae', *Studi e documenti di storia e diritto*,
III (1892) 74–86, *Codice topografico della città di Roma*, I, 207–58.

pupils, while Leto was guiding a foreign gentleman through the ancient ruins of the city.[1] The text of the *Excerpta* is, and unavoidably so, somewhat bare. It follows a set itinerary, starting at the Flavian Amphitheatre and ending at the Capitol and naturally including all the main sites. Yet despite its conciseness it is quite sufficient to give an adequate idea of Leto's grasp of ancient Roman topography. As to when the excursion which prompted the *Excerpta* took place, all we know now is that it must have occurred after 1484. Had it not been so he could hardly have said when mentioning the 'ara maxima' of Hercules, that it had been destroyed 'tempore Xysti IIII'.[2]

Despite its extreme sketchiness the *Excerpta* is not devoid of interest. For instance what is said there about the remains of an ancient sundial unearthed in the Campo Marzio,[3] is of some significance. And it is interesting to note that it includes the first accurate indication of the site of Rome's Seven Hills. Antiquarian and topographical information was also included in Leto's metrical account of the lenten stations in the Roman churches,[4] the pious aim of which did not prevent him from referring here and there to ancient remains of some interest. Nor is ancient topography absent from Leto's university courses on the Latin classics and particularly from those on Varro and Florus,[5] where a bare hint in the text is often a sufficient excuse for a substantial archaeological digression.

Leto was, one may say, a professional. Yet as an archaeologist he was outdistanced by Bernardo Rucellai, that is to say, by an amateur. But after Leto and before Bernardo Rucellai one may mention the activities of Rucellai's protegé Bartolomeo Fonzio, who in April 1472, shortly after his return to Florence from Rome, delighted in enumerating in a letter to Battista Guarino[6] those Roman monuments which had particularly impressed him. What Bartolomeo gave in this letter was very much like a catalogue. Still in spite of this it is sufficient to disclose to us that he looked at the Roman monuments quite intelligently and, furthermore, that his archaeological learning was both accurate and up-to-date. It is also clear that the Claudian aqueduct was

---

[1] De Rossi, *Note di topografia romana*, 58–64, *Codice topografico della città di Roma*, IV, 423–36.

[2] De Rossi, *Note di topografia romana*, 63.

[3] *Ibid.* 60.

[4] O. Marucchi, *Elements d'archéologie chrétienne*, III, (Paris-Rome, 1909) 63–66.

[5] Zabughin, *Giulio Pomponio Leto*, II, 112–36.

[6] B. Fontius, *Epistolarum Libri III*, ed. L. Juhasz, (Budapest, 1931) 10–12.

the subject of his special scrutiny: 'Conspexi omnium magnificentissimum aquaeductum, quem divus Claudius ad Caelium usque montem perduxit et L. Septimius Severus et T. Aurelius Antoninus Pius pluribus in locis corruptum restituerunt'.[1] Such an interest in aqueducts proved even stronger in Bernardo Rucellai,[2] who also shared Fonzio's enthusiasm for epigraphy, an enthusiasm that eventually led Fonzio to assemble a sylloge of ancient inscriptions.[3]

Bernardo Rucellai (1448–1514) was one of the sons of that Giovanni Rucellai whom we met earlier in this chapter.[4] The gap separating Bernardo from his father was, however, wider than the usual one between two generations, for Bernardo was an accomplished and up-to-date humanist, which Giovanni was obviously not. As an antiquarian, Bernardo was clearly an innovator, who combined Biondo's philological method with the practical approach of Alberti; all his work was coloured by an independent judgement of his own. To him Alberti was the greatest of all students of Antiquity and to him he was indebted not only for what he learnt from his *De re aedificatoria*, but also for his first introduction to the ruins of Rome.[5] For when Bernardo visited Rome in 1471 together with Lorenzo de' Medici and Donato Acciaiuoli, their guide through the old ruins had been none other than Alberti himself.[6] The chief pursuit of Rucellai happened to be politics. But this was an activity tempered by a friendship with Pontano and redeemed by a warm admiration for Pomponio Leto and Ermolao Barbaro, both of whom were quoted with approval in the *De urbe Roma*.[7] As far as acumen and learning were concerned, Rucellai had certainly no serious rivals among those contemporaries of his who wrote on the topography of ancient Rome. Here was a subject where he was absolutely up-to-date about archaeological discoveries and where he showed a unique competence in the examination of ancient buildings. When studying an antique ruin he was careful to compare its features with those of other monuments of the same period, even going as far as to check

[1] *Ibid.* 11.
[2] *Infra*, 79.
[3] *Ibid.* 146, n.2.
[4] *Supra*, 73-74.
[5] Bernardo Rucellai's *De Urbe Roma* is printed in J. Tartinius, *Rerum Italicarum Scriptores* ... *ex Florentinarum Bibliothecarum Codicibus*, II (Florentiae, 1748) 785–1132.
[6] *Ibid.* II, 839.
[7] *Ibid.* II, 802, 816.

whether their respective building techniques agreed with each other. Moreover Bernardo relied upon instruments in order to measure the ruins and, like Biondo, he did not appeal solely to literary texts. He also considered coins, inscriptions, and works of art in order to secure the answers he sought. He had recourse to drawing in order to set down the outlines of this or that ancient building,[1] in fact he omitted no evidence or line which struck him as potentially valuable.

In Rome Rucellai transcribed a considerable number of old inscriptions and was particularly impressed by the remains of the ancient aqueducts. On these he actually went as far as to plan a treatise[2], but this proved far more complex than he had anticipated, so that he was forced to give it up. Accordingly the antiquarian science of Rucellai is to be sought instead in his De Urbe Roma. This treatise which was warmly praised by Pietro Crinito,[3] was addressed by the author to his son Palla and composed a few years after 1495.[4] Originally it was meant as an introduction to a vast historical compilation[5] which was, however, never written. What we have is a careful commentary on the Notitia regionum Urbis, ascribed to Publius Victor, which was followed by Rucellai in the interpolated text prepared by Pomponio Leto,[6] though he did not overlook some ancient copies of the Notitia formerly belonging to Cardinal Bessarion, which he saw in Venice among the volumes bequeathed by that prelate to the Venetian Republic.[7]

After an introduction in which he discussed the foundation of Rome, its early site and shape, as well as its walls and gates, Rucellai proceeded with his commentary in the way usually adopted by humanists in the explanation of classical texts. Every entry in the Notitia was thus commented upon with the help of a very impressive array of authorities. Inscriptions unearthed only recently were often quoted in full,[8] and so were some

[1] Ibid. II, 828, 844.
[2] Ibid. II, 882.
[3] G. Pellegrini, L'umanista Bernardo Rucellai, (Livorno, 1920) 15.
[4] F. Gilbert, 'Bernardo Rucellai and the Orti Oricellari', Journal of the Warburg and Courtauld Institutes, XII (1949) 108, 110, n. 1.
[5] Tartinius, op. cit. II, 783–4.
[6] On which see supra, 76. As the text followed by Rucellai placed the 'Thermae Philippi Caesaris Augusti' in the third region, cf. Tartinius, op. cit. II, 847, the 'Graecostasis' in the eighth, ibid. II, 914, etc. it is clear that the text used by Rucellai was that interpolated by Leto.
[7] Ibid. II, 823, 1016.
[8] See for instance ibid. II, 896.

hailing from as far as Rimini and Brescia.[1] As far as inscriptions were concerned, he obviously did not rely entirely on copies taken by himself, indeed it seems fairly certain that he had under his eyes the sylloge put together by Fra Giocondo,[2] the first recension of which had been actually dedicated to Rucellai's own brother-in-law Lorenzo de' Medici.[3] Occasionally Rucellai omitted to comment upon an entry in the *Notitia* and more than once we find him referring to some particular manuscript, such as the famous Florentine Pandects,[4] or some of the manuscripts bequeathed to Venice by Cardinal Bessarion.[5] Nor is it uncommon to find him examining and discussing a particular point and weighing up the authority of one classical writer against that of another.

Needless to say, Rucellai did not invariably agree with the views put forward by other antiquaries. Thus he firmly rejected the current identification of the 'Amphitheatrum Castrense' with that of Statilius Taurus: 'Neque me latet fore plerosque, qui theatrum hoc Statilii Tauri opus fuisse putent, quod absonum est ab eo genere structurae, eaque operum magnificentia, quae per Augusti tempora claruere.'[6] The identity of the equestrian bronze figure of Marcus Aurelius challenged him. Here the right identification had been actually reached by Platina.[7] All the same Rucellai was not so far off the mark when he put forward the name of Antoninus Pius: 'Exstat etiamnum ad Laterana ex aere statua permagna insidens equo, cuius effigies, quod eadem sit quae in nummis veteris notae, adparet in honorem M. Antonini Pii percussis, eiusdem principis opus fuisse perhibetur.'[8] Concerning the 'Aedes Iovis Victoris' he pointed out that 'extat et in nummis a Domitiano percussis titulus inscriptus IOVI VICTORI',[9] and he was only too ready to intervene in the debate on the interpretation of names and surnames, particularly of imperial ones, on certain ancient inscriptions.[10]

---

[1] *Ibid.* II, 809, 1117.

[2] To give an example the inscription from Brescia, *C.I.L.* V.1, 4365, which Rucellai gives in full, cf. Tartinius, *op. cit.* II, 1117, occurs also in the sylloges of Felice Feliciano, Michele Ferrarini and Fra Giocondo.

[3] *Infra*, 150.

[4] Tartinius, *op. cit.* II, 797.

[5] *Supra*, 79.

[6] Tartinius, *op. cit.* II, 874. Such belief had been held, for instance, in Blondus, *Roma instaurata*, I, 87.

[7] B. Platyna, *Liber de vita Christi ac omnium pontificum*, ed. G. Gayda, (Città di Castello, 1913–32) 418.

[8] Tartinius, *op. cit.* II, 921.

[9] *Ibid.* II, 1054.   [10] *Ibid.* II, 796–98.

Besides the *De Urbe Roma* Rucellai was also the author of a *De Magistratibus Romanorum veterum commentarius*,[1] but his 'magnum opus' was undoubtedly the *De urbe Roma*. After it the study of Roman antiquities could no longer be conducted on the same lines as before. Sources were henceforth to be more varied; in fact an antiquarian was henceforth expected to adopt a technique really not so dissimilar from that followed by Politian in the *Miscellanea* and by Ermolao Barbaro in the *Castigationes Plinianae*. He was expected to have an eye for ancient works of art and display an active interest in excavations with archaeological aims or yielding archaeological results. These were, however, counsels of perfection, and the fact that Rucellai's treatise had only the very limited circulation of a work in manuscript in the age of printing also contributed to the failure at once and universally to conform to his exacting standards. Thus the short accounts of Rome by Fabrizio Varano and Raffaele Volaterrano do not conform with such exacting standards, but then also as scholars they did not belong to Rucellai's class.

The slender tract by Fabrizio Varano, a son of the Lord of Camerino Rodolfo IV Varano and himself bishop of this town from 1482 until his death in 1508,[2] is certainly rather disappointing. For one would have expected something more thorough from a humanist whose Latin poetry found appreciation among his contemporaries[3] and whom Egnazio called rather exuberantly 'vir de lingua latina bene meritissimus'.[4] To Egnazio Varano presented a copy of the pseudo-Publius Victor,[5] that is to say a text one would expect to be in the hands of a student of Roman topography. Such a study was not, however, carried very far by Varano, for his *De Urbe Roma Collectanea*[6] though

---

[1] *Bernardi Oricellarii de Magistratibus Romanorum Veterum Commentarius*, ed. I. E. I. Walchius, (Lipsiae, 1752).

[2] On him see particularly *Ludovici Lazzarelli Septempedani . . . Bombyx*, ed. J. F. Lancillottius, (Aesii, 1765) 44–46, A. Luzio and R. Renier, 'La coltura e le relazioni letterarie di Isabella d'Este Gonzaga', *Giornale storico della letteratura italiana*, XXXIX (1902) 249–51.

[3] Among whom Angelo Colocci, who included his name in his list of poets, cf. Vatican Library, Ms. Vat. lat. 3450, f. 56r.

[4] *Marci Antonii Sabellici annotationes . . . Joannis Baptiste Egnatii Veneti Racemationes*, (Venetiis, 1508) f. LXXVIIIv.

[5] *Ibid.* loc. cit. Varano was also the author of a commentary on Ausonius now lost, which was supposed to have been plagiarised by Mariangelo Accursio, cf. A. Campana, 'Accursio (Accorso), Mariangelo', *Dizionario Biografico degli Italiani*, I, (Roma, 1960) 128.

[6] First printed in *P. Victor. Pomponius Laetus. Fabricius Camers. R. Volaterranus. De Urbe Roma. Scribentes*, (Bononiae, 1520) ff. AA1r–BB4r, and again in *De Roma prisca et nova varii auctores*, (Romae, 1523) ff. gg3r–hh2v.

divided into headings according to the traditional classification still adopted in Renaissance descriptions of Rome, is really little more than a congeries of undigested jottings, clearly not meant for publication. The *Collectanea* includes some measurements of the circuit of the city walls taken from ancient authors, such as Pliny, Vopiscus, and the jurists Paul and Marcellus, as well as the actual length of these walls in his own time.[1] Some extremely sketchy notes are given about some of the main monuments and only once is the authority of an inscription appealed to, this being in connection with the Claudian aqueduct, where he mentioned that 'literae in tabula marmorea apud hospitalem Sancti Joannis Laterani ostendunt'.[2] Errors are, and inevitably so, not quite absent from his pages. Thus the small round temple by the Tiber is still indicated as that of Vesta,[3] while the Sistine bridge is identified with nothing less than the Sublicius.[4] But one should not blame Varano too much for what he says in a tract obviously unrevised and not really meant to be published.

The interest of Varano's little tract is fairly slight. Yet it is perhaps worth noticing, if for nothing else just as an example of the attraction exerted by the Roman ruins upon a mediocre humanist, whose main interest lay in Latin versification. It would be therefore invidious to compare his effort in the antiquarian field with that of Raffaele Maffei, better known as Volaterrano (1451–1522) not only because Maffei was a humanist of a different calibre,[5] but also because his description of Rome, though also printed separately,[6] was really part of his own 'magnum opus', the sixth book of his massive *Commentaria Urbana*, first printed in 1506.[7] As an antiquarian Maffei did not belong to the same class as Biondo and Rucellai. None the less he was endowed with a critical mind and possessed a good mastery of the Greek and Latin classics. His humanist interests show considerable leanings towards archaeology.

---

[1] *P. Victor. Pomponius Laetus . . . De Urbe Roma Scribentes*, f. AA1ʳ. Here Varano relied on Blondus, *Roma instaurata*, I, 3.
[2] *P. Victor. Pomponius Laetus . . . De Urbe Roma scribentes*, f. BB2ʳ.
[3] *Ibid.* f. AA2ᵛ.
[4] *Ibid.* f. AA2ʳ.
[5] On Maffei see now P. Paschini, 'Una famiglia di curiali—I Maffei di Volterra', *Rivista di storia della Chiesa in Italia*, VII (1953) 344–69.
[6] *P. Victor. Pomponius Laetus . . . De Urbe Roma Scribentes*, ff. GG1ʳ–III1ʳ. *De Roma prisca et nova varii auctores*, ff. hh4ʳ–kk3ᵛ.
[7] R. Volaterranus, *Commentariorum Urbanorum Libri XXXVIII*, (Romae, 1506) ff. Kiʳ–K4ʳ.

Here was a field where he certainly had a sharp eye for the relevant and where he looked with great interest at excavations. Little wonder then, that he did not omit to remember those undertaken by his brother Mario, later Bishop of Aquino,[1] who shared his antiquarian tastes. The importance of epigraphic sources did not escape him,[2] and in one case he also mentioned the reverse of a Roman coin in order to confirm a point.[3] News of the discovery of ancient statues certainly gave him a thrill! Thus that of the *Laocoon* filled him with such enthusiasm that he hastened to add a short paragraph about it in the *Commentaria*,[4] when the volume was already in the press.[5]

Maffei started his account of ancient Rome by examining the actual origin of the city's name. What he gave were not, however, his personal views on the subject; for he preferred instead to repeat the various opinions about it, which he had read in some classical writers, from whom he also gathered all the names of the early tribes of Rome that he could find. He chose to quote in full an inscription supplying the number of the urban regions,[6] and he did not hesitate to offer an emendation to the text of Varro[7] a propos of the spelling of Agonius: 'quamquam apud Varronem Aegonius scribitur.'[8] Maffei divided his description of ancient Rome according to subjects: that is to say, there were sections dealing with the gates, the bridges, the forums, and so on. The problem here was obviously to keep the description as concise as possible, which led inevitably to an extreme sketchiness, redeemed, however, to some extent by the competence with which Maffei handled his materials, as well as by his scholarly presentation of the subject matter. A deep interest in Roman antiquity was obviously behind it, such an interest being also revealed by his Virgilian hexameters, where he described the origins of Rome.[9] The poem

---

[1] *Ibid.* f. K3v.   [2] *Ibid.* f. K2 r-v etc.
[3] *Ibid.* f. K3r.   [4] *Ibid.* f. K2v.
[5] Since the discovery of the *Laocoon* only took place in January 1506, cf. *infra*, 103, and the volume was issued on 19 February 1506.
[6] Volaterranus, *op. cit.* f. K1r.
[7] Varro, *De lingua latina*, VI, 14.
[8] Volaterranus, *op. cit.* f. K2r. A short account of some monuments in Rome written in 1505 by a member of the Venetian embassy which went to Rome to bring Venice's obedience to Pope Julius II, is printed in E. Müntz, 'Les monuments antiques de Rome à l'époque de la Renaissance', *Revue Archéologique*, ser. 3, III (1884) 298–305. On its date and on its not being by Bernardo Bembo see A. Campana, 'Intorno all' incisore Gian Battista Palumba e al pittore Jacopo Rimpacta (Repanda)', *Maso Finiguerra*, I (1936) 175–76.
[9] Printed in *De Roma prisca et nova varii auctores*, ff. qq3r–rr3r.

in question, the *De origine Urbis*, was typical of the Latin verse recited in the Roman Academy on formal occasions.

To write on Rome's antiquities was not, however, a complete humanist monopoly. It had not been so in the fifteenth century, and it was still not so in the days of Varano and Maffei. There was still a clientèle for popular and semi-popular accounts, where humanist sophistication was replaced by a genuine enthusiasm, but by little else. The *Antiquarie prospetiche*, which an obscure Milanese painter addressed to no less than Leonardo da Vinci and chose to publish in Rome about 1500[1] is a case in point. For the author, who hid his identity by calling himself 'Prospectivo Melanese depictore' was not the man one would have expected to see engaged in archaeological activity. His work is in Italian verse, atrocious verse at that, and it is really in the nature of a catalogue. Yet, though he rightly styled himself 'idioto',[2] that is to say without letters, he definitely had an eye for works of art, so that whereas what he tells us about the monuments is fairly irrelevant, his remarks about Roman collections of antiques[3] are not without some interest.

By the beginning of the sixteenth century the collecting of statuary, inscriptions, and other antiques was being regarded with greater interest than hitherto. This is evident from the literary remains of Francesco Albertini (fl. 1493–1510),[4] which are also of some interest in showing how by this time the *Mirabilia* were no longer satisfying even those who were not professional antiquarians. Albertini himself cannot be considered a real scholar. He was in fact a gifted amateur with a flair for vulgarisation and an eye for works of art[5]; not for nothing had he been a pupil of Ghirlandaio in Florence,[6] which makes one wonder whether he may have been the author of the drawings of Rome and Roman antiquities now at the Escorial,[7] which clearly betray

---

[1] Reprinted in G. Govi, 'Intorno a un opuscolo rarissimo della fine del secolo XV intitolato *Antiquarie Prospettiche Romane composte per Prospettivo Milanese Dipintore*', *Atti della Reale Accademia dei Lincei*, ser. 2, III, (1876) 39–66.

[2] *Ibid.* 49.   [3] See especially *ibid.* 49–50.

[4] On Albertini see now J. Ruysschaert, 'Albertini, Francesco', *Dizionario biografico degli Italiani*, I, (Roma, 1960) 724–25 and the bibliography *ibid.* 725.

[5] This is also shown by his *Memoriale di molte statue e pitture nella città di Firenze*, (Florentia, 1510).

[6] F. Albertinus, *Opusculum de mirabilibus novae et veteris Urbis Romae*, (Romae, 1510) f. 101r. The section of this work dealing with ancient Rome may be read in *Codice topografico della città di Roma*, IV, 462–546. An edition of the section on the new Rome by A. Schmarsow was published at Heilbronn in 1886.

[7] Reproduced in H. Egger, *Codex Escurialensis—Ein Skizzenbuch aus Werkstatt Domenico Ghirlandaio*, (Wien, 1906).

Rome, Museo Lateranense. Roman urn with thirteenth century inscription in honour of St. Agnes and St. Alexander.

PLATE 1

Church of San Domenico, Orvieto, Arnolfo di Cambio, Tomb of Cardinal Guillaume de Braye, upper part.

PLATE 2

Pisa, Cathedral. Statues of Fortitude and Prudence from the pulpit by Giovanni Pisano, Prudence being modelled on ancient statue of the 'Venus de' Medici' type.

PLATE 3

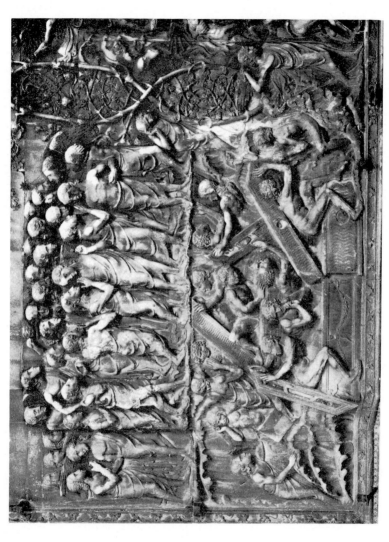

Orvieto, Cathedral. Relief on the front made c. 1330 and showing the resurrection of the flesh with the resurrected coming out of ancient Roman sarcophagi.

PLATE 4

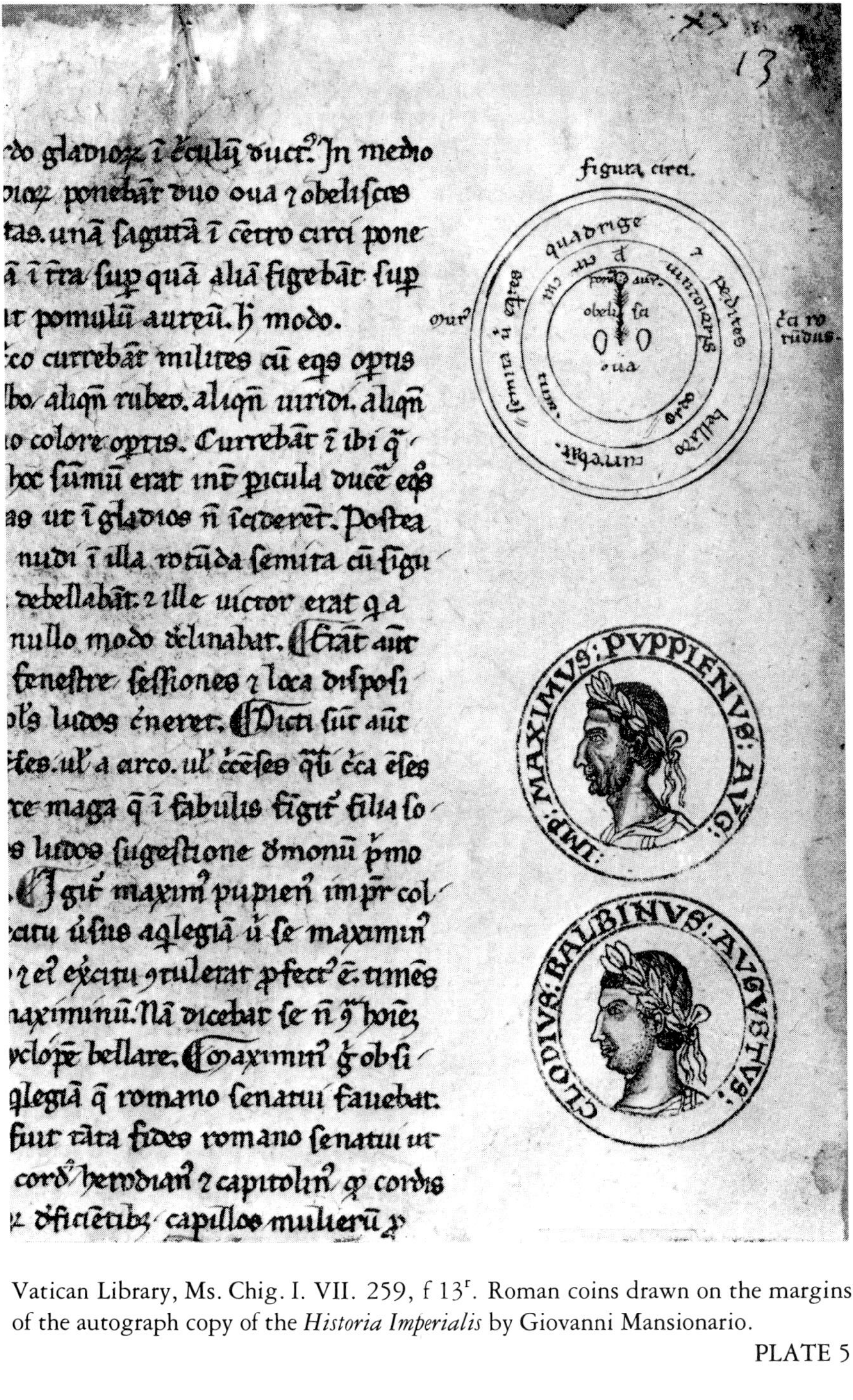

do gladioꝛ̄ ī ēcꝉū ꝺuct.ꝰ Jn medio
ꝺioꝛ̄ ponebāt ꝺuo oua ⁊ obelifcꝰ
tas. unā fagittā ī cētro circi pone
ā ī ꝼra fuꝑ quā aliā figebāt fuꝑ
ꝑ pomulū aureū. ħ modo.
:co currebāt milites cū eqs optis
ꝉbo, aliqn̄ rubeo. aliqn̄ uiridi. aliqn̄
o colore optis. Currebāt ī ibi q̄
hoc fūmū erat int̄ picula ꝺucē eqs
as ut ī gladios n̄ fecꝺeret. poftea
nudi ī illa rotūda femita cū figu
rebellabāt ⁊ ille uictor erat qa
nullo modo ꝺclinabat. ¶ Erat aūt
feneftre feffiones ⁊ loca difpofi
oꝉs ludos éneret. ¶ Dicti fūt aūt
ꝉtes. uꝉ a arco. uꝉ ācefes q̄ti ēca ēfes
re maga q̄ ī fabulis figit filia fo
⁊ ludos fugeftione ꝺmonū p̄mo
¶ Igit maximū pupien ī imp̄r col
ratu ufus aglegiā ū fe maximin
⁊ ei exciru ꝼtulerat ꝑfect ē. timēs
maximinū. Nā ꝺicebat fe n̄ q̄ hoiez
yclopē bellare. ¶ Maximin̄ g̃ obfi
glegiā q̄ romano fenatui fauebat.
fuit tāta fides romano fenatui ut
corꝺ herodiaꝛ̄ ⁊ capitoliꝛ̄ q̄ cordis
⁊ officētibꝯ capillos mulierū ꝑ

figura circi.

IMP: MAXIMVS: PVPPIENVS: AVG:

CLODIVS: BALBINVS: AVGVSTVS:

Vatican Library, Ms. Chig. I. VII. 259, f 13ʳ. Roman coins drawn on the margins
of the autograph copy of the *Historia Imperialis* by Giovanni Mansionario.

PLATE 5

Left hand section of the view of Rome in Hartmann Schedel's *Liber Cronicarum* (Nuremberg, 1493).

PLATE 6

·T· PHAEDRVS TANTO PERICVLO EREPTVS ✦

IESV CHRISTO SERVATORI

St. John Lateran, Rome, Sala Capitolare, 'Ex voto' of Tommaso Fedro Inghirami made between 1503 and 1508 and showing the Arch of Titus and the Coliseum.

PLATE 7

Sulmona.   Fifteenth century statue of Ovid.

PLATE 8

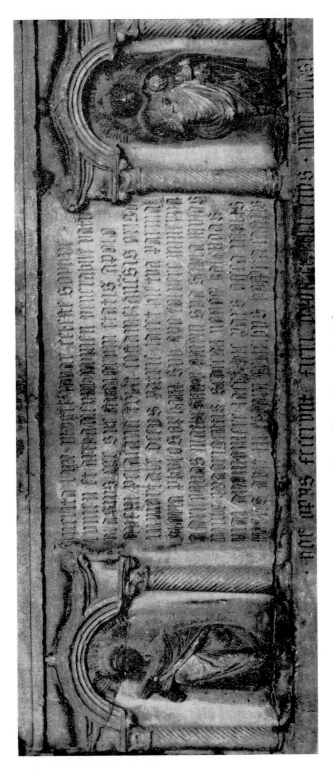

Parma Cathedral, Tomb of Biagio Pelacani with the effigy of Macrobius on the left.

PLATE 9

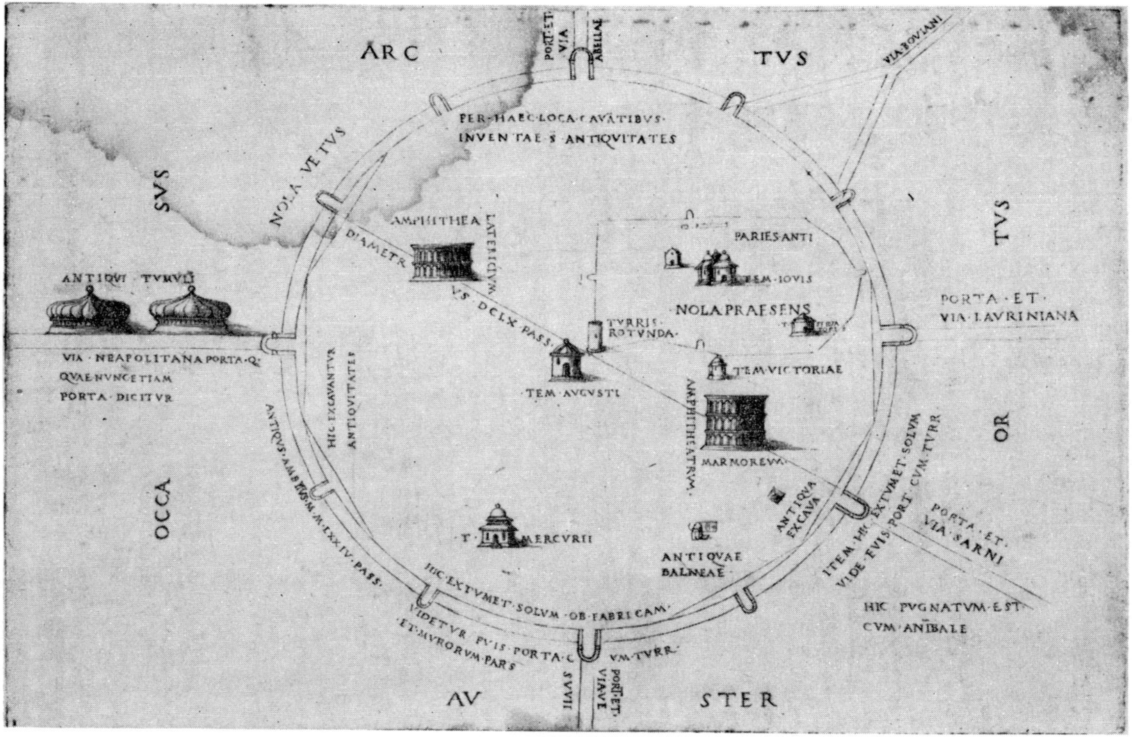

Map of ancient Nola (engraved by Girolamo Mocetto) in Ambrogio Leone, *De Nola*, (Venice, 1514)

PLATE 10

Vatican Library, Ms Chig. F. V. 110, f. 39ᵛ. View of the Plain of Troy and the
Dardanelles in Cristoforo Buondelmonti's *Liber Insularum Archipelagi.*

PLATE 11

Chiesa di San Michele, Fano. Reproduction of the Arch of Augustus at Fano made by Bernardino di Pietro da Carona in 1513.

PLATE 12

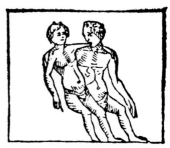

MES. MAI.	MES . IVN.
Dies.xxxi.	Dies.xxx.
Non.Septim.	Non.Quint.
Dies Hor.	Dies Hor.xv.
XIIIIS.	Nox Hor.
Nox Hor.	
VIIIIS.	VIIII.
Sol Tauro	Solſtitium
Tutela	VIII k IVL.
A Pollinis	
Segetes	Sol Geminis
Runcantur	Tutela
Oues tundunt	Mercuri
Lana lauatur	Fænific
Iuuenci iniant	Vineæ
Iuru Abul	Occantur
Secatur	
Segetes	SACRVM
Luſtrantur	Herculi
Sacrum.	Sacrum
Mercurii	Entis
Et mineruæ	Et Lunæ.
Turua VNT.	a ii

Hemerologia Romana, (Rome, c. 1510), f.2ʳ. Section of Roman epigraphic calendar.

PLATE 13

Torri del Benaco. Memorial cippus of Domizio Calderini,
erected c. 1479.

PLATE 14

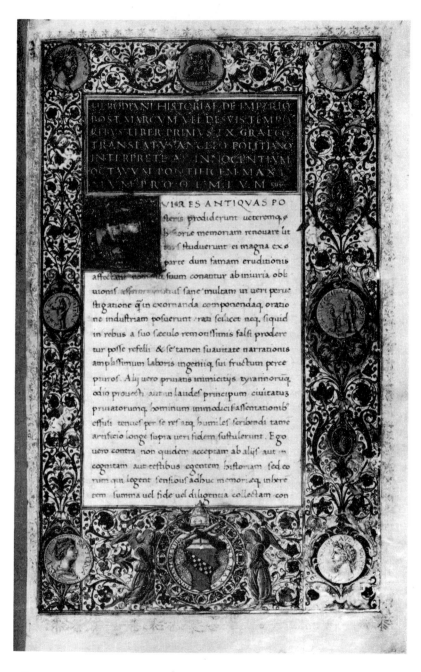

Biblioteca Vittorio Emanuele II, Rome, Ms. 1005. First page of the dedication copy to Pope Innocent VIII of Politian's Latin translation of Herodian's *Historiae* with reproductions of Roman coins illuminated in the margins.

PLATE 15

Bronze cast of an engraved amethyst formerly in the collection of Pope Paul II, showing it in a frame with the coat of arms he held when still a Cardinal.

Museo degli Argenti, Florence. Cup formerly in the collection of Lorenzo de'Medici the Magnificent.

PLATE 16

a hand trained by that painter. Had Albertini lived to-day he would perhaps have been the author of discursive guide books, packed with information and not particularly original.

It was in the household of Cardinal Fazio Santoro in Rome that Albertini composed his *Opusculum novae et veteris Urbis Romae*. But the suggestion to write it had actually come from Cardinal Galeotto della Rovere,[1] who had expressed the wish to see a reliable and up-to-date guide of the city. While the *Opusculum* is invaluable for the information it supplies on contemporary Rome, it certainly constitutes no landmark in the development of antiquarian science. Even its avowed aim to replace the *Mirabilia* had really been anticipated a couple of generations earlier by Biondo. What Albertini really achieved was a new *Mirabilia*, a handbook meant for the cultured visitor to Rome, where medieval legend was replaced by the new knowledge resulting from about a century of humanist investigation. Its structure is still that of the old *Mirabilia* with the subject matter still subdivided in the traditional way, its chapters dealing with the walls, the 'viae', the theatres, etc. It is in fact a kind of swollen catalogue, nor is such an arrangement abandoned in the second part, where Albertini dealt with the Rome of his own time. But here similarities with the *Mirabilia* cease. For Albertini did not hesitate to summon to his aid all the sources on which he could lay his hands, thus revealing the considerable range of his reading. Classical texts used by him included not only the better known authors and the catalogues of the regions, naturally in the text revised by Pomponio Leto, but also Festus, Vitruvius, and Frontinus, on whom he of course relied for his section on aqueducts. He was obviously at home with inscriptions, and besides relying on the evidence they supplied, he often quoted them in full, not hesitating to include some discovered only very recently.[2] Like other antiquarians, he did not ignore the evidence offered by ancient coins.[3] But perhaps what shows most clearly the range of his interests is his references to humanist writings. For here besides Petrarch, Biondo, Leto, and Poggio, we also find appeals to the authority of Alberti, Landino, Pietro Marsi, Beroaldo, and Raffaele Maffei. Like so many of his contemporaries, he too was taken in by Annio da Viterbo's outrageous forgeries of ancient texts and antiquities, just as he did not

---

[1] Albertinus, *op. cit.* f.A3v.   [2] *Ibid.* f. C4r.
[3] *Ibid.* ff. G2v, M1v.

escape the usual mistakes, such as the identification of the small temple by the Tiber with that of Vesta,[1] or the attribution of the well-known Dioscuri[2] to Pheidias and Praxiteles.

Albertini's account of ancient Rome is certainly valuable. It is so particularly because of what he tells us about excavations and recent archaeological discoveries, and also because of the information he gives about the Roman collections of antiques in his time. It certainly proved something of a best-seller during the first quarter of the sixteenth century, as is brought home to us by its no less than five editions between 1510 and 1523.[3] Nor did it lack at least one imitator. For his example found a follower in Fra Mariano da Firenze, who based his itinerary of Rome[4] upon Albertini's *Opusculum*. This Fra Mariano was very probably in Rome in 1516–17[5] and had almost certainly visited the city before. It was, however, not in Rome, but in the monastery of San Girolamo at Volterra, that he finished his *Itinerarium Urbis Romae* on September 1st, 1518.[6] Fra Mariano too was credulous enough to believe in the forgeries of Annio da Viterbo. It was in fact on them and on the Latin version of Plutarch's *Vita Romuli* by Tortelli, that he based his account of the origins of Rome. But despite the many sources he quoted, which ranged from Plutarch to Beroaldo's commentary on Suetonius, from Bede to Leto and Raffaele Maffei, his main guide remained Albertini, from whom he differed only in the arrangement, which is according to 'itinera' and not subject matter and by his mentioning churches alongside with the ancient remains. He also talked about recent discoveries and supplied the texts of inscriptions, though here his sources were not direct ones, but the *Opusculum* of Albertini.

To say that nothing new on ancient Rome was supplied by the *Itinerarium* of Fra Mariano is certainly true. Something new was, however, supplied instead by the works of Andrea Fulvio (c. 1470–1527),[7] whose Latin epigram in praise of Albertini figured on the frontispiece of the first edition of the *Opusculum*.

---

[1] *Ibid.* f. M1ᵛ.

[2] *Ibid.* ff. P4ᵛ–Q1ʳ.

[3] Editions of it appeared in Rome in 1510, 1515, and 1523, in Basle in 1519 and in Lyons in 1520.

[4] Fra Mariano da Firenze, *Itinerarium Urbis Romae*, ed. E. Bulletti, (Roma, 1931).

[5] *Ibid.* 111.

[6] *Ibid.* 237.

[7] On whom see R. Weiss, 'Andrea Fulvio antiquario Romano (c. 1470–1527)', *Annali della Scuola Normale Superiore di Pisa—Lettere, storia e filosofia*, ser. 2, XXVIII (1959) 1–44.

The difference between the antiquarian activity of Albertini and that of Fulvio is, however, very considerable. It is really the difference between a gifted amateur and a professional trained in the school of Pomponio Leto. Fulvio's first antiquarian work was published in 1513. But his archaeological studies had started long before in the days of Pomponio Leto, for whom he secured at least one ancient inscription,[1] and he was probably the 'Andreas Praenestinus' who contributed a Latin epigram to the *Priscorum Heroum Stemmata* of Thomas Ochsenbrunner,[2] a work published in Rome in 1494. Yet despite this and other early activity, he did not hasten to put the results of his antiquarian studies into writing. Albertini also secured some help from Fulvio.[3] On the other hand, as we saw, Fulvio waited until 1513 before producing his first work on archaeology, the *Antiquaria Urbis*.[4] A poem in Latin hexameters dedicated to Pope Leo X, the *Antiquaria*, sets out to describe the topography of ancient Rome, or, more exactly, what was still left of the old monuments and buildings without, however, overlooking altogether the more striking achievements of the new Rome of the Renaissance. Needless to say Fulvio was here indebted to some extent to both Biondo and Albertini. But he also shows in it his use of ancient inscriptions and an appreciation of some of the alterations undergone by the old monuments in the course of time. In spite of this it was certainly not, nor was it meant to be, a very full and detailed account. This was perceived by Pope Leo X, who accordingly encouraged Fulvio to prepare a much fuller prose version of it.[5] The advice of Pope Leo was duly followed by Andrea Fulvio. Several years were, however, to elapse before it materialized, for his massive *Antiquitates Urbis* appeared only in the spring of 1527,[6] just a few weeks before the troops of Charles V brought death and desolation upon Rome.

It is no exaggeration to say that the *Antiquitates* (incidentally this word already has here the modern meaning of 'antiquities'[7]) shows the results of a lifetime dedicated to the study of ancient Rome. Fulvio did not look at the ruins with the eyes of an architect, but rather with those of a historian and antiquarian,

---

[1] *Ibid.* 3.
[2] *Ibid.* 15–16.
[3] *Ibid.* 6.
[4] A. Fulvius, *Antiquaria Urbis*, (Romae, 1513).
[5] Weiss, *Andrea Fulvio antiquario Romano*, 30.
[6] A. Fulvius, *Antiquitates Urbis*, (S.L.N.A.).
[7] Momigliano, *Contributo alla storia degli studi classici*, 73–74.

just as Biondo had done before him. And, like his great predecessor, Fulvio did not limit his sources to the literary field. He
in fact made a wide use of inscriptions, of which he frequently
gave the text in full. Nor were these classical only, but medieval
and even contemporary inscriptions were also considered by
him, just as he did not overlook the evidence offered by ancient
coins.[1] The scheme followed by him is reminiscent of that
followed in Biondo's *Roma instaurata*, and really amounts to a
grouping of the various antiquities according to their nature but,
if anything, more consistently than in the treatise of Biondo.
Naturally enough Fulvio too bewailed the unceasing liquidation
of ancient remains, and to this he also added some laments for
the continuous exportation of antiques to Florence and Venice
despite papal bans.[2] More than once he rectified some of the
mistakes of Biondo and Leto.[3] On the other hand, Fulvio also
went wrong occasionally. He misunderstood for instance a
passage of Varro about the 'Lucus Fagutalis',[4] mistook the
'Porta Fontinalis' for the 'Porta Capena'[5] and talked of a 'Lucus
Larum' which never in fact existed.[6] Nor is it possible to say
that he had the depth and acumen of a Flavio Biondo or a
Bernardo Rucellai. Biondo was his main model, though one
which he did not choose to follow blindly; indeed he was not
afraid of criticizing him and assuming quite an independent
position.

The most important feature of Fulvio's *Antiquitates* is
naturally the information it furnishes about ancient remains and
inscriptions still existing when he was writing, but which have
vanished since then, and about contemporary discoveries of
antiques. Quite clearly he did not have much of an eye for style.
It is true that he could distinguish what sections of an ancient
building belonged to different epochs.[7] On the other hand, he
remained unaware that the reliefs on the Arch of Constantine
belonged to more than one period,[8] a feature which was, however, noted by Raphael[9] and later by Marliani.[10] Altogether, in

[1] Weiss, *Andrea Fulvio antiquario Romano*, 32, n.3.
[2] *Ibid.* 33.
[3] *Ibid.* 36.
[4] *Ibid.* 38.
[5] *Ibid.* loc. cit.
[6] *Ibid.* loc. cit.
[7] *Ibid.* 39.
[8] *Ibid.* loc. cit.
[9] *Ibid.* loc. cit.
[10] *Ibid.* loc. cit.

the age stretching from the early Quattrocento to the Sack of Rome in 1527, Fulvio stood at the end; indeed he ended a tradition which was still continuing in the high Renaissance the aims and methods of the fifteenth century and of Leto and his school. Between the treatise of Fulvio and that of Bartolomeo Marliani, first published in 1534, there was not only the Sack of Rome. There was also a new consciousness, which led eventually to a new archaeology.

CHAPTER SEVEN

THE TOPOGRAPHY AND THE DESTRUCTION OF ANCIENT ROME

The universal appeal of ancient Rome was also reflected by the interest taken in its topography.[1] The immense prestige of the city created an appetite for its image, so that pictorial views of it had already been executed in classical times. Views of Rome, varying in detail and shape yet invariably inaccurate, were also made during the Middle Ages, when the town was even represented in the shape of a lion, for no other reason than because the lion was the king of animals.[2] Even in the fifteenth century the earlier views and plans, showing a circular city occupied by the various monuments, often represented in a somewhat fanciful way, had not become obsolete. They are in fact behind the circular panorama of Rome frescoed in 1414 by Taddeo di Bartolo in the Palazzo Pubblico of Siena[3], and a view of a similar type is among the illuminations in the *Très Riches Heures* of the Duke of Berry executed by the Limburg Brothers about that period.[4] What we have in these representations is but a highly standardized image of Rome with groups of classical and later buildings, such as the Coliseum, the Capitol, Castel Sant'Angelo, St. Peter's, the Lateran, etc., grouped and disposed in accordance with a more or less set pattern. That by the fourth decade of the Quattrocento such a type of plan was no longer found satisfactory in some quarters, is certainly not surprising. In fact considering the enormous strides made by antiquarian studies since Petrarch, what is surprising is that they were still being made at so late a date.

What was probably the first sign that the current standardized views were no longer satisfactory to everyone, may be detected during the period 1432–34, when the presence in Rome of Leon Battista Alberti, then employed at the Curia as an apostolic abbreviator,[5] stimulated a desire among his humanist colleagues,

---

[1] The early views of Rome are collected in Frutaz, *op. cit.*
[2] *Ibid.* I, No. III, II, pl. 3.
[3] *Supra*, 6. [4] *Ibid. loc. cit.*
[5] C. Grayson, 'Alberti, Leon Battista', *Dizionario Biografico degli Italiani*, I (Roma, 1960) 703–04.

who had been deeply impressed by his experiments on optics and his study of Roman antiquities, to see the city represented in a more scientific manner. The Roman Curia had then some of the greatest names in contemporary humanism among its employees. In 1432–34 the papal secretaries and abbreviators, the latter being the officials who were entrusted with the drafting of bulls and other official documents, included Poggio, Antonio Loschi and Flavio Biondo. Moreover in 1432–33 Ciriaco d'Ancona was in Rome and we know him to have then conducted the Emperor Sigismund on a tour of the ancient remains.[1] It seems accordingly highly probable that the 'amici literati', at whose request Alberti undertook to gather data for a plan of Rome,[2] were actually his humanist colleagues at the Curia, several of whom were deeply interested in Roman topography, and perhaps included Ciriaco d' Ancona.

Alberti accepted the invitation: what he prepared was not, however, a proper plan of the town. His *Descriptio Urbis Romae*,[3] was instead a set of measurements of distances between the principal landmarks, taken with the aid of a mathematical instrument and including all the main features, such as monuments, buildings, etc., 'quo pacto quivis vel mediocri ingenio praeditus, bellissime et commodissime pingere, quantacumque voluerit in superficie, possit'.[4] The instructions formulated by Alberti were extremely simple. As was explained by Gnoli,[5] Alberti's instructions were to draw a circle, which was to be called the horizon and would be divided into forty-eight degrees, each degree being in turn subdivided into four. Then from the centre, which was to be the Capitol, a mobile radius divided into fifty degrees, each degree being in turn subdivided into four, was made so as to reach the horizon. After this it would be easy from the measurements given to fix the corresponding points on the radius and the horizon, thus reconstructing the view of Rome according to Alberti's intentions.[6] The plan resulting from these instructions had a vertical projection. But whether Alberti translated his

---

[1] E. W. Bodnar, *Cyriacus of Ancona in Athens*, (Bruxelles-Berchem, 1960) 22.
[2] *Codice topografico della città di Roma*, IV, 212.
[3] The last edition of it is *ibid*. IV, 212–22.
[4] *Ibid*. IV, 212.
[5] D. Gnoli, 'Di alcune piante topografiche di Roma ignote o poco note' *Bullettino della Commissione archeologica comunale*, XIII (1885) 66.
[6] For a modern reconstruction of a map according to Alberti's data cf. *ibid*. pl. IX–X, Frutaz, *op. cit*. I, No. LXXIX, II, pl. 151.

data into practice and made a plan of Rome, showing the various monuments at a true distance from each other, is not known, though it is not unlikely. All one can say now is that if he made such a plan, it has not reached us; nor do we know today any view of Rome which appears to have been derived from Alberti's instructions.[1]

Apparently a view of Rome closely linked with Biondo's *Roma instaurata* was also executed not long after the release of this work. In the view, which was orientated to the south, the shape of Rome was circular with the Capitol as a centre, and it showed both modern and ancient buildings, while its nomenclature appears to have conformed with that of *Roma instaurata*. Unfortunately this view has not reached us. It was, however, almost certainly the ultimate prototype, from which was derived the view drawn in Venice in 1472 by Alessandro Strozzi, as well as the panoramas of the city illuminated by the Florentine Pietro del Massaio in three manuscripts of Ptolemy, two of which are dated 1469 and 1471.[2]

Further progress in what might be called the portrayal of Rome was achieved in the panorama of the city which was probably executed by the Florentine cartographer Francesco Rosselli,[3] the brother of the painter Cosimo Rosselli, whose art perhaps appears at its best on the walls of the Sistine Chapel. Several views of Rome may be traced directly or indirectly to Francesco Rosselli's prototype. It is true that his view of Rome, made some time between 1478 and 1490 has not reached us, and that we are aware of its existence only because an inventory of his 'bottega' included among other things a 'Roma in tre pezzi in 12 fogli reali'.[4] However the remains of his cartographic activity allow us to suggest that Rosselli's Rome consisted of a view of

[1] Gnoli, *op. cit.* 67, states that some topographical studies by Alberti were discovered in the British Museum by Professor Uzielli, who intended to publish them. He never published them, and search in the British Museum has proved fruitless.

[2] For the view based on Biondo and its derivates cf. G. Scaglia, 'The Origins of an Archaeological Plan of Rome by Alessandro Strozzi', *Journal of the Warburg and Courtauld Institutes*, xxvii (1964) 136–63. For Strozzi's plan see also Frutaz, *op. cit.* I, No. LXXXIX, II, pl. 159. For those by Pietro del Massaio, cf. *ibid.* I, Nn. LXXXVII–VIII, XC, II, pl. 157–58, 160. According to Scaglia the lost view of Rome was by Biondo rather than derived from him, but this view, on which see also Fubini, *op. cit.* 14, is hardly acceptable.

[3] On Rosselli see R. Almagià, 'On the Cartographic Work of Francesco Rosselli', *Imago Mundi*, VIII (1951) 27–34.

[4] C. Huelsen, 'Die alte Ansicht von Florenz im Kgl. Kupferstichkabinett und ihr Vorbilt', *Jahrbuch der Königlich Preussischen Kunstsammlungen*, XXXV (1914) 101. The inventory also mentions 'Roma in tela innistamta del pupillo L. 3', cf. *ibid.* 101, n. 57, on which nothing is known. That Rosselli was the author is not absolutely certain, as printers and dealers of maps and engravings often acquired plates engraved by others.

the town, as it appeared during the last quarter of the fifteenth century, when seen from some high ground above the zone known as 'Alta Semita'. Needless to say, it showed both ancient and modern monuments, while houses were represented in a conventional manner. The monuments were not scattered about indiscriminately, while the centre of the city was included within a triangle formed by the Pantheon, St. Peter's, and Castel Sant'Angelo.

All the above details concerning Rosselli's work may be gathered from the many derivations of it. These range from the woodcut views in the 1490 edition of Bergomensis' *Supplementum Chronicarum*[1] and the 1493 edition of the *Liber Cronicarum* by Hartmann Schedel,[2] down to the huge panorama of Rome now at Mantua and executed not before 1538,[3] yet giving the city as it appeared during the last quarter of the fifteenth century. And on Rosselli's panorama may also have been based the view of Rome promised in 1490 by Cardinal de la Balue to King Charles VIII,[4] as well as those painted by Pinturicchio in the Vatican Belvedere[5] and by Giovanni Bellini in the 'Sala del gran consiglio' in the Doge's Palace at Venice,[6] none of which has reached us. On the other hand, it was not behind the view taken from Monte Mario and showing a row of buildings, mostly modern, included in a sketchbook by a pupil of Domenico Ghirlandaio.[7]

Although all these plans of Rome included ancient buildings and monuments, what they really meant to show was what the city looked like at the time rather than what it had looked like in the past. It is impossible to say when views of the ancient city had first been attempted; in fact a satisfactory plan of ancient Rome did not appear until 1544, when the second edition of the treatise on the topography of ancient Rome by Bartolomeo Marliani included one devised by him and executed by the famous calligrapher Giovanni Battista Palatino.[8] Marliani's plan was not, however, the earliest effort to show the ancient city. For several decades before him the Dominican Annio da Viterbo,

[1] Frutaz, *op. cit.* I, No. XCV, II, pl. 165.
[2] Pl. VI, Frutaz, *op. cit.* I, No. XCVI, II, pl. 166.
[3] *Ibid.* I, No. XCVII, II, pl. 167–69.
[4] E. Müntz, *Les arts à la cour des Papes*, IV, (Paris, 1898) 34.
[5] G. B. De Rossi, 'Panorama circolare di Roma delineato nel 1534 da Martino Heemskerck pittore olandese', *Bullettino della Commissione archeologica comunale*, XIX (1891) 337.
[6] *Ibid.* loc. cit.   [7] Frutaz, *op. cit.* I, No. XCIV, II, pl. 164.
[8] *Ibid.* I, No. XII, II, pl. 21.

now only remembered as a shameless fabricator of ancient texts, had produced a plan of the Rome of Romulus. Among the notorious forgeries by Annio, which, incidentally, were still deceiving people as late as the eighteenth century,[1] there was a *De aureo saeculo et de origine Urbis* by 'Quintus Fabius Pictor'.[2] Now, in this tract, Annio had included a description of the archaic city and its early development. Accordingly he deemed it advisable also to include a plan, illustrating the topographical information supplied by 'Fabius Pictor'. 'Nunc' he said, having reached the second part of the first book of the *De aureo saeculo*, 'depingit atque describit, qualis erat regio septicollis antequam inhabitaretur: sed pasqua bobus erat. Ad cuius intellectum descripsi in plano totum quod scribit Fabius, ut melius novi'. Modestly adding: 'Non enim profiteor artem pictoriam. Quod magis assuetus est Romae, atque melius intelligit Fabium: ipse emendat sicubi in pingendo erravi.'[3]

In accordance with the information available in the tract forged by him, Annius drew early Rome in the shape of a bow with the Tiber as its chord, the plan being orientated to the east. Very few buildings appear in it; the square city is divided into four sections, i.e. Roma, Vellia, Germallia, and the Forum, and is surrounded by typically medieval walls with battlements and towers. The Tiber shows only one bridge, the 'Pons Carmentalis', while localities indicated include the Via Sacra, the Vicus Tuscus, the Lacus Curtius, and the Capena, the last one being represented as a small castle at the foot of the Aventine.[4]

It is hardly necessary to say that the plan made by Annius is entirely fanciful. The next attempt to provide a representation of ancient Rome was an ambitious scheme which unfortunately never materialized, owing to the death in 1520 of its designer, the great painter Raphael.[5] After settling in Rome in 1509,

---

[1] R. Weiss, 'Traccia per una biografia di Annio da Viterbo', *Italia Medioevale e Umanistica*, V (1962) 438–39.

[2] J. Annius, *Antiquitates*, (Romae, 1498) ff. L4r–N3r.

[3] *Ibid.* f. Mir.

[4] *Ibid.* f. Miv. On this plan see O. A. Daniellson, 'Annius von Viterbo über die Gründungsgeschichte Roms', *Corolla Principi Hereditario Regni Sueciae Gustavo Adolpho dedicata*, (Lund, 1932) 1–16, Frutaz, *op. cit.* I, No. V, II, pl. 14.

[5] There is no positive evidence that a plan of ancient Rome was prepared by Leonardo da Vinci during his stay in the city in 1513–16. The suggestion that the 'gentile intelletto' who, according to Pietro Aretino, had made such a map and had submitted it to the courtiers of Pope Leo X who, bored by his explanations had set fire to it with the wax of their candles, was Leonardo, cf. C. Pedretti, *A Chronology of Leonardo da Vinci's architectural drawings after 1500*, (Genève, 1962) 161, is not convincing, as it is hardly credible that Aretino would have omitted Leonardo's name.

Raphael had gradually developed an enthusiastic interest in the antiquities of the town. What fascinated him above all were the architectural remains, though of course ancient sculpture and painting also made a powerful appeal to him. The non-stop destruction of the old ruins and marbles gave him considerable pain, and made him see how imperative it was to make an accurate record of what was still left before it was too late, on lines not very dissimilar from those advocated by Alberti. Furthermore he believed that their ancient structures, together with the evidence provided by Vitruvius[1] and other ancient writers, would yield enough evidence for visual reconstruction of the ancient city, in which the now ruined buildings would be shown not as they were, but as they had been.

If Raphael's letter to Baldassarre Castiglione of 1514[2] is authentic, he was already at that time seeking to establish the original shape of some ancient ruined buildings. It is anyhow certain that his interest and enthusiasm for ancient Rome eventually moved Pope Leo X to commission him about 1519 to prepare an idealized view of it.[3] In his letter, or more accurately report, to Leo X, really written in accordance with his instructions by his friend Baldassare Castiglione in 1519,[4] that is to say the very year in which he also offered to erect in St. Peter's Square the obelisk unearthed near the mausoleum of Augustus,[5] Raphael outlined his programme. His intention was to follow the account of Rome's regions then believed to be by Publius Victor,[6] thus showing that he would have dealt with one region at a time, and have considered only buildings earlier than the fall of the Roman Empire. He was going to use a compass in order to take exact measurements and he also explained the principles to be followed in drawing the ancient structures.

To Raphael's work on his pictorial reconstruction of ancient

---

[1] In fact as Vitruvius's text was too much for him, he had it turned into Italian by his friend Fabio Marco Calvo. The autograph copy of his translation is now in the Staatsbibliothek of Munich, Ms. Ital. 216. Another Italian version of Vitruvius is in the Vatican Library, Ms. Ottob. lat. 1653. The first Italian version to appear in print was that by Cesare Cesariano (Como, 1521).

[2] V. Golzio, *Raffaello*, (Città del Vaticano, 1936) 30.

[3] *Ibid*. 84, 281–82.

[4] Castiglione's authorship is established beyond doubt in V. Cian, 'Nel mondo di Baldassarre Castiglione' *Archivio storico lombardo*, N.S. VII (1942) 70–76. The text of the letter can be read in Golzio, *op. cit.* 82–92.

[5] *Ibid*. 101.

[6] *Ibid*. 84.

Rome in 1519–20 several contemporary writers testify, among them Andrea Fulvio, who was apparently the antiquarian adviser of the venture and went about with Raphael, pointing out to him what should be included in the survey; and this Raphael duly drew.[1]   But Raphael's untimely death in the spring of 1520 ended all this after he had completed no more than his sketches for the pictorial account of the first region. Thus Marcantonio Michiel writing from Rome after the death of Raphael, stated: 'el stendeva in un libro, sicome Ptolemeo ha isteso il mondo, gli edificii antiqui di Roma mostrando sí chiaramente le proportioni, forme et ornamenti loro, che averlo veduto haria iscusato ad ognuno haver veduta Roma antiqua: et già havea fornita la prima regione. Nè mostrava solamente le piante de li edificii et il sito, il che con grandissima fatica et industria de le ruine saria raccolto; ma ancora le facia con li ornamenti quanto da Vitruvio et da la ragione de la architectura et da le istorie antique, ove le ruine non lo rite-nevano, havea appreso, expressivamente designava.'[2]

The collapse of Raphael's scheme was lamented by his contemporaries in prose and verse.[3]   It was left to his devoted friend and literary adviser Marco Fabio Calvo of Ravenna, to publish a representation of old Rome though on much more modest lines. Calvo was a serious scholar,[4] not a forger of texts like Annio da Viterbo, and he relied on genuine literary sources, such as Livy, Dionysius of Halicarnassus, Pliny, and the ancient catalogues of regions in the interpolated text by Pomponio Leto. Yet, despite his scholarship and his close links with Raphael, in whose house he had actually lived,[5] his plans of ancient Rome are so naive as to be little more valuable than the plan invented by Annio da Viterbo. His set of views, which was printed in Rome only a few weeks before the terrible sack of the city in 1527, were naturally inspired by Raphael's ambitious designs. In fact by preparing his set of plans of ancient Rome he meant to carry out as far as he could the intentions of his deceased friend.

[1] Weiss, *Andrea Fulvio antiquario romano*, 11–12.

[2] Golzio, *op. cit.* 113.

[3] *Ibid.* 79–80, 281–82. Raphael's antiquarian activity was also praised in a 'canzone' written shortly after his death by Francesco Maria Molza and included in a miscellaneous manuscript of Italian poetry copied about 1525–30 and belonging to H. P. Kraus of New York.

[4] On Calvo see G. Mercati, *Notizie varie di antica letteratura medica e di bibliografia*, (Roma, 1917) 67–71, and the bibliographical indications *ibid.* 68.

[5] R. Lanciani 'La pianta di Roma antica e i disegni archeologici di Raffaello', *Rendiconti della R. Accademia dei Lincei. Classe di scienze morali, storiche e filologiche*, ser. 5, III (1894) 797.

Calvo was, however, primarily a man of letters turned anti-quarian by circumstances. Accordingly his survey was not so much the fruit of personal archaeological investigation, as the result of his study of the relevant literary sources.

The *Antiquae Urbis Romae cum regionibus simulachrum*[1] by Calvo consists of a series of plates supported by the barest text. The first plate[2] shows his idea of the 'square Rome' of Romulus. Its shape is rhomboidal with the north to the left and it has four gates, each named after one of the four hills of the city, on each of which appear only a few buildings, while four buildings are shown outside the city walls. An octagonal shape is given to the Rome of Servius Tullius,[3] which now includes all the seven hills as well as numerous gates. Only the temple of Apollo figures on the Palatine, while the temple of Diana is the only building on the Aventine. The temple of Serapis now appears on the Esquiline, while the centre of Rome, the 'umbilicus Urbis', is indicated by a pillar surmounted by a statue.

The Rome of Augustus[4] has instead a circular shape, the circle is divided into sixteen equal sectors, each with its gate and corresponding to one of the ancient urban regions, the two regions figuring besides the traditional fourteen being the 'Regio Vaticana' and the 'Campus Martius Minor'. Each sector has representations of the principal buildings of the region, while the centre of the city is now indicated by the 'milliarium aureum', which is represented here by a pillar with a statue on top. This 'milliarium aureum' also appears in the last plate of Rome, which gives the city in the time of the Elder Pliny.[5] Few build-ings are shown here and the shape of the city is still circular. But the gates are now thirty-two, while six bridges appear on the Tiber. This is followed by a plate showing the Capitol surrounded by a wall with towers, its main buildings and the 'arx' also surrounded by a wall and with soldiers inside it.[6]

Any claim to genuine topography is abandoned in the fourteen plates showing the ancient regions of Rome.[7] For Calvo here limited himself to showing in each of these plates some vertical and parallel rows of small identical houses, each

[1] On which see *ibid*. 795–99, Frutaz, *op. cit*. I, Nn. VI–X, II, pl. 14–19.
[2] F. Calvus, *Antiquae Urbis Romae cum regionibus simulachrum* (Romae, 1532) f. 3r.
[3] *Ibid*. f. 4r.
[4] *Ibid*. f. 5r.
[5] *Ibid*. ff. 6r–7r.
[6] *Ibid*. f. 8r.
[7] *Ibid*. ff. 9r–22r.

row being equidistant and similar to the next one, between which he placed in each case some of the main buildings of the locality. Accordingly, what we have here is no more than a pictorial illustration of the ancient catalogues of regions as interpolated by Pomponio Leto. Where Calvo showed himself at his most fanciful was, however, in the last two plates of the *Simulachrum*,[1] where he gave his own idea of a Roman bath and of a circus.

These last two plates are in the same tradition as the well known volume which Felice Feliciano completed in 1465 for Giovanni Marcanova and its derivates,[2] which displays a series of imaginary pictures of various parts of ancient Rome peopled by persons in fifteenth century garb.[3] If we want some faithful views of Quattrocento Rome we must turn instead to the drawings by a pupil of Ghirlandaio now at the Escorial,[4] which give several accurate views of part of the city as it still was though not for long.

Enthusiasm for Antiquity neither prevented nor even slowed down the destruction of the Roman ruins. But then it should not be forgotten that such an enthusiasm was felt only by a very small circle of people. Thus throughout the Renaissance the demolition of old remains never ceased, and the city continued to be regarded as a source of stone, an inexhaustible quarry, ever yielding materials invaluable for building or for burning into quicklime.[5] Besides the natural desire of builders and stonemasons to acquire materials as cheaply as possible—to extract marble from an old ruin was obviously much less expensive than importing it from Carrara—another threat was to be found in the modernisation of the town initiated under Pope Nicholas V. For whenever a new road was opened or an old one broadened or straightened, any monument, however ancient or important, that happened to stand in the way was quickly eliminated.

[1] *Ibid.* f. 23r, 24r.
[2] On which cf. C. Huelsen, *La Roma antica di Ciriaco d'Ancona*, (Roma, 1907), H. van M. Dennis III, 'The Garrett Manuscript of Marcanova', *Memoirs of the American Academy in Rome*, VI (1927) 113–26, C. Mitchell, 'Felice Feliciano Antiquarius', *Proceedings of the British Academy*, XLVII (1961) 207–08.
[3] See Huelsen, *La Roma antica di Ciriaco d'Ancona*, pl. I–XVIII, E. B. Lawrence: 'The Illustrations of the Garrett and Modena Manuscripts of Marcanova', *Memoirs of the American Academy in Rome*, VI (1927) 127–31.
[4] Reproduced in Egger, *op. cit.*
[5] For the demolition of ancient Rome see particularly the first volume of Lanciani, *Storia degli scavi di Roma* and the same author's *The Destruction of Ancient Rome*, (New York, 1901).

The constant lamentations of humanists and antiquarians, from Petrarch to Fulvio and from Biondo to Raphael, tell a similar tale but they invariably fell upon deaf ears. Official attempts to end or to decrease the destructions, were not only few, but also wholly unsuccessful. Despite its emphasis on classical learning the Renaissance proved undeniably far more destructive, where ancient remains were concerned, than the preceding centuries. Nor should this surprise us, since the Renaissance passion for building and town planning inevitably brought with it the sacrifice of much of the old for the new. During the Middle Ages an ancient temple was often turned into a church. But in the Renaissance when a new church was built any ancient remains which happened to be on its site would be demolished and used as materials for the new building rather than incorporated into it.

The speed at which ancient Rome was fading away is brought home vividly by the melancholy chronicle of demolition. Under Pope Eugenius IV what was still standing of the 'Zecca vecchia' disappeared for ever.[1] The ruined arch of Gratian, Valentinian, and Theodosius, followed at some time between 1451 and 1454 during the alterations made in the Via San Celso, the later Via dei Banchi.[2] That this took place under the pontificate of so enlightened a humanist as Pope Nicholas V is not altogether surprising. For his enthusiasm for the Greek and Roman classics did not extend to the tangible relics of Antiquity, and found expression in a passion for building. Indeed during his pontificate the region between the Caelian and the Capitol, as well as the Aventine, the Forum and, naturally, the Coliseum were deprived of much of their ancient stone.[3] Was all this never to stop? It seemed not. If hopes were raised by the bull of April 28th, 1462, with which Pius II sought to protect the ruins of Rome,[4] they certainly did not last long; for everything went on as if nothing had happened. In fact it was under this very Pope, whose poetic remains included an elegy bewailing the state of Rome's ruins,[5] that the eastern colonnade of the Portico of Octavia, the so-called 'Trullo', and other important

---

[1] Müntz, Les arts à la cour des Papes, I, 35.
[2] Lanciani, Storia degli scavi di Roma, I, 53.
[3] Müntz, Les arts à la cour des Papes, I, 105.
[4] Ibid. I, 352–53.
[5] Ibid. I, 266.

monuments were sacrificed in order to provide materials for buildings in the Vatican.[1]

The quarrying of stone out of the Coliseum and other places did not cease during the seven years (1464–1471) in which that enthusiastic antiquarian, Paul II, occupied the Papal throne.[2] On the other hand, one of the earliest actions of his successor Sixtus IV was the issue only a few days after his election of an order to the keeper of the castle at Ostia, enjoining him to prevent any export of marble, this to include statuary as well as blocks from buildings and other pieces.[3] Dispensations from such enactments could, however, be obtained. One was, for instance, obtained by Giulio Cesare Varano in 1488 under Innocent VIII.[4] But to go back to Sixtus IV, one can say without hesitation that, despite his foundation of the Capitoline Museum, he was not particularly concerned for the antiquities of Rome. His bull of 7 April 1474[5] was not aimed at the preservation of the ancient ruins, but at that of the city's churches. Because the sarcophagus of Constantina had been removed from a church by Paul II, shortly after becoming Pope he ordered its return to the church of Santa Costanza.[6] It is therefore hardly surprising that his pontificate witnessed the demolition of the temple of Hercules in the 'Forum Boarium'[7] and the conversion into cannon balls of what still remained of the so-called bridge of Horatius Cocles,[8] as well as countless other demolitions, which aroused the indignation of Fausto Maddaleni Capodiferro, who vented his feelings in an acrimonious Latin epigram against Pope Sixtus.[9]

In 1491 the arch by Santa Maria in Via Lata vanished away for ever during the rebuilding of that church.[10] But perhaps the most regrettable of all the destructions in the Quattrocento took place in 1499, when most of the pyramid commonly known as the 'Meta Romuli', which the *Mirabilia Romae Urbis* had indicated

---

[1] Lanciani, *Storia degli scavi di Roma*, I, 69.
[2] Müntz, *Les arts à la cour des Papes*, II. 7.
[3] *Ibid*. III, 168, n. 3.
[4] *Ibid*. IV. 287.
[5] *Ibid*. III, 152–53.
[6] *Ibid*. III, 158.
[7] *Ibid*. III, 178.
[8] S. Infessura, *Diario della città di Roma*, ed. O. Tommasini, (Roma, 1890) 147.
[9] Müntz, *Les arts à la cour des Papes*, III, 177.
[10] Infessura, *op. cit.* 268, Lanciani, *Storia degli scavi di Roma*, I, 88, A. M. Colini, 'I frammenti di architettura e di rilievi rinvenuti presso la chiesa di S. Maria in Via Lata', *Atti della Pontificia Accademia Romana di Archeologia, Rendiconti*, ser. 3, XI (1935) 41–61.

as the tomb of Romulus,[1] was pulled down.[2] Here was yet another example of a prominent monument having to give way to a new road. For it was during the building of the new Via Alessandrina that most of the 'Meta' was sacrificed, and what was then left disappeared a few years later.[3] The demolition of ruins and the destruction of old marbles did not decrease during the pontificate of Julius II.[4] Under his successor Leo X the need to straighten the road leading to the Capitol for the festivities held in 1513 in honour of Giuliano and Lorenzo de' Medici, brought with it a further sacrifice of ancient remains.[5] Indeed old Rome was disappearing so fast that a brief of 28 August 1515 empowered Raphael the painter to halt any further destructions of old marbles and particularly of inscriptions.[6] Not surprisingly also this measure had little effect, and an enactment passed by the City Council on 3 March 1520 and aimed against the destroyers of ancient monuments[7] proved hardly more effective.

Against the long tale of destruction it is, however, possible to set the occasional restorations of old monuments and the discoveries of masterpieces of ancient art. Such discoveries were invariably accidental. For excavations during the Renaissance could hardly be called archaeological. Those which took place were either made in order to dig up the foundations of new buildings or in order to secure stone; or, occasionally, for 'loot', such as metal or gems. To dig in order to reveal an ancient building was unthinkable. On the other hand, in view of the antiques which so often came to light in the course of diggings, licenses were sometimes issued giving permission to excavate in search of metal, stone, and gems,[8] or we find contracts granting permission to dig, in which the grantor reserved for himself all or a proportion of the ancient objects discovered during the operation.[9]

Excavations, demolitions, and the searching for antiquities were bound to, and in fact did bring to light several statues and other antique objects of considerable value. When Lorenzo

[1] *Codice topografico della città di Roma*, III, 35.
[2] B. M. Peebles, 'La Meta Romuli e una lettera di Michele Ferno', *Atti della Pontificia Accademia Romana di Archeologia, Rendiconti*, ser. 3, XII (1936) 21–63.
[3] *Ibid.* 37, n. 64.
[4] Lanciani, *Storia degli scavi di Roma*, I, 137.
[5] *Ibid.* I, 160.
[6] *Ibid.* I, 166, Golzio, *op. cit.* 39–40.
[7] *Lanciani, Storia degli scavi di Roma*, I, 195.
[8] *Ibid.* loc. cit.
[9] *Ibid.* I, 196, 208–09, 215, 219.

Ghiberti was in Rome he had the welcome opportunity of admiring among other things a statue of a Hermaphroditus found in a drain.[1] The demolition of the temple of Hercules in the 'Forum Boarium' under Sixtus IV revealed a statue of that demigod, which was eventually moved to the Capitol.[2] But Pope Sixtus was certainly more moved when he heard of the discovery of the sarcophagus of St. Petronilla in the very chapel dedicated to her in St. Peter's, to which it had been translated by Pope Paul I in 757.[3] So much so that he hastened to send word of the discovery to King Louis XI, who happened to be the patron of the chapel, then also called the 'Cappella Francorum'.[4] Of course this was not as much an instance of antiquarian interest as of religious zeal. Just as devotional was the enthusiasm which greeted the news of Cardinal Mendoza's discovery in 1492 of what was believed to be the actual tablet fixed on the top of the cross of the crucifixion, said to have been brought to Rome by St. Helen, the mother of the Emperor Constantine.[5] Yet when only a few years before on 19 April 1485 a sarcophagus was found containing the practically intact body of a girl, immediately identified as Cicero's daughter Tulliola, crowds flocked to see it, until Pope Innocent VIII put an end to this pilgrimage by having it secretly removed at night.[6]

Though the feeling aroused by this sudden reappearance of an ancient Roman girl was perhaps dictated more by curiosity than by antiquarian interest, there is no doubt that its popular appeal owed also much to the memory of ancient Rome, which had never faded out of the people's consciousness and was suddenly rekindled by the discovery. As for its effect on humanist opinion, this is amply testified by the number of Latin writings in both prose and poetry on the event.[7] The finding of the Belvedere Apollo, perhaps unearthed at Grottaferrata and quickly secured for himself by Cardinal Giuliano della Rovere,

[1] Ibid. I, 46. Lorenzo Ghibertis Denkwurdigkeiten, I, 61–62, II, 187–88.

[2] Müntz, Les arts à la cour des Papes, III, 177.

[3] Lanciani, Storia degli scavi di Roma, I, 79.

[4] Ibid. loc. cit.

[5] Ibid. I, 89.

[6] On this see particularly G. Mercati, Opere Minori, IV, (Città del Vaticano, 1937) 268–83, F. Saxl, 'The Classical Inscription in Renaissance Art and Politics', Journal of the Warburg and Courtauld Institutes, IV (1940–41,) 26–27, 44–45, pl. 5 b. Two accounts of this discovery, by Alessandro Cortesi and by 'cuiusdam fidedigni', are in the Biblioteca Laurenziana, Florence, Ms. Ashburnham, 1657, ff. 107v–109r.

[7] See C. Huelsen, 'Die Auffindung der römischen Leiche vom Jahre 1485', Mittheilungen des Instituts für Oesterreischische Geschichtsforschung', IV (1883) 433–49, Mercati, Opere minori, IV, 275–83.

later Pope Julius II,[1] did not cause at first the sensation it certainly deserved. Yet it had become famous enough by the last decade of the century to be sketched twice while it was in the Cardinal's Palace at San Pietro in Vincoli in the book of drawings by a pupil of Ghirlandaio now at the Escorial.[2] The enthusiasm, however, which greeted the reappearance of the *Laocoon*, the famous group found in January 1506 in the 'vigna' of Felice di Fredi 'in loco dicto le Capoce appresso la chiesa di S. Piero ad vincula'[3], could scarcely have been greater. Compared to this the discovery of the so-called Cleopatra[4] and that of the group of Hercules and Telephus in the Campo dei Fiori on 15 May 1507,[5] made much less of an impression. And even less excitement accompanied the discovery in a now unknown place in September 1514 of ancient copies of the statues sent to the Athenians by King Attalus I.[6]

Despite the destructions, some of the more important antiquities were not altogether neglected. Restorations and repairs on more than one famous relic of ancient Rome were indeed carried out during the fifteenth and early sixteenth century. It is, however, necessary, to distinguish between repairs to ancient buildings still in use, such as, for instance, the Pantheon, Castel Sant'Angelo, or the Capitol, and those to monuments of a purely artistic or archaeological interest.

---

[1] A. Michaelis, 'Geschichte der Statuenhofes im vaticanischen Belvedere', *Jahrbuch des Kaiserlich deutschen archäologischen Instituts*, V (1890) 10–11. According to a Cesena chronicle the Apollo of Belvedere was discovered in 1489, but the discovery is also recorded under the year 1493 in the same text, cf. '*Caos' Cronache Cesenati del Sec. XV di Giuliano Fantaguzzi*, ed. D. Bazzocchi, (Cesena, 1915) 30, 43. Giuliano della Rovere was also responsible for the rescue and preservation of the antique marble eagle still in the forecourt of the church of the Santi Apostoli in Rome, cf. R. Weiss, *The Medals of Pope Sixtus IV* (1471–1484), (Roma, 1961) 36, and in 1488 he prevented the export to Florence of some antiquities brought to light in Rome, cf. G. Gaye, *Carteggio inedito d'artisti dei secoli XIV, XV, XVI*, I, (Firenze, 1839) 285.

[2] Egger, *op. cit.* pl. 53, 64. Another discovery made in the late fifteenth century, that of the underground rooms of Nero's 'Domus Aurea', had a very powerful influence upon artists, who modelled their 'grottesche' on the wall paintings in them, cf. Vasari, *op. cit.* VI, 531, F. Weege, 'Das goldene Haus des Nero', *Jahrbuch des Kaiserlich deutschen archäologischen Instituts*, XXVIII (1913) 141–42, A. von Salis, *Antike und Renaissance*, (Erlenbach-Zurich, 1947) 35–60, P. P. Bober, *Drawings after the Antique by Amico Aspertini*, (London, 1957) 12.

[3] C. C. Van Essen, 'La Decouverte du Laocoon', *Mededelingen der Koninklijke Nederlandse Akademie van Wetenschappen, Afd. Letterkunde, Nieuwe Reeks, Deel* 18, No. 12 (1955) 293. On the discovery and its aftermath see M. Bieber, *Laocoon—The influence of the Group since its Rediscovery*, (New York, 1942).

[4] Michaelis, *Geschichte des Statuenhofes im vaticanischen Belvedere*, 18–20.

[5] Lanciani, *Storia degli scavi di Roma*, I, 144. An account of this discovery was given to Isabella d'Este by Giorgio da Negroponte in a letter from Rome dated 19 May 1507 in Archivio di Stato, Mantua, Archivio Gonzaga, Serie E. XXV. 3, busta 857.

[6] Lanciani, *Storia degli scavi di Roma*, I, 162–63.

Repairs to the former are not really evidence of a desire to save ancient monuments from decay just because they happened to be ancient. Those to the latter are of course quite a different matter. Now during the fifteenth century the Pantheon, the Capitol, Castel Sant'Angelo were repaired and improved several times.[1] It is, however, not until we reach the pontificate of Paul II that we find old remains without a utilitarian value being repaired. Under this Pontiff the bronze equestrian statue of Marcus Aurelius, then still at the Lateran, was extensively restored.[2] Other monuments repaired in his time included among others the arch of Titus,[3] the two horse tamers of the Quirinal,[4] as well as a column in the vicinity of the baths of Diocletian.[5] Moreover it was this very Pope who, in order to have them displayed in a worthier manner, removed the porphyry sarcophagus of Constantina from the church of Santa Costanza[6] and the large basin in front of the church of San Giacomo al Colosseo,[7] in order to place them in the piazza San Marco by the monumental palace which he had erected as a cardinal,[8] the palace now known as Palazzo Venezia and notorious as the once official residence of Mussolini.

Further work on the bronze Marcus Aurelius was carried out under Sixtus IV,[9] when the so-called temple of Vesta also underwent some repairs.[10] But after Sixtus IV, who died in 1484, the restoration of old buildings or other remains no longer in use appears to have ceased altogether. From then until the sack of the City in 1527 nothing more seems to have been done towards the preservation of even the most outstanding monuments which were not required for practical purposes. Statuary of course went on being restored and repaired and found shelter in gardens and palaces. But the ruins, the arches, the baths, the theatres, the forums, were abandoned to the ravages of the weather and the greed of the building contractors and the stonemasons. The Renaissance passion for building on classical lines was the main cause for much of the destruction of what still remained of ancient Rome.

---

[1] Müntz, *Les arts à la cour des Papes*, I, 34, 148, II, 89–90, III, 169, etc.
[2] *Ibid.* II, 92–93.
[3] *Ibid.* II, 94.
[4] *Ibid.* II, 94–95.
[5] Lanciani, *Storia degli scavi di Roma*, I, 74.
[6] Müntz, *Les arts à la cour des Papes*, II, 84.
[7] *Ibid.* II, 95–96.
[8] On which see especially F. Hermanin, *Il palazzo di Venezia*, (Roma, 1948).
[9] Müntz, *Les arts à la cour des Papes*, III, 176–177.
[10] *Ibid.* III, 174.

CHAPTER EIGHT

THE ANTIQUITIES OF ITALY: I

The antiquities of Rome alone did not monopolize the attention of humanists. The ancient remains still visible in other parts of Italy also aroused their interest, either because of their historical associations, or because of their striking appearance, or just because they were old. In an age when every town of any note claimed origins lost in the very mists of Antiquity, attempts were frequently made by local humanists to prop up with tangible evidence the legends handed down by oral tradition or too credulous chroniclers. To confirm that a city owed its foundations to a demigod like Hercules or a Trojan hero like Antenor, became an important duty. It would, however, be mistaken to assume that antiquities outside Rome were overlooked until the Renaissance. It is true that some very famous ones were still unknown long after the sixteenth century, though they were there to be seen, as was the case with the Greek temples at Paestum, which remained entirely unnoticed until the eighteenth century.[1] On the other hand, monuments such as the Arena of Verona or some of the principal Roman antiquities of Milan, were already being scrutinized during the early fourteenth century by Benzo d'Alessandria,[2] while Petrarch and Boccaccio also paid attention to some of the ancient monuments outside Rome,[3] as also did Petrarch's devoted friend Giovanni Dondi during his journey, when he went to Rome in 1375 for the Jubilee.[4]

Despite earlier references to Italian antiquities, what one might call the earliest account of the ancient monuments of a town, can be found in a letter of Leonardo Bruni, giving a brief description of those at Rimini, where he happened to be staying with the Papal Curia. Bruni, who was then a papal secretary, had

---

[1] S. Lang, 'The Early Publications of the Temples at Paestum', *Journal of the Warburg and Courtauld Institutes*, XIII (1950) 48–64. The temples had, however, been mentioned as early as 1524 by the Neapolitan humanist Pietro Summonte, cf. *infra*, 130, n.1.

[2] *Supra*, 25, *infra* 122, n. 4.

[3] *Supra*, 35, 44–46. The account of some Milanese antiquities in the *Flos Florum* of Ambrogio Bossi written at the very end of the fourteenth century is, on the other hand, somewhat fictitious, cf. Biblioteca Nazionale Braidense, Milan, Ms. AG. IX. 35, ff. 15ᵛ, 61ʳ, 62ʳ.

[4] *Supra*, 51.

been asked by his friend (later mortal enemy) Niccolò Niccoli for an account of the local Roman remains. The result was his letter to him of 20 February 1409,[1] in which he mentioned the 'Porta', i.e. the arch, of which he also emphasized the archaic diphthongs of the inscriptions, and the bridge on the Marecchia started under Augustus and completed under Tiberius.

Bruni's description of the arch and bridge at Rimini shows how he was chiefly interested in their inscriptions. But in order to find a different approach to antiquities outside Rome, an approach which was appreciative of both their spirit and their historical meaning, we must turn to the *Commentarii rerum memorabilium* of that gifted humanist Enea Silvio Piccolomini, who became Pope Pius II (1458–1464). The learning of the humanist and the sensitivity of the poet colour the descriptions of old remains in the *Commentarii*. Several centuries before Romanticism inaugurated the cult of ruins, Pius II looked at them with romantic eyes. The ruins at Albano, ancient Ostia, and Porto, what remained of Hadrian's villa at Tivoli, led to descriptions conveying the writer's delight between the lines. But whenever antiquities were to be seen, he would stop to inspect them. Not in order to copy inscriptions or take measurements, or to find out what building materials had been employed in their construction, but in order to record their decorative rôle against the green of trees and meadows and the bright coloured spring flowers and to comment on their historical associations.

The sophisticated author of Euryalus and Lucretia bore lightly his massive classical learning. Though we may find him mentioning Strabo a propos of the ruins of ancient Tusculum[2] or referring the reader to Pliny,[3] or pointing out the spot where it was alleged that Milo had killed Clodius,[4] he never loses his lightness of touch, and his erudition never degenerates into pedantry. As a describer of antiquities, he had an eye for the significant that only Alberti's could rival. Thus at Porto Ercole he was quick to notice that the huge square stone blocks of the ancient walls fitted together perfectly without mortar.[5] He

---

[1] *Leonardi Bruni Arretini Epistolarum Libri VIII*, ed. L. Mehus, I, (Florentiae, 1741) 76–83.
[2] Pius Secundus, *Commentaria rerum memorabilium*, (Romae, 1584) 570.
[3] *The Commentaries of Pius II Books X–XIII*, (Northampton, Mass. 1957) 752, Pius Secundus, *op. cit.* 556.
[4] *Ibid.* 565.
[5] *Ibid.* 33.

informs us how a marble pile, then turned into a fort and standing by the second bridge on the Aniene from Tivoli to Rome, had been the tomb of the Plautii.[1] He was really dumbfounded by what he saw of Hadrian's villa,[2] and while at Porto he was especially attracted by some unpolished blocks of stone with numerals marked on both sides, particularly as there was more than one view about their meaning.[3] What seems to have interested him most was Albano and, among the Albano monuments, the so-called tomb of the Horatii and Curiatii, (actually a monument of the Republican period) of which he rightly rejected the traditional attribution.[4]

Pius II looked at Roman antiquities with the eyes of a humanist who was also a literary artist. Leon Battista Alberti looked at them as a humanist who was also an outstanding architect anxious to master the building techniques of classical antiquity. Thus in his *De re aedificatoria* which was completed by 1452, Alberti acknowledged his inability to look at any ancient remains without feeling at once compelled to ascertain whether anything worth while could be learnt from them.[5] This, of course, is not surprising in a man like Alberti, who believed that, so far as architecture was concerned, more could be learnt from the ruins of ancient buildings than from any classical writer.[6] Nor is it surprising to find him making drawings, taking careful measurements, and investigating the materials and building techniques of any old remains he met on his travels. Thus we find him examining some ruins at Alatri[7], the tomb of Theodoric at Ravenna,[8] a small temple in Umbria,[9] and trying to find out the technique used in the paving of the old road from Tivoli to Rome.[10]

Vitruvius, the direct study of ancient building methods, and Alberti's genius made the *De re aedificatoria* the masterpiece of early Renaissance architectural literature. But, not surprisingly, it is vain to search it for a systematic description of those anti-

[1] *Ibid.* 250.
[2] *Ibid.* 251.
[3] *The Commentaries of Pius II Books X–XIII*, 752, Pius Secundus, *op. cit.* 556.
[4] *Ibid.* 564.
[5] L. B. Alberti, *L'Architettura (De re aedificatoria)*, ed. G. Orlandi and P. Portoghesi, II, (Milano, 1966) 443, 556.
[6] *Ibid.* I, 257.
[7] *Ibid.* I, 61.
[8] *Ibid.* loc. cit.
[9] *Ibid.* I, 59.
[10] *Ibid.* I, 321.

quities which came in his way, any more than in Biondo's *Italia illustrata*. But then such descriptions were not among the terms of reference of either Alberti or Biondo. For in the *Italia illustrata* it is quite clear that what was the author's intention was to furnish an account of the Italian peninsula accompanied by historical introductions and digressions, as well as mentions of the famous men, both ancient and modern, who had given fame to the various towns. Nevertheless we also read here of a visit to the ruins of Antium together with Cardinal Prospero Colonna,[1] of his delight at Albano on seeing the care with which the local relics of Antiquity were being looked after,[2] and of his great interest in the attempt to raise the sunken ships from the bottom of Lake Nemi.[3]

In order to find descriptions of Roman remains outside Rome by Biondo, it is necessary to turn to his extant letters. One of them, sent to Leonello d'Este, Marquis of Ferrara, and written at Marino on 13th November, 1444,[4] is full of admiration for some Roman ruins seen in the course of a hunt organized by Cardinal Prospero Colonna in honour of Borso d'Este. Moreover, Biondo says in it how the Cardinal, who is known to have supplied Biondo with information for the *Italia illustrata*,[5] had also taken him to Nemi, where he had the excitement of being able to inspect some pieces of Caligula's sunken ships which had been brought up from the lake, and then to Albano, where he had been most impressed by what was still left of the ancient theatre.[6] In another letter, of 12 September 1461 addressed to Gregorio Lolli,[7] Biondo included a description of some most impressive ruins, obviously those of Hadrian's villa, still to be seen about two miles from Tivoli. But to go back to the *Italia illustrata*, there is no doubt that this treatise, in which Biondo can be rightly said to have inaugurated historical geography, exerted an overwhelming influence on later topographical and geographical literature. Not only treatises like the *Geographia* of Berlinghieri, but also accounts of towns such as that of Ravenna

---

[1] Blondus, *Opera, Italia illustrata*, 311.
[2] *Infra*, 113.
[3] *Ibid. loc. cit.*
[4] Nogara, *op. cit.* 154–59.
[5] A. Campana, 'Due note su Roberto Valturio', *Studi Riminesi e bibliografici in onore di Carlo Lucchesi*, (Faenza, 1952) 15.
[6] This theatre was also described in the *Commentarii* of Pius II, cf. Pius Secundus, *op. cit.* 563.
[7] Nogara, *op. cit.* 194–202.

THE ANTIQUITIES OF ITALY: I

by Desiderio Spreti or that of Nola by Ambrogio Leone, display quite clearly the hall-mark of Biondo's treatise.

Besides Enea Silvio Piccolomini, other humanist travellers did not fail to notice the Roman arches, bridges, theatres, aqueducts, etc., dotted all over the Italian countryside. Of these travellers, Enea Silvio Piccolomini may have been the greatest artist. Archaeologically, however, by far the most important of them was Ciriaco d'Ancona (1391?–after 1453). The achievement of this indefatigable traveller lies, it is true, in the field of Greek archaeology. It would, however, be erroneous to assume that he did not also spend much energy and time on the antiquities of Italy. What has reached us about his activities in Italy does not amount, admittedly, to very much. His so-called *Itinerarium*,[1] in which he described his Italian journeys up to 1435, is unfortunately somewhat confused and only exceptionally tells us as much as we would like to know about this or that monument. Fortunately this is partially supplemented by some extant fragments of his lost *Commentaria*,[2] and also by the biography of Ciriaco written by his fellow-citizen and friend Francesco Scalamonti.[3] From all this it is obvious that during his Italian journeys Ciriaco also made copious notes and sketches of what caught his eye. Naturally his first priority on such journeys was the transcription of inscriptions: but he also sketched monuments and took measurements of ancient ruins, made drawings of coins or statues, and occasionally copied out a passage which had particularly interested him in a volume seen in some library. Needless to say, these explorations were inspired by his great enthusiasm for classical antiquity. It was therefore quite typical of this enthusiasm that when he visited Fano in 1448 or 1449 he was so impressed by the local arch of Augustus that, besides copying its inscriptions, he could not resist delivering a lecture to some of the local inhabitants on its historical significance.[4] Nor is it difficult to imagine his feelings when he saw the Arena at Verona,[5] or when in front of Trajan's arch at Benevento[6] or of

---

[1] Published in *Kyriaci Anconitani Itinerarium*, ed. L. Mehus, (Florentiae, 1742).

[2] A. Degli Abati Olivieri, *Commentariorum Cyriaci Anconitani nova fragmenta notis illustrata*, (Pisaurii, 1763). See also C. C. Van Essen, 'I Commentaria di Ciriaco d'Ancona', *Il Mondo Antico nel Rinascimento-Atti del V Convegno Internazionale di studi sul Rinascimento*, (Firenze, 1958), 191–94, Bodnar, *op. cit.* 69–72.

[3] G. Colucci, *Delle antichità Picene*, XV (Fermo, 1792), XLV–CLV.

[4] P. *Ovidii Fastorum*, (Rome, 1489) f. 91ᵛ; R. Sabbadini, *Classici e umanisti da codici ambrosiani*, (Firenze, 1933) 122. When Ciriaco went to Fano the so-called 'Basilica' of Vitruvius had already disappeared, as it had been destroyed about 1274 by St. Nicholas of Tolentino, cf. G. Berardi, *Fano Romana, Basilica di Vitruvio*, (Fano, 1967) 44–45.

[5] *Infra*, 117.   [6] Colucci, *op. cit.* XV, XCIC.

that erected in honour of the same emperor in his native Ancona.[1]

Other travellers with antiquarian tastes are also known to have recorded the antiquities they saw during their journeys. Such a traveller was Marin Sanudo, the famous Venetian diarist who was the author of, among other things, a *De antiquitatibus Italiae*[2] which has not reached us, and a statistical and geographical description of Friuli.[3] In his *Itinerario* Sanudo recorded the tour made by him in 1483 through the Venetian territories on the Italian mainland, the so-called 'Terraferma'. Thus along the shores of Lake Garda we see his attention being caught by some Roman mosaics and other antiquities, and particularly by a capital with the head of Zeus Ammon in the church of Santa Maria del Benaco.[4] Needless to say, Roman Verona impressed him very much.[5] The two places where his antiquarian enthusiasm soared highest were, however, Aquileia and Pola. What appealed to him in particular at Aquileia, apart from the very early churches, were the broken walls, a theatre, and an aqueduct among the ruins of the patriarchal palace 'mal conditionato et roto, ut dicitur, longo mia 7'.[6] At Pola it was the amphitheatre and the triumphal arch[7] that made him so enthusiastic. His enthusiasm for the monuments of Pola was shared by another humanist, that Pietro Martire d'Anghiera who spent most of his life in the Spanish service and became the historian of the New World. So much so that in his relation of the Embassy of 1501 to the Venetians and the Sultan of Egypt on behalf of Ferdinand and Isabella, he mentioned having seen at Pola two ancient theatres, an arch with inscriptions, as well as many other epigraphic texts, of which he copied about forty.[8]

One of the many problems facing antiquarians was the identification of ancient sites and the establishing whether a town or village and if so which had been built over them. An attempt to equate ancient with modern place names was made again and again by Biondo in the *Italia illustrata*, and after him it became a

[1] A. Campana, 'Giannozzo Manetti, Ciriaco e l'arco di Trajano ad Ancona', *Italia Medioevale e Umanistica*, II (1959) 483–504.

[2] Cf. M. Sanudo, *Itinerario per la Terraferma Veneziana nell'anno MCCCCLXXXIII*, ed. Rawdon Brown, (Padova, 1847) 29.

[3] *Descrizione della Patria del Friuli di Marino Sanuto fatta l'anno MDII-MDIII* L. ed., Manin, (Venezia, 1853).

[4] Sanudo, *Itinerario per la Terraferma Veneziana*, 88.

[5] *Ibid.* 99–101.

[6] *Ibid.* 143–44.

[7] *Ibid.* 153–54.

[8] S. Maffei, *Verona illustrata*, IV, (Verona, 1731) 191–92.

common practice among topographical writers. Needless to say, the identification of the site of an ancient town was not always successful. The attempts of the humanist Antonio Ivani to find the modern equivalents of some ancient place names in Lunigiana, led to many erroneous conjectures derived from his relying too much on a very corrupt manuscript of Florus, all these being clear from his letter to Leonardo Tobalio of Pontremoli of 30 January 1442.[1] In other cases it could be long before a very obvious site was identified. For instance it was only as late as 1442 that Giacomo Bracelli established in his *Descriptio orae Ligusticae* that the Gulf of La Spezia was the harbour of ancient Luni[2], an identification which was accepted by Biondo in the *Italia illustrata*[3] and Berlinghieri in the *Geographia*[4]. It could also happen that an identification did not necessarily encounter universal approval. In the *De bello hispaniensi* Bracelli refused to accept the view that Piombino was the ancient Populonia.[5] In fact a disputed identification could even lead to a debate which might drag on for centuries. In 1525, for instance, there appeared by the types of Ludovico Arrighi a Latin poem by Pietro Corsi, a humanist solely remembered now for his polemic with Erasmus, in which he sought to establish that Civita Castellana had been an 'oppidum' of the Falisci, not of the Veientes,[6] as was held by many.[7] Here was an issue which was not yet closed three centuries later, when a book was issued in Terni seeking to prove that Civita Castellana had been the ancient Veium.[8]

Of all controversies of this type, that on the Rubicon which Caesar had crossed, went on longest. Among the many rivers of Romagna the actual choice was among the Pisciatello, called Rigone in its lower reaches, the Fiumicino near Savignano, and the Uso, the last one being the 'official' Rubicon of today.[9] Of

[1] G. Sforza, 'Gli studi archeologici sulla Lunigiana e i suoi scavi dal 1442 al 1800', *Atti e memorie della R. Deputazione di Storia Patria per le Provincie Modenesi*, ser. 4, VII (1895) 81.
[2] *Ibid.* 90.
[3] Blondus, *Opera, Italia illustrata*, 299.
[4] F. Berlinghieri, *Geographia*, (Firenze, 1482) f. eei[v].
[5] C. Andriani, 'Giacomo Bracelli nella storia della geografia', *Atti della Società Ligure di Storia Patria*, LII (1924) 145.
[6] *Petri Cursii Civis Ro. Poema de Civitate Castellana Faliscorum non Veientium oppido*, (Rome, 1525).
[7] See for instance Pius Secundus, *op. cit.* 63.
[8] F. Morelli, *Dissertazione in cui si stabilisce per ipotesi che Civita-Castellana è l'antica Veio si cerca qual fu la sede de' Falisci e dove parte di questi si stabilì dopo la presa di Veio*, (Terni, 1825).
[9] A brief account of the various views on the Rubicon up to the middle of the sixteenth century is in *Dissertazione seconda dell'abate Pasquale Amati savignanese sopra alcune lettere del signor dottor Bianchi di Rimini e sopra il Rubicone degli antichi*, (Faenza, 1763) 6–8.

these the Pisciatello was the favourite among fifteenth century humanists. It was the choice of Biondo,[1] who quoted in support the so-called 'Sanctio', that is to say the apocryphal inscription placed by a bridge on this river and forbidding any army to cross in the name of the Roman senate and people.[2] This identification was accepted by Francesco Berlinghieri[3] and Raffaele Maffei (Volaterrano), who also gave the text of the 'sanctio'.[4] It was rejected, on the other hand, by Pontico Virunio, who in the dedication of his *Historiae Britannicae* completed at Reggio Emilia in 1508, denied that the Pisciatello was Caesar's Rubicon.[5] The 'Sanctio' was eventually removed in 1522 (only to be put back in 1545) at the request of the 'Decuriones' of Cesena but for the wrong reasons. For its removal was not due to its being believed to be a forgery, but because of its dilapidated condition.[6]

The removal of the 'Sanctio' in 1522 shows how anxiety for local antiquities could also be felt outside Rome. But already some sixty years earlier the gradual destruction of what still remained of Roman Luni had been arousing considerable apprehension. To stop any further damage to those ruins was clearly imperative, but how was this to be achieved? Cardinal Filippo Calandrini who as a local man viewed the situation with dismay, thought that the only way to save the ruins was to secure an order from the Pope. He may have been successful in getting a brief from the Pope, but not in ending the demolitions. For though Pius II had intervened by issuing a brief on 7 April 1461 forbidding any interfering with the remains of Luni,[7] it made, unfortunately, no difference at all. In fact when the 'Palazzo del Comune' was being built at Sarzana in 1474, stone from Luni provided a considerable part of the building materials.[8]

Against the countless destructions, the number of restorations of ancient monuments was distressingly small. The repairs

---

[1] Blondus, *Opera, Italia illustrata*, 343.
[2] *C.I.L.* XI. I, 30*. To those who gave the text of this inscription should be added Jacopo da Udine in a letter to Francesco Barbaro of 1448, cf. 'Jacobi de Utino canonici Aquilejensis De civitate Aquilejae Epistola', *Miscellanea di varie operette . . . all'illustriss. Sig. Abate D. Giuseppe Pasini . . .* , II (Venezia, 1740) 115.
[3] Berlinghieri, *op. cit.* f. ee4r.
[4] Volaterranus, *op. cit.* f. K7r.
[5] L. Ponticus Virunius, *Historiae Britannicae*, (S.L.N.A.) f. b3v.
[6] J. P. Braschius, *De vero Rubicone quem Caesar contra Romanum interdictum trajecit*, (Romae, 1733) 301. The 'Sanctio' is now at Cesena in the Museo Archeologico.
[7] The brief is printed in G. Sforza, *La patria, la famiglia e la giovinezza di Niccolò V*, (Lucca, 1884) 270–71.
[8] Sforza, *Gli studi archeologici sulla Lunigiana*, 87, n. 1.

done to the Roman aqueduct at Albano at the expense of Cardinal Ludovico Trevisan[1] and the isolation by him of other ancient remains there,[2] were unfortunately as untypical as they were infrequent. Nonetheless some care for antiquities could also be seen in neighbouring Nemi, thanks to the enlightened outlook of its feudal lord, Biondo's protector Cardinal Prospero Colonna.[3] He was responsible for what might be called the first attempt at archaeological recovery.

For a long time pieces of wood, bronze fittings, etc., belonging to two ships which could be dimly seen in clear weather lying on the bottom of the lake, had been brought up at Nemi in the nets of local fishermen. Some of these pieces had been shown to Biondo by Cardinal Colonna in 1444.[4] One can accordingly wonder how much the Cardinal's eventual decision to salvage the ships was due to Biondo's powers of persuasion. Whether or not this was so, the Cardinal decided in due course to salvage the ships and commissioned Alberti, then a papal abbreviator, to proceed with it. That the choice of Alberti, who was obviously the man best qualified for the task, had been suggested by Biondo, then a colleague of his in the Papal Chancery, cannot be confirmed but seems likely enough. What is, however, important is that Alberti had divers and the necessary machinery sent from Genoa, and set about the task. The raising of the first ship, which took place not later than June 1450, was something of an occasion, as the papal court had come to Nemi to watch the operation. But one of the ships had already been lifted out of the water when the rotten wood gave way, so that it went back to the bottom,[5] after which no further attempt was made. What was salvaged nonetheless proved of some value to both Biondo and Alberti. Thanks to it, the former was able to give a detailed account of how the ships had been built and attribute erroneously their construction to Tiberius on the strength of an inscription on a lead pipe.[6] The latter also investigated their structure, but by assigning their construction to Trajan[7] he also proved quite

[1] Blondus, *Opera, Italia illustrata*, 319.
[2] *Ibid*, loc. cit.
[3] *Supra*, 108.
[4] Nogara, *op. cit.* 155.
[5] Blondus, *Opera, Italia illustrata*, 326. The passage concerning the Nemi ships in Pius Secundus, *op. cit.* 566–67 derives from Biondo. The account in *Lilii Gregorii Gyraldi Ferrariensis de re nautica libellus*, (Basileae, 1540) 47, comes entirely from Alberti, *op. cit.* I, 389.
[6] Blondus, *Opera, Italia illustrata*, 326.
[7] Alberti, *op. cit.* I, 389.

wrong. On the other hand, one would search Alberti's extant
writings in vain for any mention of his salvage attempts, perhaps
because the operation had been a failure.[1]

Compared to the attempted rescue of the Nemi ships, the
haphazard excavations occasionally attempted outside Rome
seldom proved exciting. Also because rather than proper searches
with an archaeological aim, they really were diggings made in
the course of agricultural work, or while laying the foundations
of a new building, or while searching for buried treasure. An
exception was the spectacular dig which took place at Viterbo
in the autumn of 1493, during which the statues of some of
the more flamboyant characters connected with the mythical
history of the city were unearthed. Unfortunately on this
occasion the ground had been previously 'salted' by the notorious Giovanni Nanni, better known as Annio da Viterbo,
who promptly lectured on the exceptional historical significance of these wonderful finds.[2] Needless to say, what
Annio brought to light was a series of miserable fakes
manufactured for the occasion. Genuine discoveries were,
however, far from being uncommon. Apart from the immediate
neighbourhood of Rome, one hears of a bronze Hercules half a
cubit in height and a cornaline with a man's head found at
Luni or thereabout in 1474 by a peasant, who ceded them to
the famous sculptor Matteo Civitali.[3] In 1510 the Sarzana city
council presented a marble triton found at Luni to the French
governor of Genoa.[4] In 1489 one learns of some golden ornaments, certainly Etruscan, being unearthed at Corneto, the ancient
Tarquinia.[5] Excavations also seem to have been carried out at Este
during the Quattrocento. We know this thanks to the priest
Girolamo Atestino, who mentioned in his vernacular chronicle
how gold rings, engraved gems, and bronze weapons, were
constantly being found in old tombs in Este and its territory,
mosaics, marble pillars, and gold and silver coins also coming to
light there very frequently.[6] But talking of Este, it may be worth
mentioning that an antique lamp, allegedly still burning when

---

[1] Perhaps Alberti's now lost *De Nave*, on which cf. Alberti, *op. cit.* I, 389, was connected
with the Nemi ships.

[2] Weiss, *Traccia per una biografia di Annio da Viterbo*, 434.

[3] Sforza, *Gli studi archeologici sulla Lunigiana*, 85.

[4] *Ibid.* 102.

[5] M. Pallottino, 'Tarquinia', *Monumenti antichi pubblicati per cura della R. Accademia
Nazionale dei Lincei*, XXXVI (1937) 20.

[6] H. Atestino, *La cronica de la antiqua cittade de Ateste*, (S.L.N.A.) ff. a4r, b3r.

discovered, was found at Este about 1500. Our source for this extraordinary piece of information is the humanist Francesco Maturanzio, who tells us that he eventually became the owner of so unique a piece and left a description of it.[1] Whether he invented the story or was made to believe it, is unknown. But one may well wonder whether we have here a distant echo of the story concerning another ancient lamp 'still burning', found in the tomb of Pallas in Rome and handed down to us by William of Malmesbury.[2]

Thanks to Elia Caprioli we learn that a considerable number of statues and small bronzes were being unearthed at Brescia in his own time.[3] Particularly noteworthy among these was a bronze figure of Mars, found among the ruins of a temple dedicated to this god just outside the city.[4] The discovery of Etruscan antiquities near his native Volterra was recalled by Raffaele Maffei, who mentioned in particular a recently found stone image with an Etruscan inscription,[5] this being one of many which were continually being found there. Further south, the countless tombs, cinerary urns, bronze arms, and gold rings which were continually found outside Vasto, were mentioned by Antonio Galateo in the *De situ Iapigiae*.[6] But in order to find an investigation of ancient sites prompted by definite antiquarian aims one has to turn to Sigismondo Tizio, whose explorations of ancient underground passages at Chiusi, in which he found and inspected tombs and inscribed pottery,[7] speak for his enthusiasm.[8]

---

[1] See on this F. Scardeonius, *De antiquitate urbis Patavii*, (Basileae, 1560) 55–6, G. B. Vermiglioli, *Memorie per servire alla vita di Francesco Maturanzio oratore e poeta perugino*, (Perugia, 1807) 50–3. Scardeonius, *op. cit.* 56 gives the inscriptions on the urns inside which was found the lamp, and which are an obvious humanist forgery, this being shown by the non-classical name Olibius on both inscriptions and some words from Plautus, *Aulularia* 41 on l. 2 of the second inscription.

[2] *Supra*, 10 n.6.

[3] H. Capreolus, *Chronica de rebus Brixianorum*, (Brixiae, s.a.) f. A6ʳ.

[4] *Ibid.* f. B4ᵛ.

[5] Volaterranus, *op. cit.* f.G8ᵛ.

[6] A. Galateus, *Liber de situ Iapygiae*, (Basileae, 1558) 96.

[7] P. Piccolomini, *La vita e l'opera di Sigismondo Tizio* (1458–1528), (Siena, 1903) 137.

[8] It is worth pointing out that ancient remains also attracted the attention of Leonardo da Vinci who was, incidentally, the owner of a volume with drawings of ancient buildings, cf. Pedretti, *op. cit.* 79, L. Reti 'The Two Unpublished Manuscripts of Leonardo da Vinci in the Biblioteca Nacional of Madrid-II', *Burlington Magazine*, CX (1968) 81, 86, n. 100. But his drawings of some remains near Civitavecchia, on which/cf. L. H. Heydenreich, 'Studi archeologici di Leonardo da Vinci a Civitavecchia', *Raccolta Vinciana*, XIV (1930–34) 39–53, were aiming at a reconstruction of them for ends not necessarily antiquarian.

CHAPTER NINE

THE ANTIQUITIES OF ITALY: II

Antique remains were often used as evidence for the identification of ancient sites or buildings, etc. Thus a letter of Antonio Ivani to his fellow humanist Antonio Medusei written on 15 July 1473, informs us how after having seen an inscription on its wall, which suggested that the abbey church of San Venanzio at Ceperana stood on the site once occupied by the temple of Jupiter Sabatius, he had carried out an exploration of the church, which was rewarded by the discovery of an ancient pillar in the choir and three similar ones in the crypt, which confirmed his suspicions.[1] This discovery gave him also an excuse for a dissertation on the cult of Jupiter Sabatius in the same letter,[2] while in another written to Niccolò Michelozzi in 1472,[3] he maintained that the ancient theatre at Luni had really been an amphitheatre and that ancient Luni had been far larger than the medieval city.

Another humanist, Desiderio Spreti, having noticed on two of the mosaics of Sant'Apollinare Nuovo at Ravenna representing the palace of Theodoric and the town of Classe, that churches and other buildings had curtains instead of doors, thought he could confirm the veracity of this detail by referring to some ancient bronze hooks still on the top of the two entrances of the church of San Vitale.[4] The Arena of Verona and a passage in Juvenal enabled the humanist Giovanni Antonio Panteo to assert that this city had been a Roman 'municipium';[5] just as the marbles, pillars, mosaics, coins and inscriptions found at Este, enabled Girolamo Atestino to assert that the town had once belonged to the Roman Emperors.[6] Stone carvings and inscriptions also enabled Elia Caprioli to identify the existence of some

---

[1] Sforza, *Gli studi archeologici sulla Lunigiana*, 77–9.
[2] *Ibid.* 79.
[3] *Ibid.*, 84–5; G Targioni Tozzetti, *Relazioni d'alcuni viaggi in diverse parti della Toscana*, XI, (Firenze, 1777) 21.
[4] D. Spretus, *De amplitudine, de vastatione et de instauratione urbis Ravennae*, (Venetiis, 1489) f. a6v.
[5] *Annotationes Joannis Antonii Panthei Veronensis*, (Venetiis, 1506) f. P2r.
[6] Atestino, *op. cit.*, f. b3r.

particular cults as well as temples in the Brescia countryside.[1]
And this same humanist had enough enthusiasm to travel all
the way to Milan, just in order to examine the columns of the
church of San Lorenzo and thus confirm his suspicions that some
buildings at Brescia had been erected by the Emperor Maximian.[2]

The antiquity and size of ancient Lupiae were assumed by
Antonio Galateo on the evidence of an arch, passages, vaults,
and foundations of buildings which could still be seen underground.[3] It was left to Benedetto Giovio, the humanist brother
of the far more famous Paolo, to conjecture from the presence
of mosaic pavements in Borgovico at Como, just where the
Convent of the Umiliati was standing, that this must have been
the situation of the villa of Caninius Rufus mentioned by the
younger Pliny[4]; at the same time the pillars in the Como baptistery led him to wonder whether they were all that was left of the
porch of Calpurnius Fabatus, the existence of which had been
revealed to him by the younger Pliny's letters.[5] Needless to say,
some of the ancient monuments outside Rome aroused particular
interest.   As the most important Roman building in north
Italy, it was inevitable that the Arena of Verona should have
been viewed with both awe and admiration during the Middle
Ages.[6] During the first half of the fifteenth century the Arena,
which an anonymous account, probably late medieval, had
called 'altum lambyrintum in quo nescitur ingressus et
egressus',[7] was visited by Ciriaco d'Ancona, who declared that
it had been built by Augustus in the year 3 B.C., giving at the
same time a description of it full of admiration for the way in
which it had been built.[8] According to Giovanni Antonio
Panteo's De laudibus Veronae of 1483, the Arena struck one as a
superhuman construction.[9] As for the builder of it, who could
he have been but Vitruvius? Such an attribution seemed quite
obvious to Marin Sanudo, who on being shown by the local
humanist Giusto dei Giusti the inscription with the name L.
VITRVVIVS on the arch of the Gavi, which was locally believed

[1] Capreolus, op. cit. f. B4r-v.
[2] Ibid. f. A2r-v.
[3] Galateus, op. cit. 82–83.
[4] B. Giovio, Opere scelte edite per cura della Società storica Comense, (Como, 1887) 231; C.
Plinius Secundus, Epistularum Libri Decem, I, iii.
[5] Giovio, Opere scelte . . ., 233; Plinius Secundus, op. cit. V. xi.
[6] Cf. Maffei, op. cit. IV, 79–88.
[7] Biblioteca Vaticana, Ms. Vat. lat. 5108, f. 30r.
[8] Colucci, op. cit., XV, XCIII.
[9] Annotationes Joannis Antonii Panthei Veronensis, f. P4v.

to have been part of the Arena, jumped to the conclusion that this Vitruvius, whom he felt certain was the great architect, had also been responsible for the building of it.[1]

Other monuments, such as the arch of Augustus and the bridge of Tiberius at Rimini, the 'Porta Aurea' at Ravenna, the arch of Augustus at Fano, were locally regarded with enough pride to be reproduced on the seals of their respective towns.[2] Furthermore the Fano arch was the subject of a lecture by Ciriaco d'Ancona;[3] and after the destruction of its upper part during the siege of 1464, it was at least twice represented as it was before being damaged, first about 1475 on a capital of the Loggie of San Michele, and again in 1513 on the front of the new church of San Michele,[4] lest the original appearance of so important a monument be forgotten. Some particular sites also seem to have exerted an unusual appeal. During the second half of the fourteenth century, the ruins at Sirmione on Lake Garda, the so-called 'Grotte di Catullo', were noticed by Benvenuto da Imola, who said in his commentary on Dante's *Divine Comedy* how he had seen there the remains of ancient buildings underground and how nothing grew there except olives.[5] During the fifteenth century some passing references to the Roman remains at Sirmione were made in the *De laudibus Veronae* by Giovanni Antonio Panteo,[6] the commentary on Catullus by Antonio Partenio da Lazise,[7] and the emendations on Catullus and the *Priapeia* by Girolamo Avanzi, who was full of admiration for the 'structuram latericiam Triplici fornice concuneatam' which he saw there.[8] All this shows, of course, that for obvious geographical reasons the Sirmione ruins were well known to the humanists of Verona. Yet it was a humanist from Milan, Stefano Dulcinio, who furnished in a letter of 31 October 1502 prefixed to his *Sirmio*[9] the first description of any length of those remains. Dulcinio's description of the Sirmione ruins does not add to our

---

[1] Sanudo, *Itinerario per la Terraferma Veneziana*, 101.
[2] G. C. Bascapé, 'I sigilli dei Comuni Italiani nel medio evo e nell'età moderna', *Studi di paleografia, diplomatica, storia e araldica in onore di Cesare Manaresi*, (Milano, 1953) 89, 91–2, pl. II, 23.
[3] *Supra*, 109.
[4] For these 'reproductions' see R. Weiss, 'L'arco di Augusto a Fano nel Rinascimento', *Italia Medioevale e Umanistica*, VIII (1965) 351–58, PL. XIV-XV.
[5] *Benevenuti de Rambaldis de Imola Comentum super Dantis Aldigherii Comoediam*, II, 181.
[6] *Annotationes Joannis Antonii Panthei Veronensis*, f. P4[v].
[7] Catullus, *(Carmina)*, (Venetiis, 1491) f. gi[v].
[8] *Hier. Avancii . . . in Val. Catullum et in Priapeias Emendationes*, (Venetiis, 1495) f. a5[r].
[9] S. Dulcinius, *Sirmio*, (Mediolani, 1502) ff. a3[v]-6[r].

knowledge of them except in this, that they appear to have been then in the same state as they still were before the site was thoroughly excavated and restored a few decades ago.

Another famous site, that of ancient Tarquinia, did not find a Dulcinio to describe it. Passing references to it may on the other hand be found as early as Petrarch, who after mentioning Corneto in the *Itinerarium Syriacum*, stated that within its boundaries was Tarquinia, now but a name and ruins.[1] Also Domenico Bandini reflected similar sentiments about Tarquinia.[2] But although some diggings, doubtless prompted by the hope of treasure, were occasionally made there during the Quattrocento,[3] several centuries were to elapse before Tarquinia was really discovered. It was during the early sixteenth century that the discovery of ancient Etruria started. But the real discoverer of the Etruscans was the Scotsman Thomas Dempster in the early seventeenth century with his *De Etruria Regali*, a work which had to wait for over a century before appearing in print.[4]

Already Flavio Biondo had shown some interest in the Etruscans, one of the digressions in his *Italia illustrata* being an attempt to show what the Romans had owed to them.[5] Here Leon Battista Alberti went further. For besides noticing the Etruscan remains that came his way during his wanderings through the territories of ancient Etruria, he was also keen enough to inspect various ruins, cemeteries, and tombs recently brought to light.[6] He also saw, it is interesting to note, how the lettering of their inscriptions, though close to the Greek and Latin characters, was something quite different and, moreover, quite unintelligible.[7] The Etruscan language may have appeared so to Alberti. On the other hand, it appeared to his contemporaries to have no mysteries for the notorious Annio da Viterbo, whose shameless fabrications included some texts in an obvious gibberish, which he claimed to be Etruscan and found no

---

[1] Petrarca, *Opera*, (Venetiis, 1503) f. c5r.

[2] *Supra*, 56.

[3] *Ibid*. 114. The underground passages, tombs with figures, and statues at Tarquinia were mentioned in a Latin poem by Lorenzo Vitelli or Vitelleschi, written during the second half of the fifteenth century and addressed to Francesco Filelfo, cf. Pallottino, *Tarquinia*, 19.

[4] T. Dempster, *De Etruria Regali libri VII*, (Florentiae, 1723–24). On interest in the Etruscans during the Quattrocento see A. Chastel, 'L' "Etruscan Revival" du XVe Siècle', *Revue Archéologique*, (1959) I, 165–80.

[5] Blondus, *Opera*, *Italia illustrata*, 300.

[6] Alberti, *op. cit*. II, 697.

[7] *Ibid*. loc. cit.

difficulty in turning into Latin.[1] No one to-day believes in the 'discoveries' of Annio, though as late as the mid-eighteenth century the Lisbon Academy was still deeming it advisable to warn scholars against his forgeries. But even some of his contemporaries were not deceived by his claims. Raffaele Maffei, for instance, not only dismissed his discoveries[2] but, furthermore, as was fitting to a native of Volterra, that is to say a town where Etruscan antiquities were continually brought to light, went as far as to examine the problem of Etruscan origins and to sketch a history of this people in his *Commentaria Urbana*.[3] The greatest effort in this field was, however, that of Sigismondo Tizio, the chronicler of Siena. If Tizio is still remembered, it is certainly not because of his critical powers, which were decidedly weak, to the point that he never suspected the authenticity of the texts published by Annio.[4] Hence when he dealt with the origins of the Etruscans and Siena, his conclusions were certainly very dubious.[5] It is all the same undeniable that he felt an irresistible attraction towards the Etruscan civilization. To learn Etruscan soon became his principal aim, and though he naturally failed, nonetheless he honestly thought he had found the way to understand the many inscriptions he had so sedulously transcribed.[6]

The origins of a town, the identity of its founder or founders, when had its foundation taken place, who had been its most illustrious citizens, were questions which were already being asked and answered during the Middle Ages and continued to be posed during the Renaissance. Civic pride had naturally stimulated such an interest, and if a town happened to be the birthplace of one of the great men of Antiquity some monument or at least an alleged tomb was often provided. Here Mantua had probably been the first with its thirteenth century statue of Virgil in the garb of a medieval university teacher, still to be seen to-day on the front of the 'Broletto'. Of another statue of Virgil in the town, all we know is that it was removed in 1397 by Carlo Malatesta as an object of superstitious cult, thus

---

[1] Cf. O. A. Danielsson, 'Etruskische Inschriften in handschriftlicher Ueberlieferung', *Skrifter utgivna av K. Humanistika Vetenskap-Samfundet i Uppsala*, 25:3, (Uppsala-Leipzig, 1928) XIII–XX, R. Weiss, 'An unknown epigraphic tract by Annius of Viterbo', *Italian Studies presented to E. R. Vincent*, (Cambridge, 1962) 101–20.

[2] *Volaterranus, op. cit.* f. RR5r.

[3] *Ibid.* f. G8v.

[4] Biblioteca Vaticana, Ms. Chig. G.I. 31, ff. 10v, 32r, etc.

[5] Piccolomini, *op. cit.*, 151–52.

[6] Cf. Biblioteca Vaticana, Ms. Chig. G. I. 31, ff. 39v–42r, 48r, 51v–52r, etc.

arousing the indignation of humanist Italy.[1] And that a Virgil 'cult' existed in Mantua is also brought home to us by the presence of his effigy on the local coinage.[2] But this and the statue on the 'Broletto' still seemed inadequate to Isabella d'Este, the very intellectual wife of Francesco Gonzaga, Marquis of Mantua. Thus in 1499 we find her in touch with both Gioviano Pontano the humanist and Mantegna the painter about a monument to Virgil to be erected in Mantua,[3] a scheme which came to nought, probably because of lack of money.

What Virgil meant to Mantua Ovid meant to Sulmona. Apart from his appearing on the local seals, more than one statue of Ovid was to be seen there during the fifteenth century. One of these, erected in 1477 by Polidoro Tiberti of Cesena during his term as 'Capitano' of Sulmona and still preserved in the local museum, shows the poet in the attire of a 'doctor'.[4] The cult of Ovid at Sulmona was, however, equalled by that of Livy at Padua. The tomb of Antenor, the alleged founder of the city, had been erected there as early as 1283-84. Visible evidence for a local cult of Livy started later. The discovery of the inscription of another Livy, immediately identified as the great historian, made between 1318 and 1324 was followed in 1413 by that of some bones believed to be his own. Eventually in 1428 these bones were placed with an inscription and bust on one of the outer walls of the Salone della Ragione. Not for long, however, for in 1457 they were removed into the interior of the building, together with the presumed tombstone and a new bust.[5] It was left to Como to place statues of the two Plinies on each side of the main entrance of the Cathedral at the very end of the fifteenth century at the instigation of Benedetto Giovio.

The tomb of an illustrious citizen could occasionally lead to some confusion. This is what happened at Parma, where the supposed remains of the tomb of Macrobius, then believed to have been born in the town, could still be seen in the fourteenth century. The date of their final disappearance is unknown.[6]

[1] *Supra*, 50-51.

[2] A. Magnaguti, 'Numismatica Virgiliana', *Numismatica Mantovana*, I (1927) 11-3, 27-31, 61-2.

[3] E. Tietze Conrat, *Mantegna*, (London, 1955) 207.

[4] Pl. VIII, A. Campana, 'Le statue quattrocentesche di Ovidio e il capitanato sulmonese di Polidoro Tiberti', *Atti del Convegno internazionale Ovidiano*, I, (Roma, 1959) 269-88.

[5] Ullman, *Studies in the Italian Renaissance*, 55-8.

[6] A. Mancini, 'Macrobio Parmense', *Archivio storico per le Province Parmensi*, N.S. XXVIII (1928) 1-9.

What we instead know is that after the death in 1416 of the celebrated philosopher and astronomer Biagio Pelacani, the sculptor responsible for his tomb, still to be seen on the front of the Cathedral, represented Pelacani on the right end of it and Macrobius on the left. With the result that already not so many years later, scholars like Ciriaco d'Ancona and Flavio Biondo were led to believe that the tomb was that of Macrobius, to which Pelacani's remains had been added.[1] Monuments such as the stone marking the spot at Rimini where Caesar was believed to have harangued his troops after crossing the Rubicon,[2] or the 'Sanctio' by the bridge near Cesena on what was believed to be that river,[3] are further instances of civic pride, accompanied by an interest in Roman characters and events.

Normally the origins of a town were dealt with in the initial chapters of local chronicles. Another place where they were often discussed was in medieval descriptions of cities. These accounts of cities were not, broadly speaking, conspicuous for the display of critical powers on the part of their authors. The description of Milan by Benzo d'Alessandria written about 1316[4] is an exception. For not only do we find raised and discussed here some problems connected with the origins of this town, but also because they are treated with a thoroughness unusual for his time.

Benzo's methods anticipate in several ways those of the humanists of the next two centuries, when the origins and early history of towns or regions were often the subjects of works of varying size and character. Some of these, such as the long Latin letter on the antiquities and nobility of Aquileia sent to Francesco Barbaro in 1448 by Jacopo da Udine,[5] the *De origine Fulginatum*[6] written after 1453 by the Aristotelian Niccolò Tignosi (1402–1472), who was one of the teachers of Marsilio Ficino, the *De antiquitatibus Carneae* by Fabio Quintiliano Ermacora,[7] the *De origine urbis Venetiarum* by Bernardo Giustinian[8] or the *Carmen in Utini originem* by Marco Antonio Sabellico,[9] were really straight-

[1] *Ibid.* 2–5. See also N. Burtius, *Bononia illustrata*, (Bononiae, 1494) f. a 8ᵛ, Pl. IX.
[2] Campana, *Il cippo riminese di Giulio Cesare.*   [3] *Supra,* 112.
[4] 'Bentii Alexandrini de Mediolano civitate opusculum', ed. L. A. Ferrai, *Bullettino dell'Istituto Storico Italiano*, no. 9 (1890) 15–36.
[5] Printed in *Miscellanea di varie operette . . . all'illustriss. sig. Abate Don Giuseppe Luca Pasini*, II, 105–34.
[6] Biblioteca Nazionale Vittorio Emanuele II, Rome, Ms. 112, ff. 1r–10v.
[7] In Biblioteca Comunale, Udine, Fondo Joppi, Ms. 66.
[8] B. Giustinian, *De origine urbis Venetiarum*, (Venetiis, S.A.).
[9] M. A. Sabellicus, *Opuscula*, (S.L.N.A.), ff. K3ʳ–L9ᵛ.

forward histories. Others, like the same author's *De vetustate Aquileiensis patriae*[1] composed about 1483 or shortly afterwards,[2] combined history and topography, while more or less topographical were the same Sabellico's *De Venetae Urbis situ* written in 1491–92,[3] the account of Palermo by Pietro Ranzani (1428–1492),[4] the *De patria illustrata*[5] by Jacopo da Porcia, this being an account of Friuli sent to Lorenzo de' Medici, Duke of Urbino, and therefore between 1516 and 1519, and perhaps the now lost *De agro Ariminensi* by Roberto Valturio.[6] Some of these treatises, however, also found room for some mention of local antiquities. Thus the *De origine et antiquitate Urbis Senae* by Francesco Patrizi, Bishop of Gaeta,[7] a tract which was one of the sources used by Sigismondo Tizio in his chronicle,[8] mentioned also some of the local antiquities[9], as also did the *De situ Iapigiae* by Antonio Galateo.[10]

Also individual churches were occasionally the subject of what might be called short monographs. To the fourteenth century belongs an account of the foundation of the church of San Giovanni Evangelista at Ravenna.[11] But it was during the sixteenth century that the early churches of this city appear to have been the subject of particular study. Of this kind was the detailed description of the Basilica of Sant' Apollinare in Classe, which the Camaldolese Monk Vitale Acquedotti addressed in

[1] *Ibid.* ff. A3r–F9v.

[2] This date is suggested by a note by Pilade Boccardo on behalf of Marin Sanudo, and therefore written in 1483 or thereabouts, when Boccardo was Sanudo's secretary, in which Sabellico is asked to send the *De vetustate* 'quam primum'. The letter is in Sanudo, *Itinerario per la Terraferma Veneziana*, XLIII.

[3] Sabellicus, *op. cit.*, ff. A2v–D4v; for its date see G. Mercati, *Ultimi contributi alla storia degli umanisti—Fascicolo II*, (Città del Vaticano, 1939) 14, n.1.

[4] *Petri Ranzani Panormitani . . . opusculum de auctore, primordiis et progressu felicis urbis Panormi . . .* (Panormi, 1737).

[5] In Biblioteca Comunale, Udine, Fondo Joppi, Ms. 66.

[6] Campana, *Due note su Roberto Valturio*, 12–17. Also strictly topographical was the description of Bergamo and its countryside written in 1516 by Marcantonio Michiel and printed in *De origine et temporibus Urbis Bergomi Francisci Bellafini liber: Agri et Urbis Bergomatis descriptio Marci Antonii Michaelis Patricii Veneti*, (Venetiis, 1532) ff. e4r -f2r.

[7] Biblioteca Riccardiana, Florence, (Biblioteca Moreniana) Ms. Pecci, 11, ff. 8r–22v.

[8] Vatican Library, Ms. Chig. G.I. 31, f. 175r.

[9] Biblioteca Riccardiana, Florence, (Biblioteca Moreniana) Ms. Pecci, 11, ff. 18v–20r.

[10] Printed in Galateus, *op. cit.* As for the archaeological pursuits of Fra Francesco Colonna, the author of the *Hypnerotomachia Poliphili*, it has been established that the antiquities described in his work are of literary origin, i.e. derived from the works of classical and Renaissance writers, and only very occasionally from ancient remains in the Venetian territory, cf. M. T. Casella and G. Pozzi, *Francesco Colonna–Biografia e opere*, II, (Padova, 1959) 32–77.

[11] The *Tractatus de dedicatione Ecclesie S. Ioannis Evangeliste* in Biblioteca Classense, Ravenna, Ms. 406.

1511 to Cardinal Francesco Soderini,[1] or the tracts on the churches of San Giovanni Evangelista, San Vitale, and the tomb of Galla Placidia, by Gian Pietro Ferretti (1482–1557).[2] The connexion of churches with ancient sites was also not overlooked. Already Giorgio Merula had stressed in the *Antiquitates Vicecomitum* the connexion between the church of San Lorenzo at Milan and the temple of Hercules erected by Maximian.[3] This was also stressed in what was, despite its brevity, the most important study on the archaeology of churches produced in the early sixteenth century, this being the *De templo D. Eustorgii, Tribus Magis, D. Laurentii templo et alii scitu dignis* by Andrea Alciati,[4] to whom we also owe a straightforward early history of Milan[5], written while he was still studying under Giano Parrasio, in which local antiquities were not overlooked.

Among the accounts of towns or regions including some antiquarian information, a few stand out on account of their particular thoroughness or interest. Chronologically, the first one deserving some special mention is the *De amplitudine, de vastatione et de instauratione Urbis Ravennae* by Desiderio Spreti (1414–c.1474). Already in 1457, while seeking refuge in the countryside from the plague, Spreti had found time to address a Latin tract in letter form to the Venetian praetor of Ravenna, Pietro Zorzi[6], in which he gave a narrative of the events which led to the city's coming under Venetian rule in 1441. This tract eventually became part of the second and third books of the *De amplitudine*, which was completed after 1461[7] and posthumously printed in Venice in 1489. Whereas the tract sent to Zorzi was a straightforward historical narrative, this was not so with Spreti's major work. Although its main purpose is also historical, Spreti also found room in it for talking about the city and its most notable monuments. The ancient walls and the 'Porta Aurea',

---

[1] Printed in M. Mazzotti, *La Basilica di Sant'Apollinare in Classe*, (Città del Vaticano, 1954) 243–71.

[2] Cf. Vatican Library, Ms. Vat. lat. 5835, ff. 7r–18v, 58v, Ms. Vat. lat. 5836, ff. 2r–25r.

[3] G. Merula, *Antiquitates Vicecomitum Libri X*, (Mediolani, 1630) 4.

[4] Printed in *Analecta Bollandiana*, XI (1892) 207–11.

[5] *Rerum Patriae Andreae Alciati I.C. celeberrimi libri IIII*, (Mediolani, 1625).

[6] Biblioteca Marciana, Venice, Ms. Lat. XIV. 251 (4685), 6th fascicle, ff. 1r–15v.

[7] Although its composition is given as c. 1459 in *Historiarum Hieronymi Rubei Libri X*, (Venetiis, 1572) 397, its letter of dedication to Vitale Lando, who was podestà of Ravenna in 1461, cf. G. Fabri, *Effemeride sagra et istorica di Ravenna*, (Ravenna, 1675) 412, written after Lando was no longer occupying this office, shows that it must have been completed after that date. A copy of Spreti's work appears in the inventory of books of Giovanni Marcanova drawn up in 1467, cf. L. Sighinolfi, 'La biblioteca di Giovanni Marcanova', *Collectanea variae doctrinae Leoni S. Olschki*, (Monachii, 1921) 218.

which he rightly attributed to Claudius, are mentioned in it,[1] and so are San Vitale, the tomb of Galla Placidia, and the other main churches. And when writing about San Vitale he delighted in mentioning a block of a rare stone to be seen in it which was transparent in spite of its thickness, the two marble figures of boys, then believed to be by no one less than Polycletus, as well as a mosaic on the ceiling with the Agnus Dei, which always appeared as facing one, whichever the angle from which it was observed.[2]

Following what he had learnt from the chronicle of Agnellus, Spreti asserted that the city walls had been enlarged by Galla Placidia and Valentinian III.[3] Of the tomb of Theodoric, he stated that it was now called Sancta Maria Rotunda,[4] and he also mentioned a gilt statue of this king removed by Charlemagne.[5] He also informs us that a church built by the Goths and dedicated to St. Andrew had been recently levelled down by the Venetians in order to make room for their new fortress;[6] but all this is but a sample of what we are told by Spreti, whose interest in mosaics was wide enough for him to use them as sources of antiquarian information.[7] The same applied to local inscriptions and here he struck a new note by giving a substantial group of them at the end of his treatise.[8]

Spreti's volume is still invaluable to the student of the antiquities of Ravenna. The writings on his own native town by Giovanni Nanni, better known as Annio da Viterbo, proved instead a curse to historians and antiquarians for several centuries. What Annio wished to establish was that Viterbo had been the very cradle of civilization. Now the traditional link of the town with Hercules was hardly out of the ordinary. So he decided to improve on it, and in a series of public lectures Annio told his fellow citizens how Isis and Osiris, as well as a host of heroes and heroines indiscriminately drawn from classical mythology, had taken part in its foundation and early development.[9] Evidence for such claims was soon to follow. Thus

[1] Spretus, *op. cit.* f. a4v.
[2] *Ibid.* f. a5r.
[3] *Ibid.* f. a4v.
[4] *Ibid.* f. a5r.
[5] *Ibid.* loc. cit.
[6] *Ibid.* loc. cit.
[7] *Ibid.* f. a6r-v.
[8] *Infra*, 152.
[9] Weiss, *Traccia per una biografia di Annio da Viterbo*, 432.

between 1488 and 1492 he produced a history of Viterbo from the beginning to the time of Pope Innocent VIII (1484–1492),[1] where he gave his own incredible version of its early history. Another of his works, already completed in February 1491 and now lost but for a few fragments, dealt with the illustrious men of Viterbo,[2] its historical reliability being shown by his making the Farnese family descend from Osiris and be brought to Tuscany by prince Tyrrhenus. Furthermore between 1490 and 1492 he manufactured some epigraphic evidence in pseudo-Etruscan and Greek, showing what had happened to Atlas, Electra and Co., after settling in Viterbo, as well as a decree of the Lombard King Desiderius giving details about the territories subjected to the town.[3] Only a fraction of the writings of Annio has reached us. These also include two tracts in which he expounded his epigraphic discoveries[4] and the *Alexandrina lucubratio*, which he dedicated in 1495 to Cardinal Alessandro Farnese, the future Pope Paul III, for which he had selected the very ambitious theme of the origins of Italy.[5]

Annio's forgeries, both literary and epigraphic, accompanied by ample comments, were eventually assembled together in his 'magnum opus', the *Antiquitates*, which were printed for the first time in Rome in 1498. Even by then his enthusiasm for the antiquities of his birthplace had not cooled down. Witness his petition to Pope Alexander VI,[6] in which he begged to be placed in charge of the antiquities of the Viterbo countryside. Whether his petition was successful, we do not know; but one may be left to wonder what his contribution might have been if he had directed his energies and talents to an honest illustration of the genuine antiquities of Viterbo and its adjacent country.

Genuine and straightforward antiquarian enthusiasm backed by a critical and inquisitive mind were instead behind the history of his native Brescia by Elia Caprioli. Also this humanist was very proud of the long history of his city. But, unlike Annio, Caprioli was an honest man, who did not approve of the fabrication of historical evidence. In his day several legends, mostly

[1] The *Viterbiae Historiae Epithoma* in the Vatican Library, Ms. Vat. lat. 6263, ff. 346ʳ–371ᵛ.
[2] Weiss, *An unknown epigraphic tract by Annius of Viterbo*, 102.
[3] *Ibid*. 101–20.
[4] *Supra*, 120, n.1.
[5] Biblioteca Estense, Modena, Ms. Gamma Z 3, 2, ff. 1ʳ–9ᵛ.
[6] A. Mercati, 'Comunicazioni antiquarie dall'Archivio Segreto Vaticano', *Atti della Pontificia Accademia Romana di Archeologia, Rendiconti*, ser. 3, XIX (1942–43) 415–18.

connected with Hercules, were circulating about the origins of Brescia. These he had no hesitation in repudiating.[1] On the other hand, he erroneously believed that the Emperor Maximian had been responsible for some of the ancient buildings in the town.[2] He agreed of course with the view that Brescia had been a Roman colony,[3] and quoted an inscription seen near Toscolano on Lake Garda,[4] in order to prove the connexion between the town and Julius Caesar. The many Roman statues and small bronzes unearthed at Brescia were a source of pride to him. Hence he quoted with obvious pleasure a statement by the well-known antiquarian Michele Ferrarini, asserting that no other town could display so many Roman remains.[5] Another humanist he was delighted to quote was Girolamo Campagnola a propos of two leading local antiquities, namely a very ancient temple and the amphitheatre, then believed to have been built by the Emperor Maximian.[6] He also strove to show with the help of epigraphic evidence, that the church of San Giovanni Battista stood on the site of the oracle of Pallas,[7] and that the church of San Barnaba used to be the temple of Hercules.[8]

The archaeological sections in Caprioli's history show his unusual competence as an antiquarian. In order to find a systematic account of the antiquities of an Italian town we must, however, wait until 1514, when the *De Nola* of Ambrogio Leone was first published in Venice, two years after being completed by the author. Ambrogio Leone (1457–1525), a humanist physician who had settled in Venice because his native town of Nola near Naples had turned down his claims to nobility,[9] is only remembered now as a correspondent of Erasmus, who honoured him with his praise in the *Adagia*.[10] Actually he was also a translator from the Greek of some distinction and belonged to the côterie of Aldus, then the leading humanist circle of Italy. The aim of the *De Nola* was decidedly humanistic. Not only did it include an account of the ancient topography of Nola and its 'ager', but it also strove to show at all costs how the way of life

[1] Capreolus, *op. cit.* ff. A2r–A3v.
[2] *Supra*, 117.
[3] Capreolus, *op. cit.* f. A5r.
[4] *Ibid.* f. Biv.
[5] *Ibid.* f. A6r.
[6] *Ibid.* ff. A4v–A5r.
[7] *Ibid.* f. B4r.
[8] *Ibid.* loc. cit.
[9] G. Remondini, *Della Nolana ecclesiastica storia*, I, (Napoli, 1747) 629.
[10] Erasmus, *Adagiorum Chiliades*, (Basileae, 1515) f. f2v.

of its inhabitants was a direct continuation of that of their ancient forbears.

Leone's description of the 'ager Nolanus' and its boundaries,[1] where following Biondo's example he strove to furnish the location and modern names of various ancient sites, is a very creditable though not invariably accurate effort. He may have been more or less near the mark when he identified Herculanum with Torre del Greco.[2] But he certainly went wrong when he declared that Torre Annunziata was on the site of the ancient Stabia,[3] Castellamare di Stabia being instead the actual one. The topography of Nola in classical times was also the subject of careful study by Leone, a study which indicates his familiarity with the old monuments of the city and local inscriptions. Thus we find him pointing out that the 'Fossae' had protected it from floods,[4] and supplying the size of the ancient city and its gates.[5] He investigated the building materials which had been employed in the ancient remains,[6] nor did he omit, as had been long 'de rigueur', to bewail the ceaseless destruction of what ruins were still left.[7] The description of ancient Nola by Leone includes two amphitheatres, one of which he identified as being part of an already ruined castle,[8] and added furthermore that Orso Orsini, a former feudal lord of the town, had enlarged the 'Regia' with stones removed from one of them.[9] Many other local antiquities still visible, such as the famous 'Tumuli', were described by Leone,[10] who also indicated the sites of ancient temples and streets.[11] As was only natural, Leone drew considerably from inscriptions and classical writers. Excessive reliance on literary texts was actually a source of weakness in his case, since he often failed to interpret correctly their topographical indications. What, incidentally, proved utterly beyond him were the hagiographic problems connected with St. Paulinus, which he completely failed to unravel.

[1] On which see A. Maiuri, 'Sul *De Nola* di Ambrogio Leone', *Studi in onore di Riccardo Filangieri*, II, (Napoli, 1959) 261–71.

[2] A. Leo, *De Nola*, (Venetiis, 1514) f. c4r.

[3] *Ibid.* ff. c3v–4r. The ubication of Pompei, Stabia, and Herculanum had already been discussed by Francesco Pucci in his commentary on Cicero's letters 'Ad Atticum', cf. M. Santoro, *Uno scolaro del Poliziano a Napoli: Francesco Pucci*, (Napoli, 1948) 96.

[4] Leo, *op. cit.* ff. c1v–c2r.

[5] *Ibid.* f. b6v.

[6] *Ibid.* f. b7r.

[7] *Ibid.* loc. cit.

[8] *Ibid.* ff. b4v, b7r-v.

[9] *Ibid.* ff. b7r, e6v.

[10] *Ibid.* f. b7r-v.

[11] *Ibid.* ff. b7v, c1r-v.

The antiquarian interest of the *De Nola* is not confined to its text. For at the author's request the noted painter and engraver Girolamo Mocetto supplied four engraved plates as illustrations. Of these two are of particular interest for our purpose, one of them because it shows the old 'ager Nolanus', that is to say the Gulf of Sorrento and its adjacent territory with their ancient place names,[1] the other because it is a plan of Nola in classical times with its 'viae' and monuments etc. as known to Leone,[2] this being the earliest archaeological plan of an Italian town (Rome excepted, of course), which has reached us.

Though not comparable in importance with the *De Nola*, the *Antiquitatum Bellunensium sermones quattuor*[3] which Pierio Valeriano completed in 1522, are nonetheless worthy of some special mention. It is true that this work, in which the author investigated the origins of Belluno, is almost entirely based on literary and epigraphic sources and does not really deal with the ancient remains of Belluno and its countryside. All the same its discussion of the early settlements is not without interest, and its topographical account of the course of the Piave is done with remarkable accuracy. The last of the 'Sermones', together with Valeriano's Latin poem *Urbis patriae Genethliacon*,[4] are a celebration of the 'Familia Flavia', to which Belluno was believed to owe its past greatness, a greatness which Valeriano was anxious should not be forgotten.

Although it really shows no serious attempt at reconstructing the topography of Como in classical times, the chapter entitled 'De prisco urbis situ et publicis aedificiis' in the *Historiae Patriae Libri Duo* of Benedetto Giovio (1471–1544)[5] is still of some significance. In fact the identification of some remains in the town or its neighbourhood with buildings mentioned in the letters of the younger Pliny,[6] makes this chapter a contribution to archaeology which should not be overlooked. The *Historiae Patriae*, it is interesting to note, were accompanied by an account of the town from the chronicle of Benzo d'Alessandria and the letter of Cassiodorus to Gaudiosus,[7] and give the history of Como until 1532. Yet from what we know about the antiquarian

---

[1] *Ibid.* facing f. iiiiʳ.
[2] Pl. X, Leo, *op. cit.* f. b5ʳ.
[3] J. P. Valerianus, *Antiquitatum Bellunensium Sermones Quattuor*, (Venetiis, 1620).
[4] Printed *ibid.* 110–14.
[5] Giovio, *Opere scelte* . . . , 225–34
[6] *Supra*, 117.
[7] Giovio, *Opere scelte* . . . , XIV.

activity and enthusiasm of Benedetto Giovio, it is certain that they embody the researches of almost a lifetime, and as such they could hardly be omitted from this survey.[1]

From the fourth decade of the Cinquecento onwards, accounts of local antiquities became less and less an exception. It was then that works like Giovanni Crisostomo Zanchi's *De origine Orobiorum sive Cenomanorum libri tres* (1531), Paolo Giovio's *Descriptio Larii Lacus* published in 1558 but completed not long after 1536, the *Antiquitates Valentinae* of Francesco Alighieri (1537), the *De origine et amplitudine civitatis Veronae* of Torello Saraina (1540), etc., bore witness to a new flourishing of local antiquarian studies, which would have been unthinkable a few decades earlier. That even Biondo's *Italia illustrata* was no longer found adequate was typical of the new climate, which found in Leandro Alberti's *Descrittione di tutta l'Italia* (1550) a far better answer to present needs.

[1] One should also mention as of considerable interest, in view of their use of local antiquities as evidence, the history of Milan started in 1494 or shortly after by Tristano Calchi, printed in *Tristani Calchi Mediolanensis Historiae Patriae Libri Viginti*, (Mediolani, 1627), on which see E. Fueter, *Histoire de l'historiographie moderne*, (Paris, 1914) 132–34, and the still unpublished *Historia Ferrariensis* by Pellegrino Prisciani, dedicated to Ercole I, Duke of Ferrara (1471–1505). The *Historia* is available in several manuscripts, e.g. Vatican Library, Ms. Ottob. lat. 2773. Nor should one omit to notice the mention of ancient buildings and ruins in Naples and its neighbourhood in the letter written by Pietro Summonte to Marcantonio Michiel on 24 March 1524, cf. F. Nicolini, *L'arte napoletana del Rinascimento e la lettera di Pietro Summonte a Marcantonio Michiel*, (Napoli, 1925) 173–75. At 174 Summonte gives what must be the earliest Renaissance mention of the temples at Paestum. Superficial descriptions of some ancient remains in Naples and its neighbourhood were also given by Gioviano Pontano, cf. *Johannis Ioviani Pontani De Liberalitate . . . De Magnificentia . . . Libri*, (Neapoli, 1498) ff. K2r–K3v, *Pontani de bello neapolitano et de sermone*, (Neapoli, 1509) ff. G5r–G6v.

THE DISCOVERY OF THE GREEK WORLD

Our knowledge of Greek antiquity began rather late. By the middle of the fifteenth century Roman antiquity had already been the object of study for nearly a century and of indiscriminate admiration for much longer. On the other hand, despite Crusades and trade, Latin rule and missionary effort, the archaeological study of the Greek world during the Renaissance practically began and ended with Ciriaco d'Ancona, and by 1455 Ciriaco was dead. After him the Turkish conquest of Byzantine lands put an end to antiquarian travel in Greek territories for about a century; and when Pierre Gilles went to Constantinople in 1546 as antiquary to the French ambassador, the Renaissance was nearly over. Gilles's two treatises appeared in print only in 1561 and deal with the topography of Constantinople and the Bosporus.[1] No account of the topography of Athens, which is shown as a typically German city in the great Nuremberg chronicle of 1493,[2] was published until 1624, when the *Athenae Atticae* of Johannes Meursius was issued for the first time. This Leiden professor had deemed it more comfortable to rely on literary sources than to go over to Greece to see for himself. His handbook remained the indispensable guide of every cultivated traveller to Athens for over a century.

If little was known about Greek architectural remains, even less was known about Greek sculpture, though antiquarians honestly believed themselves to know a good deal about it. But then, though from the Renaissance onwards the West was full of alleged Greek pieces, very few of them happened to be genuine. At Oxford there were, of course, the Arundel marbles. But until the arrival of the Elgin marbles, there cannot have been many to be seen in London. In this visitors to Venice were at an advantage. For among the tangible results of the Venetian genius for looting, they could see the famous four bronze horses of St. Mark's, removed from Constantinople in 1204 and so

---

[1] The *De Bosporo Thracio libri III*, (Lugduni, 1561) and *De Topographia Constantinopoleos et illius antiquitatibus libri IV* (Lugduni, 1561).

[2] H. Schedel, *Liber Cronicarum*, (Nuremberge, 1493) f. XXVIII[r].

fittingly placed on the upper front of a church where even the venerated body of the patron saint was stolen property. In the West what passed for Greek sculpture were as a rule either Hellenistic copies or Roman imitations. Whether even Winckelmann ever set eyes upon a Greek original, must be open to doubt.

The numerous remains still scattered all over the Greek world occasionally intrigued some travellers during the fourteenth century. As a rule such an interest did not stray beyond the more glamorous antiquities of Athens or Constantinople. Like Constantinople, Athens was regarded as belonging to a special class. But while a late antique account of the former, the *Notitia urbis Constantinopolitanae*, had not been altogether unknown to the medieval West[1], nothing of the kind had been available for Athens. Like Shakespeare's Padua, Athens was considered 'Mistress of all arts', the city out of which, in Dante's words, 'ogni scienza disfavilla'.[2] On the other hand, whereas Constantinople remained a great capital, medieval Athens was but a sad relic of its departed glory. Those ancient temples which had survived had been turned into places of Christian worship. That of Hephaistos in the Agora had become the church of St. George, while the very Parthenon was turned into a cathedral dedicated to the Panaghia, and it was known as St. Mary of Athens during the Frankish rule.

The legends linked with Roman monuments which fill the *Mirabilia Romae Urbis*, had their counterpart in Athens. Thus from the writings of a twelfth century metropolitan of the city, Michael Acominatus, we learn how in his time the choregic monument of Lysicrates was commonly known as the λύχνος τοῦ Δημοσθένους,[3] while what was still left of Hadrian's aqueduct was probably already believed to have been the school of Aristotle.[4] Yet the pride of medieval Rome in the relics of its past greatness, a pride which did not prevent its inhabitants from using them as building materials, was much less noticeable in Athens. The Frankish, Catalan, and Florentine rulers of Athens took no greater interest in the ancient monuments of their

---

[1] See *Notitiae Regionum Urbis Romae et Urbis Constantinopolitanae, Glossarium Latino-Theotiscum Codex Vindobonensis* 162, ed. F. Unterkircher, (Umbrae Codicum Occidentalium II), (Amsterdam, 1960) IX, XIII.

[2] Dante, *Purgatorio*, XV, 99.

[3] J. Morton Paton, *Chapters on Mediaeval and Renaissance Visitors to Greek Lands*, (Princeton, 1951) 5.

[4] *Infra*, 134.

capital, than the Venetians, the Genoese, and the Knights of Rhodes took in those to be found in their own Greek domains, which means just about nil. It is therefore somewhat surprising to learn that in a letter written in 1380 King Peter IV of Aragon referred to the Acropolis as 'la pus richa joia què al mont sie e tal que entre tots los Reys de chrestians envides lo porien fer semblant',[1] a sentiment perhaps shared by the Acciaiuoli dukes, though strategic reasons may also have been instrumental in their erecting a palace there.

Both the first two travellers who left some information about Greek antiquities were pilgrims travelling to the Holy Land. What we are told by one of them, the German Priest Ludolf von Südheim, who was writing about 1350, is not only very little, but also wildly inaccurate. We thus learn from him that the city of Genoa had been entirely built out of remains brought from Athens.[2] About the site of ancient Troy or, more exactly, what he believed it to be, he only said that no remains could now be seen. But he also related how some of the city's foundations were now under water, and also that as soon as any of its remains were dug up they were exported at once. Furthermore what he had said about Genoa and Athens, he now repeated about Venice, which he believed to have been entirely built from materials brought over from Troy, going as far as to record that there was not one single pillar or carved stone in Venice, which was not of Trojan origin.[3]

What we are told by Südheim is both trivial and inaccurate, and doubtless reflects the garbled tales which he was told during his pilgrimage. On the other hand, the information supplied by the *Liber peregrinationis ad Loca Sancta*, written one generation later by the notary Nicolò Martoni of Carinola near Capua, describing the pilgrimage on which he set out on 17 June 1394, is definitely more exciting, not so much for what he tells us about some leading monuments, as because he also relates some of the wonders connected with them. It was on his journey home from Egypt and Palestine that Nicolò Martoni visited Greece. Thus in February 1395 he was able to spend a couple of days in Athens, which enabled him to inspect

[1] On which see A. Rubió i Lluch, 'Significació de l'elogi de l'Acròpolis d'Atenes pel Rei Pere 'l ceremoniós', *Homenaje ofrecido a D. Ramón Menéndez Pidal: Miscelánea de Estudios lingüísticos, literarios, y históricos*, III (Madrid, 1925), 37–56.
[2] Morton Paton, *op. cit.* 29.
[3] *Ibid.* loc. cit.

the principal local antiquities. Here some residents acted as his guides[1] and told him a lot of nonsense about some of the ancient remains, which he accepted quite uncritically. 'Et primo accessimus' he tells us, 'ad illos duos fontes aquarum de quibus oportebat quemlibet scolarem bibere pro aquirenda scientia . . . qui fontes erant duo pulcerime laborati et fabricati cum lapidibus marmoreis'.[2] He also tells us that he saw the ruins of the school of Aristotle,[3] all this being probably what was left of the aqueduct built by Hadrian and completed by Antoninus Pius. He admired the 'magnum hospitium' of Hadrian and was duly impressed by the size of the twenty pillars still standing, so much so, that he stated that four men would have had to join hands with fully stretched arms in order to encircle one of them.[4]

The beauty of the Propylaea built by Mnesicles quite definitely moved him, to the point of making him admit that they were as handsome as Frederick II's bridgehead of his own city of Capua.[5] Similarly the church of the Panaghia or St. Mary of Athens as it was called by the Latins, i.e. the Parthenon, struck him as being of the same size as the church, that is to say the cathedral of Capua.[6] Particularly interesting for our purpose is what he said about its gates: 'In dicto introytu sunt porte de illis portellis qui steterunt in portis civitatis Troye, quando civitas Troye fuit destructa. Portelli portarum ipsius civitatis fuerunt portati ad Acthenas et facte fuerunt porte in dicta ecclesia Sancte Marie.'[7]

As a devout Christian, Nicolò also made a note of the most striking Christian relics in the 'Panaghia', these including a volume of the Greek gospels, written in gold letters by no less a person than the very mother of Constantine the Great, St. Helen,[8] a scribal attribution which one may perhaps be allowed to view with scepticism. He also has a wonderful story, really a medieval legend, connected with the 'Gorgoneium': on the top of the two Roman columns still standing to-day up the southern ramp of the Acropolis, just a little above the choregic monument of Thrasyllus, there was a niche with an idol, which had the

[1] Ibid. 32.
[2] Ibid. loc. cit.
[3] Ibid. loc. cit.
[4] Ibid. 33.
[5] Ibid. loc. cit.
[6] Ibid. loc. cit.
[7] Ibid. loc. cit.
[8] Ibid. 34.

power to sink any ships approaching Athens with hostile intentions.[1] Had such a wonder been in Naples, it would certainly have been attributed to Virgil![2] Similarly at Port Raphty, about twenty-two miles from Athens, he learnt that two marble statues of a man and a maid had originally been alive, but had been turned into stone by the gods in answer to the girl's prayer, when her chastity was threatened.[3] Eleusis too was visited by Nicolò, who saw and inspected there 'hedificia et multe columpne et marmores qui iacent ibi' as well as the remains of an aqueduct.[4]

The main interest of the narrative of Nicolò Martoni resides not so much in the details that he gives us about some Athenian antiquities, as that he is so often our sole source for some of the medieval legends concerning them. Moreover for his time he was certainly quite exceptional in taking such an interest in these old remains, which attracted him for two reasons: because they were both ancient and Athenian. On the other hand, the Venetians who were exploring the 'Labyrinth' of Gortyn in Crete already in the very early fifteenth century,[5] were merely moved by curiosity and nothing else.

During the fifteenth century some interest in Greek antiquities was developed further thanks to the new interest in geographical travel. The Florentine teaching of Emanuel Chrysoloras (1397–1400) had led to a knowledge of the *Geography* of Ptolemy,[6] and consequently to an interest in geography in general, particularly in the humanist circle of Niccolò Niccoli.[7] Contact with Niccoli, and perhaps access to the *De Insulis* of Domenico Silvestri[8] as well as to Ptolemy, were thus probably instrumental in inducing Cristoforo Buondelmonti, a Florentine priest, to move to Rhodes in 1414 in order to explore the islands of Greece. This meant a long odyssey which lasted for some sixteen years at

[1] *Ibid*. loc. cit.
[2] For the wonders attributed to Virgil in Naples see D. Comparetti, *Virgilio nel Medio Evo*, II, (Firenze, 1946) passim.
[3] Morton Paton, *op. cit.* 31.
[4] *Ibid*. 35.
[5] A. M. Woodward, 'The Gortyn "Labyrinth" and its Visitors in the Fifteenth Century', *The Annual of the British School at Athens*, XLIV (1949) 324–25. For fifteenth and sixteenth century visitors to it see also J. Pitton de Tournefort, *Relation d'un voyage de Levant*, I, (Paris, 1717) 66.
[6] R. Weiss, 'Jacopo Angeli da Scarperia', *Medioevo e Rinascimento—Studi in onore di Bruno Nardi*, II, (Firenze, 1955), 811 n. 50, 812, 824.
[7] G. Zippel, *Niccolò Niccoli*, (Firenze, 1890), 50.
[8] Which was available to humanists in early fifteenth century Florence, cf. D. Silvestri, *De insulis et earum proprietatibus*, ed. C. Pecoraro, (Palermo, 1955), 6–8, 24.

least,[1] during which Buondelmonti found ample time to learn Greek and write a Latin description of Crete addressed to Niccoli (1417), as well as an itinerary of the islands in the same language (1420), accompanying both these works with maps.[2]

Besides pursuing his geographical interests, Buondelmonti searched for Greek manuscripts. What, however, concerns us are his archaeological interests, which are so clearly reflected in his geographical writings. Needless to say, Crete proved to him a veritable antiquarian's paradise; his companions in some of his wanderings through this island also included a humanist, Rinuccio da Castiglione Fiorentino,[3] who later was one of Lorenzo Valla's teachers of Greek. In Crete the so-called tomb of Zeus at Mount Juktas certainly impressed him.[4] And though he was still medieval enough to refer to the statuary as 'idols' he was nonetheless fully appreciative of their beauty. Mosaics particularly appealed to him, and he was therefore delighted to discover during a visit to what was 'Olim Philopolim hodie Macriticho . . . musaicum pavimentum immaculatum omnium figurarum sub magnis maceriebus'.[5] Reference to some Roman ruins suggests that Buondelmonti was able to distinguish Greek from Roman monuments. But whether Greek or Roman, ancient remains aroused his admiration. It is therefore not surprising to find him writing, not without some concern: 'In portum olim Penicis hodie Lutro intravimus et destructam civitatemque vetustissimam cum columnis prostratam videmus: inter eas candidissimi marmoris sepulcra prope casas illorum rusticorum inveni, in quibus sues polentum comedebant et sculpturas circum nobilissimas laniabant. Lacerata multa vidi ydolorum busta inter quae marmorum hedifitia sparsa iacebant.'[6] Indeed the dazzling loveliness of one marble head that he found at Romelus, particularly moved him, though he could not quite decide whether it represented Venus or Diana,[7] while the so called 'Labyrinth' at Gortyn filled him with wonder tempered by awe.[8]

[1] R. Weiss, 'Un umanista antiquario—Cristoforo Buondelmonti', *Lettere Italiane*, XVI (1964), 105.
[2] Pl. XI. The *Descriptio Insulae Cretae* is printed in F. Corner, *Creta Sacra*, I, (Venetiis, 1755) 77–109, the book on the islands is in C. Buondelmonti, *Liber Insularum Archipelagi*, ed. G. R. L. De Sinner, (Lipsiae et Berolini, 1824).
[3] Corner, *op. cit.* I, 94.
[4] *Ibid.* I, 97.   [5] *Ibid.* I, 96.
[6] *Ibid.* I, 84.
[7] *Ibid.* I, 85.
[8] *Ibid.* I, 103–104.

Some notable antiquities were also mentioned by Buondelmonti in his book on the Greek islands. Here the chapter on Rhodes gave him an opportunity to include a short digression on the 'Colossus' drawn entirely from literary sources.[1] In that on Delos he tells us not only about the ruins still to be seen, but also how he vainly endeavoured with the assistance of a large crowd and some ship's ropes to replace the colossal archaic statue of Apollo on its former pedestal.[2] Ciriaco d'Ancona could scarcely have done better here!

As a rule Buondelmonti was ready to accept as true what they told him about monuments: yet though he 'swallowed' the so-called 'tomb of Zeus' in Crete,[3] he preferred not to commit himself to its authenticity, when shown the alleged remains of the sepulchre of Homer at Chios.[4] Besides the Archipelago, the handbook on the Greek islands also dealt with Crete, Rhodes, the Jonian Islands, those on the Sea of Marmara, and Constantinople. In the Byzantine capital Buondelmonti was particularly busy inspecting antiquities. Thus not only did he describe, but he also took measurements of the Hippodrome and Haghia Sophia[5] and recorded such principal monuments as the equestrian statue of Justinian, the horse of which he rightly claimed came from a statue of Theodosius,[6] the four pillars on which, according to him, had once stood the bronze horses of St. Mark's Venice, the 'Agulia', etc.,[7] as well as the more impressive Christian relics. Of the 'Agulia' he also copied the metrical Latin inscription,[8] which is not surprising, in view of his taste for epigraphy, a taste which made him, among other things, carve his own epitaph on a rock while stranded at Furni,[9] and have some sentences attributed to Greek philosophers inscribed in a Latin version on a small pillar, now in the Rhodes Museum.[10]

Buondelmonti was the first western traveller who looked at Greek antiquities with a really appreciative and sensitive eye. Here his immediate and by far greater successor was Ciriaco

---

[1] Buondelmonti, *op. cit.* 72.
[2] *Ibid.* 92.
[3] *Supra*, 136.
[4] Buondelmonti, *op. cit.*, 112.
[5] *Ibid.* 122.
[6] Weiss, *Un umanista antiquario*, 115.
[7] Buondelmonti, *op. cit.* 123.
[8] *Ibid.* loc. cit.
[9] *Ibid.* 110.
[10] G. Iacopi, 'Italiani insigni nella Rodi del passato. Il ritrovamento d'una epigrafe di Cristoforo Buondelmonti', *L'Universo*, XI (1930), 17–21.

d'Ancona. The exploits of Ciriaco as a traveller in Greek lands soon cast the achievement of Buondelmonti into the shade. And Filelfo's remark 'nunquam quiescit Kiriacus',[1] shows how his restless travelling struck his contemporaries, who fully appreciated his unique contribution to antiquarian science. Ciriaco had a mercantile upbringing relieved by travel along the Italian coast as well as to Greece and Egypt, which gave him the opportunity of seeing several monuments of the ancient world. The result of these travels was that he soon succumbed to the spell of the classical sirens, so that he was already copying some of the old inscriptions which came his way[2] before he was able to understand what he took down.

What eventually led Ciriaco to give himself entirely to the study of Antiquity, was the greatest ancient monument of his native city, Trajan's arch at Ancona.[3] For it made him realize more and more that what still remained of the ancient world was doomed to perish sooner or later, and that it was therefore his imperative duty to try to rescue, or at any rate to record, its relics for posterity before it was too late. In order to carry out such a plan, a knowledge of Greek and Latin was obviously needed. Thus Virgil and the now forgotten Tommaso Seneca opened the gates of Latin to him in 1421,[4] while four years later he started, while stranded in Constantinople, to learn Greek from Homer.[5]

From about 1423 onwards the journeys of Ciriaco were mainly occupied by archaeological activity, his diplomatic and business pursuits taking definitely a second place in his concern. Antiquity was now his ruling passion. Yet he was not altogether indifferent to medieval relics,[6] while his enthusiastic account of a triptych by Roger van der Weyden, which he admired at Ferrara in 1449,[7] indicates how he could also look at contemporary art with an appreciative eye.

During his many visits to Greece Ciriaco tirelessly searched for and recorded as many antiquities as he could. His notes included descriptions of places, odd passages from manuscripts, but above all transcripts of inscriptions and sketches of notable

[1] Bodnar, op. cit. 17.
[2] Ibid. 19.
[3] Cf. Campana, Giannozzo Manetti, Ciriaco e l'Arco di Traiano ad Ancona, 485.
[4] Bodnar, op. cit. 20.
[5] Ibid. 22.
[6] Degli Abati Olivieri, op. cit. passim.
[7] Colucci, op. cit. XV, CXLIII-IV.

monuments. Greece had already been visited by him several times, when Ciriaco saw Athens for the first time in 1436. Here he lodged in the house of the Genoese Antonello Balduino on the Acropolis,[1] whence he set forth to explore the city. Needless to say, the Parthenon made an enormous impression upon him, and he made a careful sketch of its west front.[2] He also made a drawing of the ancient city walls;[3] walls and huge pillars invariably appealed to him, and he also duly copied the inscriptions recording the city of Theseus and the later one of Hadrian.[4] Many other Athenian antiquities were also recorded by him. Nor were his interests restricted to the ancient Greek aspect of the city: Roman Athens engaged his attention too, since his notes and sketches also deal with many remains of the Antonine age.

Ciriaco made a unique contribution to archeological science not only by saving for us the text of countless inscriptions, but also by his drawings, measurements, and descriptions of buildings, statues, monuments, and other antiquities all over a substantial part of the Greek world. Just to give an idea of the magnitude of his contribution, his sketch of the impressive sepulchre of Philopappos on the Museion hill shows much of the building that has since disappeared.[5] His drawings and measurements of Hadrian's temple at Cyzicus[6] are, apart from coins, the only visual records that we possess of what was counted the eighth wonder of the ancient world and is now a mound covered with briars. His other drawings included Haghia Sophia,[7] the so-called 'tower of the winds', really the 'Horologium' of Andronicus of Cirrha, which he drew on his second visit to Athens,[8] etc.

Ciriaco's identifications of sites and monuments were not always correct, just as his drawings are not very accurate by modern standards. Thus he thought Katsingri to be the citadel of Mycenae,[9] a spot near the promontory of Taenarum the Pylos

[1] Bodnar, op. cit. 40.
[2] B. Ashmole, 'Cyriac of Ancona', Proceedings of the British Academy, XLV (1959) pl. II, IV, V.
[3] Bodnar, op. cit. 37.
[4] Ibid. 39.
[5] Ibid. 38.
[6] Cf. B. Ashmole, 'Cyriac of Ancona and the Temple of Hadrian at Cyzicus', Journal of the Warburg and Courtauld Institutes, XIX (1956), 179–91.
[7] Ashmole, Cyriac of Ancona, pl. XV.
[8] Huelsen, La Roma antica di Ciriaco d'Ancona, fig. 30.
[9] Bodnar, op. cit. 64.

of Nestor,[1] and inferred the temple of Zeus at Dodona to be
located in the neighbourhood of Nicopolis.[2] The choregic
monument of Thrasyllus before the cave of the Panagia on the
south wall of the Acropolis and that of Lysicrates were believed
by him to be theatre seats,[3] and he quite misunderstood the
representations on the running Ionic frieze of the Parthenon.[4]
On the other hand, at Gythium he refused to accept the local
ruins as the remains of the palace of Menelaus.[5] And it is
interesting to recall how during his 'navigatio pontica' he went
ahead with his plan to explore an abyss, though warned by the
local peasants that its entrance was guarded by an awesome
dragon.[6]

   To Ciriaco, and indeed, for that matter, to every cultivated
European until the age of Romanticism, Greece was no more
than a museum inhabited by people beyond contempt. Thus, but
for one exception, he regarded the Spartans of his time as utterly
degraded.[7] This did not, however, stop him from making
friends with several Greeks. The most famous of them was
Gemisthos Pletho, the humanist whose esoteric Platonism
coloured the last stages of Byzantine philosophy, and he constantly saw him when he spent the winter of 1447–48 at Mistra.[8]
Other Greek friends ranged from the Despot Constantine, who
became the last Byzantine emperor, to the deacon Agallianos,
who in 1447 completed a copy of Strabo[9] for Ciriaco. The Greek
friends of Ciriaco could prove very valuable to him. One of
them, George Cantacuzenus, lent him a Herodotus and other old
books in 1437.[10] At Vitylo John Palaeologus, the Despot
Constantine's local deputy, pointed out to him the ancient
remains employed to build part of the fortress, and proved
invaluable in the discovery of an inscription of the Emperor
Gordian, which made it possible to identify the place with the
ancient Bitylon.[11] Equally valuable as sources of information

[1] Ibid. 58–9.   [2] Ibid. 29.
[3] K. M. Setton, Catalan Domination of Athens 1311–1388, (Cambridge, Mass., 1948) 233.
[4] Ibid. 235.
[5] Bodnar, op. cit. 60.
[6] Sabbadini, Classici e umanisti da codici Ambrosiani, 27.
[7] Ibid. 31.
[8] Bodnar, op. cit. 57, 61–2. If we are to believe Iacopo Zeno, it was actually Ciriaco who
induced Pletho to go to Italy to attend the Council for the union between the Greek and
Latin Churches, cf. L. Bertalot and A. Campana, 'Gli scritti di Iacopo Zeno e il suo elogio
di Ciriaco d'Ancona', La Bibliofilia, XLI (1939) 374.
[9] Now Mss. Eton College 141 and Biblioteca Laurenziana, Florence, XXVIII. 15.
[10] Bodnar, op. cit. 42.
[11] Ibid. 59.

were monasteries, which often provided useful intelligence about ancient sites. His passion for the visible relics of Antiquity did not, however, make Ciriaco neglect the search for manuscripts, and though his quest for them was not that of a Poggio or an Aurispa, he certainly did not omit to inspect a monastic library whenever an opportunity arose.

Ciriaco was above all an antiquarian, whose main aim was to collect information and record ancient monuments. Little wonder, then, that his literary remains consist mainly of a few tracts in Latin and Greek, and a Latin version of the slim pseudo-Aristotelian *De Virtutibus* addressed to Paolo della Pergola.[1] He also wrote some Italian verse,[2] probably because he found Latin versification difficult, as well as some Latin inscriptions, as for instance those composed in honour of Janus, King of Cyprus, or of Francesco Gattilusio.[3] Nor was he above concocting a few apocrypha, like the inscription of Heliodorus the mad Carthaginian, which he claimed to have found on his tomb near Gades,[4] a 'memento mori' to anyone considering travel beyond the pillars of Hercules. It was quite characteristic of his approach and his inability to systematize his materials, that he never achieved or even planned a '*Graecia illustrata*'.

During Ciriaco's lifetime the history of the Eastern Roman Empire ended for ever. A crusade against the Turks and a union between the Greek and Latin churches had been envisaged as the only means to save what was still left of Justinian's empire. Both the crusade and the union were very much in Ciriaco's thoughts, and he was very active on behalf of these causes. Yet this did not prevent him from being on good terms with the Sultans as well as with the Byzantine Emperors. A safe conduct from the Sultan, allowing him to proceed everywhere,[5] made his progress through the Greek world easier. And it is scarcely surprising that we last hear of Ciriaco in conquered Constantinople acting as secretary to Mohammed II.[6] To Ciriaco the

[1] B. Nardi, 'Letteratura e cultura veneziana del Quattrocento', *La civiltà veneziana del Quattrocento*, (Firenze, 1957) 137, n. 26.

[2] As for instance his sonnet on Sparta in Sabbadini, *Classici e umanisti da codici Ambrosiani*, 32–33. For his participation in the 'Certame coronario' see F. Flamini, 'La lirica toscana del Rinascimento', *Annali della R. Scuola Normale Superiore di Pisa*, XIV (1891) 5, 34, n. 1.

[3] Colucci, *op. cit.* XV, LXXX, CXXXVII–XL.

[4] *C.I.L.* II, 149*.   [5] Colucci, *op. cit.* XV, CLIV.

[6] Bodnar, *op. cit.* 68. The view that Ciriaco made a study of the equestrian statue of Justinian after the fall of Constantinople cannot be accepted any longer, cf. F. Babinger, 'Note on Cyriac of Ancona and Some of his Friends', *Journal of the Warburg and Courtauld Institutes*, XXV (1962) 322–23. About Ciriaco reading Thucydides to Mohammed II during the siege of Constantinople see R. Weiss, 'Ciriaco d'Ancona in Oriente', *Venezia e l'Oriente fra tardo Medioevo e Rinascimento*, (Firenze, 1966), 336.

conqueror of Greece was certainly a master well worth serving.

After Ciriaco d' Ancona some information about the monuments of Athens was included in Τὰ Θέατρα καὶ Διδασκαλεῖα, a tract by an unknown author[1] generally referred to as the 'Vienna Anonymous', who was in the city about the time when Mohammed II visited it, that is about 1458, but was in all probability not a native of it. It is obvious that this writer was anxious at all costs to identify as many of the extant remains as possible with ancient schools, theatres, and palaces. Thus, just to give a few examples, he believed the 'tower of the winds' to have been the school of Socrates,[2] while he located that of Aristotle in the Stoa of Eumenes.[3] This shows that he was not acquainted with the local tradition, which identified it with some of the ruins of Hadrian's aqueduct.[4] He also believed the temple of Olympian Zeus to have been a royal palace,[5] and delighted in emphasizing the magnificence of the various buildings on the Acropolis,[6] adding here that the Parthenon, which he called the temple of the Mother of God, had been built and dedicated to the unknown God by Apollos and Eulogius.[7]

The identifications of the 'Vienna Anonymous' were, of course, fanciful. One is, however, left to wonder how much he relied on his own imagination and how much on local popular tradition. Yet, in spite of everything, his tract is not altogether without value as a witness to the existence of many monuments. On the other hand, from an archaeological point of view, his description is definitely inferior to that of a Venetian, whose name has also been denied to us, who left some notes on the city, which he very probably visited about 1470.[8] This Venetian scholar was not only enraptured by the beauty of what he saw, but he had furthermore a strong interest in epigraphy, and was ready to copy an inscription whenever the opportunity arose. Next to Ciriaco d'Ancona he was undoubtedly the fifteenth

[1] Printed in L. De Laborde, *Athènes aux XVe, XVIe, et XVIIe Siècles*, I, (Paris, 1854) 17–20. On it see now S. G. Mercati, 'Noterella sulla tradizione manoscritta dei Mirabilia Urbis Athenarum', *Mélanges Eugène Tisserant*, III, (Città del Vaticano, 1964), 77–84.

[2] De Laborde, *op. cit.* I, 17.

[3] *Ibid.* I, 18.

[4] *Supra*, 134.

[5] De Laborde, *op. cit.* I, 19.

[6] *Ibid.* I, 20.

[7] *Ibid.* loc. cit.

[8] The fact that he visited also other places in Greece and Constantinople suggests that he cannot have been a member of the Venetian expedition which held Athens in 1466, as has been stated, cf. Morton Paton, *op. cit.* 177.

century traveller who proved most enthusiastic about what was still left of ancient Greece, and he was honest enough not to invent a fancy name when unable to identify a monument. Thus he assigned no name to the Athenian temple of Olympian Zeus, of which he was able to count twenty columns.[1] He was, however, more fortunate with some other Athenian antiquities, though his identifications are sometimes questionable. Thus on reaching the arch of Hadrian, of which he took care to copy two inscriptions, he said that near it 'dicono li homini grossi esser stato il studio di Aristotele, ma non è alcune vestigie del aedificio antiquo. Ma credo più presso fusse quello edificio, dove sono le 20 colonne grande, reaedificato in memoria del studio antiquo di Aristotele et altri antiqui phil(osophi), perchè è in f(orm)a de portico aperto da ogni banda, ma parre, come è detto, che fusse coperto de marmore et non è alcuna scraja del muro'.[2] He also did not fail to notice the two Roman pillars above the theatre of Dionysus[3] and the choregic monument of Lysicrates, the meaning of which clearly baffled him, though he made a partial copy of its inscription.[4] Of the monument of Philopappos he left a careful description. Yet, though he could clearly see the names of Philopappos and Antiochos upon it, he judged it to have been erected in honour of Trajan.[5] Other monuments which did not escape his scrutiny included the so-called 'tower of the winds',[6] and he also left some appreciative notes on the Parthenon, 'molto mirabile tutto de marmore con col(on)ne a torno . . . e la fazza davanti nel fronto sono infiniti imagini di tutto relievo et copert(i) tutti di marmori'.[7] Outside Athens, he was struck by the size of the marble lion at Piraeus,[8] now in Venice; at Corinth he thought that the fortress was highly impressive.[9] Sparta, on the other hand, rather disappointed him. 'In lacedaemone non è aedificii antiqui excepto alcuni muri ex lapidibus quadratis'; yet about a quarter of a mile from it 'trovai 5 belli sassi grandi con epigrammati e lettere grece belle,

[1] E. Ziebarth, 'Ein griechischer Reisebericht des XV. Jahrhunderts', *Mittheilungen des Kaiserlichen Deutschen Archaeologischen Instituts Athenische Abtheilung*, XXIV (1899) 74; the whole text occupies, pp. 72–88.
[2] *Ibid*. 75.
[3] *Ibid*. 76.
[4] *Ibid*. 75.
[5] *Ibid*. 76.
[6] *Ibid*. 77.
[7] *Ibid*. 73–74.
[8] *Ibid*. 77.
[9] *Ibid*. 78.

dei li quali ne tolto 4, non trovai altro di bono'.[1] No antiques of
interest were seen by him at Mistra, Malvasia, Modone, etc.,
which he also visited. In Constantinople instead he was certainly
not disappointed, and while there he took measurements of
Haghia Sophia and the Hippodrome.[2] The Constantinople
obelisk was also duly appreciated by him and described as a
'colonna quadra come la guchia di San Pietro da R(om)a et è
pocho menor che quella, et è per ogni fazza characteri agyphici
over phaenici dal pè fino alla summità'.[3]

The antiquarian interests of the anonymous Venetian were
certainly not shared by the Florentine Benedetto Dei, who had
travelled extensively in the Sultan's domains from 1460–67. Yet
even Dei was aroused when he saw what he was told was the site
of Troy and the very tomb of Achilles, which made him write
with evident pride: 'Sono istato a la gran città di Troia la grande
in sulla Turchia e ò visto la sepoltura d'Achille e in somma ella fu
più di fama che di fatti per Dio verace'.[4] One is left to wonder
what was passed off to him as the tomb of Achilles!

After the 1470s the curtain fell over Greek archaeological
studies for nearly a century. This was mainly due to the Turkish
domination of the Greek world; but not entirely so, since travel
in those lands never ceased and some Greek islands, Rhodes,
Cyprus, and Crete among them, remained in Christian hands for
some time, so that perhaps the principal cause was apathy among
scholars rather than impossibility of access to the remains of
ancient Greece. This apathy is not alsogether surprising, when
we recall that, despite its thin Greek veneer, the humanism of the
Renaissance was essentially Latin.[5]

[1] *Ibid.* loc. cit.
[2] *Ibid.* 80.
[3] *Ibid.* loc. cit.
[4] M. Pisani, *Un avventuriero del Quattrocento—La vita e le opere di Benedetto Dei*, (Genova, 1923) 93.
[5] In 1486 or 1487 the ruins of Persepolis were visited by Giosafatte Barbaro, who left a description of them in his *Viaggio della Tana e della Persia* completed on 21 December 1487, cf. [G. Ramusio], *Secondo volume delle navigationi et viaggi*, (Venetia, 1559) f. 107ᵛ. Apart from obelisks and hieroglyphs, Egyptian antiquities aroused little interest. See on this subject Weiss, *Ciriaco d'Ancona in Oriente*, 329–32, K. H. Dannenfeld, 'Egypt and Egyptian Antiquities in the Renaissance', *Studies in the Renaissance*, IX (1959) 7–27.

CHAPTER ELEVEN

THE RISE OF CLASSICAL EPIGRAPHY

An interest in ancient inscriptions was not altogether absent in the earlier Middle Ages. The later Middle Ages fostered it and the Renaissance gave it increase. The earliest anthologies of Latin epigraphic texts were prompted by rhetorical preoccupations, those very motives which also led to the collecting of Latin letters and speeches, that is to say a desire to gather fine stylistic examples which might prove useful. The rise of humanism stimulated a new epigraphy modelled on classical examples. But already by the second half of the fourteenth century ancient inscriptions were also considered of value as historical, literary, and linguistic documents, yielding important antiquarian and philological information, as well as useful formulas and phrases, besides being appreciated merely because they were ancient. Humanists had indeed been quick to see that epigraphic texts proclaimed Roman greatness, revealed many a facet of the Roman way of life, showed the antiquity of a town, and could be invaluable to prove a grammatical point or a disputed spelling and to confirm the veracity of a legend.

From the beginning of the fifteenth century onwards sylloges of inscriptions became increasingly numerous. In Italy many were the humanists who compiled a sylloge of inscriptions or secured one to which they added more texts, or included inscriptions in their commonplace books, or assembled anthologies in which short poems, letters, orations, etc., were interspersed with epigraphic material. Generally these humanist sylloges consisted of copies taken from the original stones. Or, as was often the case, these humanists may have embodied another sylloge or sylloges, or at any rate part of them, into their own alongside with transcripts taken from the originals. Such transcripts were generally made from local monuments or during travels and, sometimes, even under difficult conditions. For instance in 1464 an expedition consisting of Felice Feliciano, the great painter Andrea Mantegna, Samuele da Tradate and Giovanni Antenoreo, the latter very probably to be identified with the humanist physician Giovanni Marcanova, spent two September days (23rd and 24th) along the shores of Lake Garda, searching for Roman inscriptions and copying all those which they could find.[1] While returning to Florence from Rome with his patron Francesco Sassetti, Bartolomeo Fonzio is known to have stopped and alighted from his horse, in order to copy an old inscribed stone which had caught his eye.[2] We find Marin Sanudo and his secretary Pilade Boccardo while visiting Aquileia in 1484, rubbing hard with water an ancient stone behind the choir of the church of Santa Maria extra muros, in order to read and take down what was engraved upon it,[3] and Fra Giocondo copying an inscription placed near St. Paul's, Rome, 'inter urticas et spineta'.[4] Some inscriptions proved, moreover, particularly popular, so that they occur again and again in the sylloges. Such were, for instance, that of Claudia Homonoea,[5] and the one on Trajan's arch at Ancona.[6]

The first humanist sylloges show no particular arrangement. Thus the one gathered by the Roman city clerk (scribasenato) Nicola Signorili and completed in 1409 'ad delectationem legentium', formerly believed to be the work of Cola di Rienzo[7] and of which there are also two later recensions made during the pontificate of Martin V (1417–1431),[8] shows not much order in its arrangement. It consists almost entirely of monumental texts from Rome, though it also includes a few from other places, which are placed at the end, these including the Greek inscription on the now destroyed temple of the Dioscuri at Naples, followed by a Latin translation of it.[9]

---

[1] The account of the expedition written by Feliciano may be read in L. Pratilli, 'Felice Feliciano alla luce dei suoi codici', *Atti del Reale Istituto Veneto di scienze, lettere ed arti*, XCIX (1939–40) 54.

[2] Saxl, *op. cit.* 21. Fonzio's sylloge is studied *ibid.* 19–46.

[3] Sanudo, *Itinerario per la Terraferma Veneziana*, 145. In the *Itinerario* Sanudo mentions a *De antiquitatibus et epitaphia* and a *De antiquitatibus Italiae*, both by him and perhaps one work, which have not reached us, cf. *ibid.* 29, 154. Part of a sylloge gathered by Sanudo is in the Biblioteca Marciana, Venice, Ms. Lat. XIV. 260, (4258), ff. 11ʳ–18ᵛ.

[4] I. Carini, 'Sul codice epigrafico di fra Giocondo recentemente acquistato dalla Biblioteca Vaticana', *Dissertazioni della Pontificia Accademia Romana di Archeologia*, ser. 2, V (1894) 227.   [5] *Supra*, 44, n.4.

[6] On the 'fortuna' of this inscription see Campana, *Giannozzo Manetti, Ciriaco e l'Arco di Traiano ad Ancona*.   [7] Silvagni, *op. cit.* 175–83.

[8] Signorili's first recension is in the Vatican Library, Ms. Barb. lat. 1952, the second is in Mss. Vat. lat. 10687 and Chig. I. VI. 204 of the same library, where is also the third recension in Ms. Vat. lat. 3851. On Signorili's sylloges see *Inscriptiones Christianae Urbis Romae*, N.S.I., XXX–XXXI.

[9] Ms. Barb. lat. 1952, f. 174ᵛ. This inscription had already been turned into Latin by Niccolò da Reggio during the early fourteenth century, cf. *supra*, 27, but the version given here is a different one. That the translator of it was not Signorili is certain, for no Latin version follows a Greek inscription from Rome also given by him, cf. Ms. Barb. lat. 1952, f. 170ᵛ. Signorili's sylloge also includes a few early medieval inscriptions, cf. *ibid.* ff. 172ʳ–174ʳ.

The inscriptions of Rome had also aroused the interest of Poggio during his early years in that city, an interest which proved particularly valuable to him when writing the *De varietate fortunae*, where not a few are quoted.[1] Thus as early as 1403 Poggio had prepared a small sylloge of inscriptions to be found in Rome which he had sent to Coluccio Salutati.[2] This was later amplified by him. Moreover while at the Council of Constance he found a fragment of an ancient sylloge similar to the one now at Einsiedeln,[3] as well as at least a part of a text invaluable to epigraphists, namely the *Notae juris* of Probus.[4] But not much now remains of Poggio's sylloge, which was used by Ciriaco d'Ancona, and of which only part has reached us.[5] Among the humanists who searched for and copied inscriptions, Ciriaco was certainly the most indefatigable and enthusiastic. In his career as an antiquarian, epigraphy had certainly first place among his interests and it was in this field that his achievement proved greatest. Italy and the Greek world were sedulously searched for inscriptions, the result of his labours being assembled in the six volumes of his *Commentaria*,[6] which probably perished, save for some fragments,[7] in the fire which destroyed the Sforza library at Pesaro in 1514.[8]

The majority of the inscriptions gathered by Ciriaco were found during his travels in Greece and Asia minor.[9] But the inscriptions of Italy were not overlooked by him, and he assembled a larger collection of them than anyone had before him. He was perhaps the first to copy non-monumental inscriptions and he is known to have collated the sylloges of Signorili and Poggio with the original stones while in Rome in 1433.[10] His copies were generally preceded by details about ubication, the conditions of the stone if damaged, and occasionally its size. Such details were not always given, and although his transcriptions were, on the whole, accurate, they were not invariably so. One of his main weaknesses was his casual approach to line

---

[1] *Supra*, 63, n.5.   [2] *Ibid.* 55.

[3] *Inscriptiones Christianae Urbis Romae*, II. 1, 11–13.

[4] Weiss, *The Medals of Pope Sixtus IV* (1471–1484), 35, n.3.

[5] In Ms. Vat. lat. 9152 of the Vatican Library.

[6] On which see *supra*, 109.

[7] As for instance those in ff. 101–24 of Ms. Trotti 373 of the Ambrosian Library, on which see Sabbadini, *Classici e umanisti da codici ambrosiani*, 1–52.

[8] *Ibid.* 46.

[9] See for example for his copies of Athenian inscriptions Bodnar, *op. cit.* 121–85.

[10] E. Ziebarth, 'De antiquissimis inscriptionum syllogis', *Ephemeris Epigraphica Corporis Inscriptionum Latinarum Supplementum*, IX (1905) 188.

division, especially when copying Greek inscriptions. Nor was he above fabricating a text, perhaps the best known of his apocrypha being the inscription of Heliodorus the Carthaginian, which he claimed to be near Gades.[1] Yet the debt which classical epigraphists owe to him could scarcely be greater, since so many inscriptions have only reached us through his copies; while the fact that most of the sylloges assembled during the Renaissance drew materials from him, speaks for the immediate popularity of Ciriaco's labours.[2]

The sylloges of Signorili and Poggio, and even more those of Ciriaco were very extensively used by later epigraphists. Thus an important source of the sylloge of the humanist physician Giovanni Marcanova (d. 1467), of which there are two recensions, one of 1457–60[3] and another of 1465,[4] were the texts collected by Ciriaco in 1435–37.[5] Another source was Felice Feliciano, who was actually responsible for the transcription and the numerous illustrations of the presentation copy to Malatesta Novello of Marcanova's second recension.[6] Apart from its imaginary views of ancient Rome,[7] the importance of Marcanova's collection lies in its being the first substantial and well arranged sylloge got up since Ciriaco, and in its providing many drawings of ancient monuments,[8] some of which, alas, have not reached us.

Felice Feliciano (1433–1480), whom his contemporaries called 'Antiquario' 'per aver lui quasi consumato gli anni soi in cercare le generose antiquità de Roma, de Ravena e de tutta l'Italia'[9] was more than anyone else instrumental in the divulgation of Ciriaco's epigraphic collections.[10] He himself copied all

---

[1] *Supra*, 141.

[2] Ciriaco's Rome sylloge, for instance, was circulating in Rome and Milan before 1461, cf. A. Luzio and R. Renier, 'I Filelfo e l'umanesimo alla corte dei Gonzaga', *Giornale storico della letteratura italiana*, XVI (1890) 159. Ciriaco's enthusiasm was shared by some of his Dalmatian friends. Pietro Cippico at Trau and Giorgio Begna at Zara collected as many texts of local inscriptions as they could get hold of. Their achievement was, however, limited, as their searches never went beyond their home territories. See G. Praga, 'Indagini e studi sull'umanesimo in Dalmazia-Ciriaco de Pizzicolli e Marino de Resti', *Archivio Storico per la Dalmazia*, XIII (1932) 262–80, G. Praga, 'Il codice Marciano di Giorgio Begna e Pietro Cippico, *Archivio Storico per la Dalmazia*, XIII (1932) 210–18.

[3] Bürgerbibliothek, Bern, Ms. B.42.

[4] Biblioteca Estense, Modena, Ms. Alpha. L.5.15. On it and two other versions of this Ms. see *Supra*, 98, nn. 2–3.

[5] Bodnar, *op. cit.* 100.

[6] *Ibid.* 99, n. 4.

[7] *Supra*, 98.

[8] See Huelsen, *La Roma antica di Ciriaco d'Ancona*, figg. 5–20.

[9] G. S. Degli Arienti, *Le Porretane*, ed. G. Gambarin, (Bari, 1914) 17.

[10] On him see now Mitchell, *Felice Feliciano Antiquarius*.

the ancient inscriptions he could, and asked friends to communicate to him as many as possible. On hearing that Callisto Montano was contemplating a business journey to Greece, he hastened to write to him in the hope of securing books and copies of whatever inscriptions he saw.[1] To Feliciano inscriptions were particularly valuable because of the evidence they provided about the accurate spelling of classical Latin.[2] No wonder then, that besides actively collaborating in those of Marcanova, he also prepared a sylloge of his own, the last and most complete recension of it being addressed, by him in 1464 to the painter Andrea Mantegna.[3] This recension like the earlier ones, follows no order, except when Feliciano transcribes from someone else's sylloge. It consists mostly of texts collected by Feliciano in Verona and its countryside, but it also incorporates materials from Ciriaco as well as from Marcanova and other sources, his inscriptions of Rome coming from the sylloges of Signorili and Poggio. Nor was he above including false inscriptions fabricated by him, just as his drawings of antique stones and sculptures owed much to his imagination.[4]

A wide selection of inscriptions occur also in the sylloges of the Carmelite Michele Ferrarini who died not later than 1492.[5] Here the texts are often accompanied by the drawings of the monuments, cippuses or stones on which they were to be found, as well as some not very convincing cinerary urns with inscriptions.[6] Besides many from north Italy, Ferrarini gave also inscriptions from Rome, south Italy, Spain, Germany, Athens, etc. Needless to say many of the inscriptions he gives came from other sylloges. The Greek inscriptions given by him derive of course from Ciriaco; others were taken from the collection of Feliciano, whose account of an expedition on lake Garda to gather epigraphic texts, the so-called 'Jubilatio', was also included by Ferrarini in his sylloge.[7]

In his letter of dedication to Ludovico Rodano, written at Bologna and dated 13 February 1477, Ferrarini urged him to read the sylloge again and again in order to absorb the elegance

---

[1] *Ibid.* 204.
[2] Pratilli, *op. cit.* 50.
[3] Biblioteca Marciana, Venice, Ms. Lat. X. 196 (3766).
[4] Cf. Mitchell, *Felice Feliciano Antiquarius*, pl. XXX–XXXI, XXXIII–XLI.
[5] On Ferrarini see G. Tiraboschi, *Biblioteca Modenese*, V (Modena, 1782) 277–79, *C.I.L.* VI, 1, XLIII–XLIV, *Inscriptiones Christianae Urbis Romae*, N.S.I, XXXIV–XXXV.
[6] Vatican Library, Ms. Vat. lat. 5243, ff. 39v, 41r, 45r.
[7] *Ibid.* f. 33r-v.

and the correct spelling of those texts.[1] As an antiquarian and epigraphist his reputation could hardly have stood higher among his contemporaries. A decree of the 'Anziani' of Reggio Emilia issued in 1493 and forbidding his sylloge to be taken out of the local Carmelite convent,[2] speaks for itself, while the passages about him in Caprioli's history of Brescia[3] confirm his fame in humanist circles.

These immediate followers of Ciriaco did not introduce any new methods into epigraphy. It was left to Fra Giovanni Giocondo (1443–1515)[4] to improve on the methods followed before him. Fra Giocondo, whose antiquarian activity was accompanied by the practice of architecture and the editing of Vitruvius, Caesar, and the letters of the younger Pliny, was fascinated by inscriptions not only because of their historical significance, but also because of the concision of their phraseology, the elegance of their spelling, and the admirable symmetry of their lettering. Their continuous destruction moved him therefore to attempt a rescue operation, that is to say to transcribe as many inscriptions as possible before it was too late, a scheme in which he was encouraged by Lorenzo de' Medici the Magnificent, through Alessandro Cortesi.[5]

Besides being arranged topographically and being as comprehensive as possible, Giocondo's epigraphic collection included also an important innovation; for it had separate sections for the texts copied directly by him from the original stones and those which he had found in other sylloges or had been communicated to him by friends.[6] These features already occur in the first recension (1478–c. 1489) which was dedicated to Lorenzo de' Medici. They are also present in the second, which was dedicated to Ludovico Agnelli, Archbishop of Cosenza (1497–1499).

[1] *Ibid.* f. 2^r.

[2] Tiraboschi, Biblioteca Modenese, V, 277–78. Perhaps this decree was prompted by the sale of the inscribed stones collected by Ferrarini by the friars on January 6th, 1493, cf. *ibid.* V. 279.

[3] Capreolus, *op. cit.* f. A6^r.

[4] The latest study on him is L.A. Ciapponi, 'Appunti per una biografia di Giovanni Giocondo da Verona', *Italia Medioevale e Umanistica*, IV (1961) 131–58. For his sylloges see especially Carini, *op. cit.*

[5] The letters of dedication to Lorenzo de' Medici were printed several times, cf. for instance the text in A. F. Gorius, *Inscriptiones antiquae Graecae et Romanae in Etruriae Urbibus*, III (Florentiae, 1743) 39–46. On Cortesi collecting inscriptions and having them copied see P. Paschini, 'Una famiglia di curiali nella Roma del Quattrocento: I Cortesi', *Rivista di storia della Chiesa in Italia*, XI (1957) 18.

[6] Carini, *op. cit.* 255–56. Originally Fra Giocondo had meant not to include inscriptions in his sylloge which he had not copied personally.

Here Giocondo's assistant was instead of Cortesi the famous scribe Bartolomeo Sanvito,[1] who was also responsible for writing and decorating partly or completely all the copies of the various recensions of the sylloge which have reached us.[2] The difference between the two recensions is not so great. The dedication to Lorenzo was replaced by an identical one to Agnelli. Some of the texts in the first recension have now disappeared, while new ones from Rome and Padua have been introduced. No dedicatory letters were included in the third recension (c. 1502),[3] which shows a new section consisting of texts communicated by friends and found in Rome as well as Italy, France, etc., the use of 'schedae' of Pomponio Leto and Pietro Sabino being also quite evident here.

Giocondo searched for inscriptions wherever he could. Though his task was to rescue what was left of Antiquity, he also did not overlook early Christian inscriptions. Occasionally he was deceived by a spurious one, such as the notorious decree of Desiderius.[4] On the other hand, when he had doubts about one he would note 'modernum puto'.[5] He would also say if he did not know the whereabouts of a text,[6] or if the stone was about to be destroyed,[7] if it was difficult to read,[8] when physical difficulties prevented him access to one,[9] or if it had just been unearthed.[10] Also the sylloge of Fra Giocondo included drawings of some of the original stones. As a collection it proved immediately popular and was extensively used in later sylloges. Now since the times of Ciriaco the aim of most sylloges was to provide a selection of texts from the whole of Italy as well as other European countries, particularly France and Spain. Apart from Rome and the Dalmatian collections of Ciriaco's friends there were, however, no humanist collections dealing exclusively with epigraphic materials from one town and its countryside. Despite its emphasis on Verona and its territory, the sylloge of Feliciano[11] was not really a collection of Veronese inscriptions.

[1] Biblioteca Nazionale Centrale, Florence, Ms. Magl. XXVIII.|5, f. 23ᵛ.

[2] J. Wardrop, *the Script of Humanism*, (Oxford, 1963) 27-29.

[3] For Mss. of the various recensions see *Inscriptiones Christianae Urbis Romae*, N.S. I, XXXV–XXXVI.

[4] Museo Correr, Venice, Ms. Cicogna 1632, ff. 160ᵛ–61ᵛ. He was also deceived by some forged inscriptions, allegedly found at Este, *C.I.L.* V. 194*, which he also accepted as antique, cf. Ms. Cicogna 1632, f. 224ʳ.

[5] Biblioteca Marciana, Venice, Ms. Lat. XIV. 171 (4665) f. 162ᵛ.

[6] *Ibid.* 163ʳ.   [7] *Ibid.* ff. 39ᵛ, 42ᵛ.

[8] *Ibid.* f. 51ʳ.   [9] *Ibid.* f. 130ᵛ.

[10] *Ibid.* f. 76ᵛ.   [11] *Supra*, 148-149.

We must therefore arrive at Desiderio Spreti, whose interest in inscriptions was already evident in 1455,[1] to find a collection of inscriptions entirely drawn from one town, this being the selection of epigraphic texts from Ravenna which he gave as an appendix to his account of that city.[2] A collection of inscriptions from Brescia and its neighbourhood got up during the late fifteenth century was probably made for Zaccaria Barbaro,[3] while outside Italy twenty-two Roman inscriptions of Augsburg and its territory were assembled and published by the well-known humanist Konrad Peutinger in 1505.[4] Local collections such as these were, however, eclipsed by the sylloge of Roman inscriptions of Milan and its 'ager' put together by the young Andrea Alciati.

What makes Alciati's sylloge so remarkable is the effort behind it to make it a *corpus epigraphicum* of his native city as comprehensive as possible. It was while he was writing his history of Milan, (1504–05) so Alciati tells us, that he decided to collect the local inscriptions and explain the more obscure ones, adding how he had been encouraged in his task by those who had done so before him.[5] The outcome of this decision was his sylloge,[6] where each text was preceded by an introduction of varying length, in which he illustrated its historical significance, archaic spellings, mentions of offices or institutions, etc., by reference to the classical writers. Sometimes his explanation of an office really was, as in the case of 'Comes',[7] a brief dissertation on the subject, or his introduction could be also an excuse for singing the praises of a powerful man who happened to own the stone, such as Gian Giacomo Trivulzio or Giovanni Francesco Marliani.[8]

---

[1] When he transcribed the epigraphic 'elogia' of C. Marius and Fabius Maximus (*C.I.L.* I, 1, 2nd ed. 193, 195) on f. 32r-v of his transcript of Leonardo Bruni's *De Militia* completed at Ravenna on 5 June 1455 and now Ms. Urb. lat. 1125 of the Vatican Library.

[2] Spretus, *op. cit.* ff. c3r-c6v.

[3] Biblioteca Marciana, Venice, Ms. Lat. X. 197 (3612). At f. 3r it has the Barbaro arms with Z on the left and B on the right, the whole within a wreath.

[4] In *Romanae vetustatis fragmenta in Augusta Vindelicorum et eius diocesi*, (Augustae Vindelicorum, 1505). In his preface Peutinger says that he collected these inscriptions having been ordered to do so by the Emperor Maximilian I and that he was assisted by the 'Sodalitas Litteraria Augustana', the canons of the Cathedral and his fellow citizens, cf. *ibid.* f. 1v.

[5] Ambrosian Library, Milan, Ms. D. 425 inf., p. 1.

[6] On which see D. Bianchi, 'L'opera letteraria e storica di Andrea Alciato', *Archivio storico lombardo*, ser. 4, XX (1913) 47–57, and Billanovich, *Il Petrarca e i retori latini minori*, 157–58. There are two recensions of the sylloge represented by Mss. D. 425 inf. and Trotti 353 of the Ambrosian Library.

[7] Ms. D. 425 inf., p. 32.

[8] *Ibid.* pp. 72, 82.

Alciati collected inscriptions wherever he could. Of one he says that it was shown to him by a friend who had dug it up in his garden.[1] Of another one he states how the original had been presented to him.[2] Occasionally he also gave a drawing of the stone[3] and he never omitted to give the exact location of the original or tell when it was difficult to decipher. Needless to say, the collection of Alciati showed a considerable progress from the earlier ones. And though he was not above occasionally giving a literary polish to his pieces and assigning a Roman origin to some Milanese families, he showed none the less such an insight and command of the relevant sources in his introductions, that one can easily forgive him such venial sins.

Also dealing with local epigraphic texts, this time those of the Como territory, was Benedetto Giovio. Also in his sylloge,[4] already completed but for a few additions in 1497, each text was accompanied by a short commentary and, moreover, there was in each case a drawing of the original. Giovio, though learned, was far from possessing the acumen of Alciati, this being plainly evident in his commentaries. The original stone was also, though only occasionally, drawn in the epigraphic collections of Mariangelo Accursio (1489–1546),[5] who was also responsible for the introduction of stricter standards of accuracy. But then he had soon realized the various weaknesses of the preceding sylloges and of the necessity to reproduce faithfully the line division of the originals, furnish drawings, provide more accurate topographical data and, above all, to collate again the texts with the originals whenever this was possible. In his epigraphic collections he furnished such details as the ubication of the stone, when it was found, and occasionally its size[6] and whether the original was faulty. Thus for the inscription of the arch of Augustus at Fano, he rightly preferred to give the complete text not from earlier sylloges, but from the reproduction of the arch on the front of the local church of San Michele.[7] Accursio's new

---

[1] *Ibid.* p. 39.
[2] *Ibid.* p. 86.
[3] Cf. for instance Ms. Trotti 353, ff. 79ʳ, 81ʳ, 84ᵛ, 85ʳ, etc. We also find him once criticising Ciriaco's reading of an inscription, cf. *ibid.* f. 16ᵛ.
[4] F. A. Zachariae S.I., 'De Benedicti Iovii Comensis Collectaneis inscriptionum', *Raccolta d'opuscoli scientifici e filologici*, XL (Venezia, 1749) 419–30, A. Soffredi, 'Codici epigrafici di Benedetto Giovio nelle biblioteche milanesi', *Comum-Miscellanea di scritti in onore di Federico Frigerio*, (Como, 1964) 379–88.
[5] See Campana, *Accursio (Accorso) Mariangelo*, 126–32.
[6] Ambrosian Library, Milan, Ms. D. 420 inf., ff. 41ʳ, 44ᵛ.
[7] *Ibid.* f. 132ʳ: 'In arcu, semiconuulso tormentis bellicis bello pii. ij. contra fanenses M.CCCC.LXIII. ut in pictura prope expressa arcus indicatur'. For the reproduction of the arch see *supra*, 118 and Pl. XII.

standards are already evident in the errata-corrige of the corpus of inscriptions from Rome issued by Mazzocchi in 1521,[1] which was almost certainly his, and was based on a comparison, whenever possible, with the original stones. Perhaps, as has been pointed out,[2] he meant to issue at a later date a supplement to the corpus|of Mazzocchi, in which case the Roman sylloge among his manuscripts[3] should refer to this.

The epigraphic collections of Alciati and Giovio had been accompanied by commentaries on the epigraphic texts. Commenting the texts was carried even further by another humanist, Girolamo Bologni of Treviso, (1454–1517), whose *Antiquarius*[4] sought to give a kind of epigraphic treatise. We thus find him already giving in the preface addressed to his own son Giulio, some examples of ancient inscriptions used on various occasions, such as in honour of a god or a well deserving personage, on a restored building, to promulgate a law, or in memory of a dead person,[5] as well as a digression on cremation among the ancient Romans.[6] There follows an account of Treviso[7] and a selection of inscriptions accompanied by historical and philological commentaries often very long, one of which, for instance, explains every single word in the inscription.[8] Doubtless this work of Bologni would have proved invaluable had it enjoyed a wide divulgation, which it did not.[9] And it seems somewhat ironical that what really could be called the earliest treatise on epigraphy was the *De marmoreis volturrhenis tabulis* of 1492–93 by Annio da Viterbo,[10] which entirely dealt with his own epigraphic forgeries!

The collecting of inscriptions was not an Italian monopoly for very long. Some of the German humanists who had studied or resided in Italy soon followed the example set by their Italian

---

[1] *Epigrammata Antiquae Urbis*, (Romae, 1521) ff. aair–aa8r.

[2] Campana, *Accursio* (*Accorso*), *Mariangelo*, 127.

[3] *Ibid.* loc. cit.

[4] In the Biblioteca Marciana, Venice, Ms. Lat. XIV. 168 (4571) ff. 1r–55r. His sylloge of inscriptions in Museo Correr, Venice, Ms Cicogna 2393, is later than 1508, cf. *ibid.* f. 54r.

[5] Ms Lat. XIV. 168 (4571) ff. 3v–5r.

[6] *Ibid.* f. 5.v

[7] *Ibid.* ff. 6v–9r.

[8] *Ibid.* f. 9r.

[9] Occasionally Bologni went wrong. In the *Antiquarius* he mistakenly identified Asolo with 'Acelum', which he calls 'Acilium', this place being instead Ceneda, and stated that the Piave and the Sile were the same river, which is by no means certain, cf. *Supplementi al Giornale de'Letterati d'Italia tomo secondo*, (Venezia, 1722) 141.

[10] Published and studied in Weiss, *An unknown Epigraphic Tract by Annius of Viterbo*, 101–20.

colleagues, perhaps the most important of these being the *Opus de antiquitatibus cum epitaphiis* by Hartmann Schedel, who completed it in 1505, and which drew to a very great extent from preceding collections.[1] As a rule pieces gathered in the humanist sylloges were ancient Roman inscriptions. At first Greek inscriptions were extremely rare exceptions, often followed by Latin translations of them.[2] This of course changed with Ciriaco, whose travels in the Greek world had enabled him to gather a very considerable collection of Greek epigraphic texts.[3] But after him his only follower in this field was the unknown Venetian who visited Athens about 1470[4] and whose collection had no divulgation. It is therefore not so rash to assume that, apart from a few existing in Italy, all the Greek inscriptions given in sylloges got up after Ciriaco were derived from him. Inscriptions in other languages attracted less attention for two reasons: because they were less plentiful and because they were unintelligible. The discovery at Andros in 1419 of the treatise of Horapollo on hieroglyphs by Cristoforo Buondelmonti[5] aroused some interest in them, especially in Florence, where Buondelmonti had almost certainly sent his find to Niccoli,[6] and a copy of Horapollo was taken with him by Ciriaco when he went to Egypt in 1435.[7] It was during this very visit that Ciriaco sent a transcript of a hieroglyph inscription on one of the pyramids, which he believed to be in Phoenician characters,[8] to Niccoli and, from what we know of his tastes, one can safely assume that other such inscriptions were copied by him on this occasion. It seems therefore highly probable that the hieroglyphs in the copies of Ferrarini's

---

[1] On it see especially G. B. De Rossi, 'Dell *'opus de antiquitatibus* di Hartmann Schedel Norimberghese', *Nuove memorie dell'Istituto di corrispondenza archeologica*, (Lipsia, 1865) 500–14.

[2] *Supra*, 147, n.9.

[3] *Ibid.* 139–140.

[4] *Ibid.* 142–143.

[5] Weiss, *Un umanista antiquario*, 111.

[6] The copy discovered by Buondelmonti is now at Florence in the Laurentian Library, Ms. 69.27. The tract of Horapollo was only turned into Latin during the second half of the fifteenth century by Giorgio Valla. His version is in Biblioteca Trivulziana, Milan, Ms. 2154. Another version is in the Vatican Library, Ms. Vat. lat. 3898, ff. 1r–16r. To these should be added the Latin versions by Willibald Pirckheimer made in Linz in 1514 at the request of the Emperor Maximilian I, cf. L. Volkmann, *Bilderschriften der Renaissance*, (*Leipzig*, 1923) 84, Bernardino Trebazio of Vicenza, first printed at Strassburg in 1515, and Filippo Fagianini, printed at Bologna in 1517. The Greek original (accompanied by a Latin version) was only published in 1505 by Aldus in Venice.

[7] C. C. Van Essen, 'Cyriaque d'Ancone en Egypte', *Mededelingen der Koninklijke Nederlandse Akademie van Wetenschappen, Afd. Letterkunde*, Nieuwe Reeks, Deel 21, n. 12 (1958) 302–03.

[8] *Kiriaci Anconitani Itinerarium*, 52.

sylloge now at Naples and Paris[1] derive from a transcript by Ciriaco.[2]

In the field of epigraphy Egyptian hieroglyphs could scarcely have aroused less interest.[3] The same can be said of Semitic inscriptions, though these could be translated by Jewish scholars, as one of them who came from Pisa but was residing in Palermo actually did for the Dominican Pietro Ranzani, when the latter was anxious to secure the version of a 'Chaldean' inscription on one of the gates of Palermo.[4] Marin Sanudo was therefore something of an exception when he recalled the ancient Hebrew inscriptions he had seen in the Jewish cemetery at Cividale,[5] some of which are now in the town's museum. Slightly greater interest appears to have been aroused by epigraphic texts in the pre-Roman dialects of Italy. It is true that some twelve years after the famous *Tabulae Iguinae* had been found in a cave near Gubbio in 1444,[6] the town authorities were glad to purchase them from their owner, Paolo Gregorio da Signa, in exchange for some pasture and wooding rights for two years valued at twenty florins.[7] But in order to find any further notice of pre-Roman texts we must really wait until the late fifteenth and early sixteenth century. It cannot have been later than 1493, when Ermolao Barbaro died, that Antonio Galateo sent copies to him, Pontano, Sannazzaro, Summonte, and others in order to have their opinion about an inscription recently discovered near Vasto, which they unanimously judged to be Messapian[8] and which Galateo later included in his *De situ Iapygiae*.[9] Two Italic inscriptions from Perugia figure in one of the epigraphic manuscripts of Mariangelo Accursio.[10] But the first who really took a

---

[1] Biblioteca Nazionale, Naples, Ms. VE 5, ff. 249v–50r, Bibliothèque Nationale, Paris, Ms. Lat. 6128, ff. 130r–31v.

[2] *Inscriptiones Christianae Urbis Romae*, II. 1, 382, n. 6.

[3] On the interest in hieroglyphs during the Renaissance, which was not part of epigraphical studies, see especially K. Giehlow, 'Die Hieroglyphenkunde des Humanismus in der Allegorie der Renaissance', *Jahrbuch der kunsthistorischen Sammlungen des Allerhöchsten Kaiserhauses*, XXXII (1915) 1–222, Volkmann, *op. cit.*, E. Iversen, *The Myth of Egypt and its Hieroglyphs in European Tradition*, (Copenhagen, 1961) 57–87.

[4] *Opuscoli di autori siciliani tomo nono*, (Palermo, 1767) 30–32.

[5] *Descrizione della Patria del Friuli di Marino Sanuto fatta l'anno MDII–MDIII*, 35.

[6] E. Giovagnoli, *Gubbio nella storia e nell'arte*, (Città di Castello, 1932) 6, *Tabulae Iguinae editae a Iacobo Devoto*, (Romae, 1937) 5; the reverse of the fifth 'tabula' was printed at Parma as early as 1519 in the Latin version of the *Vita di S. Ubaldo data fuori dal padre Stefano da Cremona canonico regolare*.

[7] See the unsigned article 'Stromento di compera delle Tavole Eugubine', *Giornale di erudizione artistica*, I (1872) 177–81.

[8] Galateus, *op. cit.* 98.

[9] *Ibid.* 97.

[10] Ambrosian Library, Milan, Ms. D. 420 inf., f. 238r.

serious interest in pre-Roman epigraphy was Sigismondo Tizio, who gave the text of a considerable number of Etruscan inscriptions in his history of Siena.[1]

Until the end of the fifteenth century the collecting of epigraphic texts had been limited to classical ones, though early Christian and later inscriptions had occasionally crept into more than one sylloge. Here a pioneer was one of the pupils of Pomponio Leto, Pietro Sabino, who in 1495 offered to King Charles VIII a collection of early Christian inscriptions.[2] To the year 1498 belongs a collection of medieval inscriptions in the churches of Rome assembled by Giovanni Capocci and now lost.[3] It was left to the Florentine Battista di Pietro Brunelleschi to complete in 1514 a sylloge of modern Latin inscriptions to be found in Rome.[4] Modern inscriptions were also to be found in Francesco Albertini's *Epythaphiorum libellus*,[5] which though about to be published by the Roman printer Mazzocchi in 1510[6] never saw the light, and they also occur very often in his book on Rome issued in 1510 by the same printer.[7]

In view of the great interest in epigraphy shown by humanists and antiquarians it is not surprising that collections of inscriptions eventually became available in print. Apart from a slim anthology, in which short poetic texts in Latin were interspersed with some inscriptions, mostly apocryphal,[8] the first epigraphic collection to be printed was that of Desiderio Spreti, which appeared in Venice in 1489.[9] After that we have to wait until 1502, when the Erfurt humanist Nicolaus Marschalk saw to the printing in his own home of a small collection,[10] mostly consisting

---

[1] *Supra*, 120, n.6. For Etruscan inscriptions in Mss. collections see Danielsson, *Etruskische Inschriften in handschriftlicher Ueberlieferung.*

[2] Biblioteca Marciana, Venice, Ms. Lat. X. 195 (3453) ff. 276ʳ–324ʳ. On it cf. *Inscriptiones Christianae Urbis Romae*, II. 1, 410–52.

[3] *Ibid.* N.S.I, XL.

[4] On this sylloge see G. De Nicola, 'Iscrizioni romane relative ad artisti o ad opere d'arte', *Archivio della Società Romana di storia patria*, XXXI (1908) 220–25. See also on the collecting of 'modern' inscriptions C. Hülsen, 'Eine Sammlung römischer Renaissance-Inschriften aus den Augsburger Kollektaneen Konrad Peutingers', *Sitzs. der Bayerischen Akad. der Wissenschaften, Philosophische-philologische und historische Klasse, Jahrgang* 1920, 15. *Abhandlung*, (München, 1921.)

[5] Albertinus, *op. cit.* ff. Ziʳ, Z2ʳ⁻ᵛ, etc.

[6] *Ibid.* f. R3ᵛ.

[7] *Ibid.* passim.

[8] On which see L. Bertalot, 'Die älteste gedruckte lateinische Epitaphiensammlung', *Collectanea variae doctrinae Leoni S. Olschki*, (Monachii, 1921) 1–28.

[9] *Supra*, 152.

[10] See C. Huelsen, 'Die Inschriftensammlung des Erfurter Humanisten Nicolaus Marschalk', *Jahrbücher der Königlichen Akademie gemeinnütziger Wissenschaften zu Erfurt*, Neue Folge-Heft, XXXVIII (1912) 161–85.

of apocrypha and adorned with woodcuts showing the so-called
'arch of the sybil'[1] copied from the 1499 edition of Probus's
Notae and some imaginary cinerary urns.[2] This was followed in
1505 by the collection of Augsburg inscriptions by Peutinger[3]
and during the same year there appeared in Fano a small
anthology assembled by Lorenzo Astemio, in which the *Ilias
Latina*, Vegio's *Astyanax*, and Latin epigrams were accompanied
by several epigraphic texts, both genuine and apocryphal. The
anthology proved popular enough to be reprinted a few years
later at Erfurt and again in 1515 at Fano.[4] On the other hand,
Rome started comparatively late to print epigraphic texts. For
it was only about 1510 that the epigraphic calendars in the third
recension of Fra Giocondo's sylloge were published in a slim
tract, almost certainly by Mazzocchi.[5] But this same printer,
who was still advertising in 1515 the sylloge of Albertini as
shortly to appear,[6] already had in all probability by then a much
greater editorial scheme in view, this being a corpus of all the
ancient inscriptions of Rome.

Already in 1517 Mazzocchi had secured from Pope Leo X a
privilege for such a book.[7] It was, however, only in 1521 that the
Epigrammata antiquae Urbis[8] saw the light. It is not very clear who
were the scholars who were responsible for this impressive
collection. That it grew out of Albertini's sylloge seems
scarcely credible, since this seems to have been a slender volume,
and containing furthermore non-classical texts as well as some
from outside Rome.[9] That Mario Maffei, Bishop of Aquino, to
whom the volume was dedicated,[10] Mariangelo Accursio, who

---

[1] *Epitaphia quaedam mirae vetustatis*, (Erfurt, 1502) f. 1.v

[2] *Ibid*. f. 4r-v. Similar 'urns' occur in the sylloge of Michele Ferrarini, cf. Vatican Library, Ms. Vat. lat. 5243, ff. 39v, 41r, 45r, and in that of Giacomo Gigli, cf. ibid. Ms. Vat. lat. 5238, f. 19r.

[3] *Supra*, 152, n.4.

[4] For this anthology and its editions see L. Bertalot, 'L'antologia di epigrammi di Lorenzo Abstemio nelle tre edizioni sonciniane', *Miscellanea Giovanni Mercati*, IV (Città del Vaticano, 1946) 305–26

[5] Pl. XIII, *Hemerologia Romana*, (S.L.N.A.).

[6] F. Albertinus, *Opusculum de Mirabilibus nove et veteris Urbis Rome*, (Romae, 1515) f. R 3v.

[7] *Epigrammata antiquae Urbis*, f. 10r.

[8] On which see *C.I.L.* VI. 1, XLVI–VII, G. B. De Rossi, 'Note sur le recueil d'inscriptions latines, intitulé *Epigrammata antiquae Urbis*', *Revue Archéologique*, XIII (1856) 51–53.

[9] *Supra*, 157.

[10] *Epigrammata antiquae Urbis*, f. 1v. On Mario Maffei see L. Pescetti, 'Mario Maffei', *Rassegna Volterrana*, VI (1932) 65–91, Paschini, *Una famiglia di curiali*: *I Maffei di Volterra*, 356–76, R. Lefevre, 'La *vigna* del cardinale Giulio de Medici e il vescovo d'Aquino', *Strenna dei Romanisti-Natale di Roma 1961*, (Roma, 1961) 171–77.

edited the text of Probus included in it[1] and was almost certainly responsible for its errata corrige,[2] and Andrea Fulvio had a hand in it seems highly likely. The principal sources of it were, however, besides new material, some earlier sylloges—chiefly the third recension of that of Fra Giocondo, that of Pietro Sabino and perhaps those of Signorili and Poggio also contributing to it.

The *Epigrammata antiquae Urbis* also included several illustrations. It is evident here that Mazzocchi 'mobilized' for the occasion all the woodblocks in his printing works. It is true that the illustrations showing monuments or other small antiquities were made expressly for this book. But the ornamental frames surrounding many of the inscriptions have a familiar air, and had already been used as the frontispieces of several of Mazzocchi's publications. One year before Mazzocchi's collection saw the light the inscriptions of Mainz had been published there by Huttich,[3] his edition also showing woodcuts of local antiquities. It was, however, left to the Venetian printer Giovanni Tacquini to issue in 1525 the last epigraphical collection published before the sack of Rome of 1527.[4] Epigraphically this small sylloge, entirely derived from the third recension of Fra Giocondo, is of small importance. It is, on the other hand, not entirely insignificant, as being the first edition of the *De notis literarum* of Peter the Deacon and some short tracts on metrology.

The influence of epigraphy soon became felt in book production. The use of monumental capitals, the attempt to imitate an ancient inscription in a title or a colophon, the placing of a title within a cippus, became fairly frequent features in fifteen and early sixteenth century manuscripts.[5] This was a feature which was also taken over by the printers. Thus cippuses occur in Ferrarini's edition of Probus's *Notae* printed at Brescia in 1486[6] and a superb cippus figures also on the title page of the first edition of Caprioli's history of Brescia,[7] while the colophons

---

[1] *Epigrammata antiquae Urbis*, ff. 2r–9v.

[2] Supra, 154.

[3] *Collectanea Antiquitatum in Urbe et Agro Moguntino repertarum*, (Moguntiae, 1520).

[4] *Hoc in volumine continentur M. Val. Probus de notis Roma. Ex codice manuscriptu castigatior . . . Petrus Diaconus de eadem re . . .*, (Venetiis, 1525).

[5] See for instance M. Meiss, 'Toward a More Comprehensive Renaissance Palaeography', *The Art Bulletin*, XLII (1960) figg. 1, 3, 29, 30, Wardrop, *op. cit.*, pl. 3, 11, 21, 36, the item in pl. 36 given as 'whereabouts not recorded' is Ms. Holkham Hall 496, U. Meroni, *Mostra dei Codici Gonzagheschi—La Biblioteca dei Gonzaga da Luigi I ad Isabella*, (Mantova, 1966) pl. 119–20.

[6] V. Probus, *De litteris antiquis opusculum*, (Brixiae, 1486), ff. aiv, a2v, a3v.

[7] Capreolus, *op. cit.*, f. 1r.

of the octavo editions of Latin and Italian classics issued by the Paganini at Toscolano on Lake Garda aim at reproducing an ancient inscription.[1] But to return to classical epigraphy, it is certain that as time went on greater accuracy was expected. Here new standards were certainly introduced by Accursio and are also evident in the handwritten corrections which Anton Lelio Romano (Podager) inserted in his copy of Mazzocchi's *Epigrammata antiquae Urbis*.[2] There is no doubt that faith in the value of inscriptions was by then universal in the humanist world. Or almost so, for when opposing Politian's spelling 'Vergilius' instead of 'Virgilius', Battista Mantovano emphasized his own faith in literary rather than epigraphic evidence.[3]

Interest in inscriptions was not limited to their text or lettering. The original stones were collected with as much enthusiasm as they were being destroyed.[4] Many famous humanists, one can mention Pomponio Leto and Platina, Pontano and Pandolfo Collenuccio, and these are but a few of them, did so.[5] Ancient inscriptions were also set up on public or other buildings. Thus by order of Pope Martin V, an 'Epitaphium Lucretie' allegedly found in Rome behind the church of San Sisto in August 1426, was placed 'in sala que dicitur de la fortuna'.[6] After the famous inscription of 'Fortuna Redux'[7] was brought to light among the ruins of the temple of Fortune at Ascoli Piceno about 1496, the Bishop of the city, Prospero Caffarelli, himself a keen epigraphist,[8] had it set up on one of the outside walls of the cathedral, with underneath it another inscription in which he recorded his own rôle in its preservation.[9]

---

[1] U. Baroncelli, *La stampa nella Riviera Bresciana del Garda nei secoli XV e XVI*, (Brescia, 1964) 33.

[2] See for instance Vatican Library, Ms. Vat.! at. 8442. On Podager see E. Pèrcopo, 'Di Anton Lelio Romano e di alcune pasquinate contro Leon X', *Giornale storico della letteratura italiana*, XXVIII (1896) 45–77.

[3] E. Bolisani, 'Vergilius o Virgilius'? L'opinione di un dotto umanista', *Atti dello Istituto Veneto di scienze, lettere ed arti*, CXVII (1958–59) 132–34.

[4] On 27 August 1515 the painter Raphael was empowered to acquire ancient stones in Rome, particularly in order to prevent the destruction of old inscriptions, cf. Golzio, *op. cit.* 38–40. For his failure in this field see Lanciani, *Storia degli scavi di Roma*, I, 166.

[5] For such collections see for instance *ibid.* I, passim. For the collection of Pomponio Leto see Zabughin, *Giulio Pomponio Leto*, II, 186–94. For that of Pandolfo Collenuccio see Ziebarth, *De antiquissimis inscriptionum syllogis*, 231, n. 1.

[6] Ambrosian Library, Milan, Ms. Trotti 373, f. 90ᵛ, *C.I.L.* VI. 5, 13*. Needless to say, it was a spurious inscription!

[7] *C.I.L.* IX. 5177.

[8] Weiss, *An unknown epigraphic tract by Annius of Viterbo*, 117, n. 29. On Caffarelli see G. Fabiano, *Ascoli nel Quattrocento*, (Ascoli Piceno, 1950) 15–18 and passim.

[9] S. Andreantonelli, *Historiae Asculanae libri IV accessit Historiae Sacrae Liber Singularis*, (Patavii, 1673) 308–09, B. Orsini, *Descrizione delle Pitture Sculture Architetture ed altre cose rare della insigne città di Ascoli nella Marca*, (Perugia, 1790) 29, G. Carducci, *Su le memorie e i monumenti di Ascoli nel Piceno*, (Fermo, 1853) 224.

At Brescia some Roman inscriptions were placed on the walls of the palace of the Monte di Pietà in Piazza della Loggia,[1] but these are only a few instances among very many.

Needless to say, classical inscriptions exerted a tremendous influence on Renaissance epigraphy. The monumental capitals used on buildings were clearly derived from them, an important rôle being played in this field by Leon Battista Alberti.[2] The lettering of the inscriptions he placed on the front of his buildings confirms their reliance on ancient Roman models, though here he also contributed some innovations of his own. As an architect he naturally appreciated their functional value; because of this his lapidary capitals were taller than their Roman prototypes, this being due to their more or less playing the rôle of caryatids, the fact that they were meant to be seen from below having also been taken into account. As far as Renaissance monumental inscriptions are concerned, the place where, despite earlier efforts in other places, they can be said to have started was Rimini, where Matteo de Pasti the medallist and Agostino di Duccio the sculptor were responsible for the carving of several of them in the Malatesta Temple and the Castle, while the supervision of Alberti himself seems likely in the design of the inscription on the front of the actual Temple.[3] Examples at Florence and Mantua show Alberti's later development of his monumental lettering.[4]

In view of the great popularity of these letters it is not surprising that pattern books showing how to construct them geometrically soon appeared. As far as it is known the earliest of the kind, apart from some wooden tablets 46 x 30.5 cm in size now at Mantua, on which were pasted sheets with models of letters,[5] was the pattern book by Felice Feliciano, which was accompanied by instructions on how these letters were to be made.[6] To shortly after 1480 belongs the small handbook on

---

[1] *C.I.L.* V. 1, 4318–19, 4325, 4328, 4361. The decision to place inscriptions there was taken in 1465 'pro maiori ornamento nostrae principalis plateae' and again in 1480, cf. B. Zamboni, *Memorie intorno alle pubbliche fabbriche più insigni della Città di Brescia*, (Brescia, 1778) 30.

[2] For the use of 'Roman' monumental capitals by Alberti and others see G. Mardersteig, 'Leon Battista Alberti e la rinascita del carattere lapidario Romano nel Quattrocento', *Italia Medioevale e Umanistica*, II (1959) 285–307, Meiss, *op. cit.* passim.

[3] Mardersteig, *op. cit.* 287–92. It is interesting to note that Matteo de Pasti possessed a Ms. of Ciriaco, cf. *Inscriptiones Christianae Urbis Romae*, II. 1, 371, n. 1.

[4] Mardersteig, *op. cit.* 293–95.

[5] *Ibid.* 297–98.

[6] Reproduced in Felice Feliciano Veronese, *Alphabetum Romanum*, ed. G. Mardersteig, (Verona 1959).

the same subject printed at Parma by Damiano da Moyle,[1] the patterns in which look, as was pointed out,[2] like a kind of typographic adaptation of those of Feliciano. On the other hand, Alberti's influence is visible in the patterns included in the *De divina proportione* of Fra Luca Pacioli published in Venice in 1509.[3] After him others also studied the construction of Roman lapidary characters. But by the second decade of the Cinquecento, when the booklets on the subject by Francesco Sigismondo Fanti and Francesco Torniello came out,[4] there was little of value to add to the foundations laid down by Alberti, Feliciano, and Pacioli.[5]

The influence of the Roman lapidary capitals was also felt outside the sphere of epigraphy. Renaissance medallists, for instance, were quick in adopting them, the lettering on the pieces by the artist known to us as Lysippus Junior, being the best produced in this field.[6] Renaissance calligraphers were also much influenced by them.[7] But besides this the formulas of classical epigraphy were very much employed during the Renaissance, when the aim of every humanist composing an inscription was to make it appear as classical as possible. Some of the inscriptions composed by Ciriaco,[8] Pomponio Leto,[9] Aldus,[10] just to give a few examples, had such an aim, which is also present in countless others, from the 'graffiti' scratched on the walls of the Catacombs by the Roman academicians,[11] down to the

---

[1] S. Morison, *The Moyllus Alphabet*, (Montagnola di Lugano, 1927).

[2] Mardersteig, *op. cit.* 305.

[3] S. Morison, *Fra Luca de Pacioli of Borgo S. Sepolcro*, (New York, 1933) 29–73.

[4] F. Torniello, *Opera del modo de fare le littere maiuxole*, (Milano, 1517); S. Fanti, *Theorica et pratica de modo scribendi fabricandique omnes litterarum species*, (Venetiis, 1514).

[5] Roman capitals also seem to have attracted the attention of Leonardo da Vinci, cf. R. Bertieri, 'Gli studi italiani sull' alfabeto nel Rinascimento, Pacioli e Leonardo da Vinci', *Gutenberg Jahrbuch*, IV (1929) 269–86, A. Uccelli, 'Sopra due presunte carte vinciane esistenti nella raccolta C. L. Ricketts di Chicago', *Raccolta Vinciana*, XV–XVI (1934–39) 185–90. The construction of capitals was considered during the third decade of the Cinquecento by Dürer, cf. A. Dürer, *Unterweysung der Messung*, (Nürnberg, 1525), A. Dürer, *On the just shaping of letters*, (New York, 1917), by Giovanni Battista Verini in his *Luminario* printed at Toscolano in 1527, on which see *Luminario or the third book of the Liber Elementorum Litterarum on the construction of Roman Capitals by Giovanni Baptista Verini in an English version by A. F. Johnson with an introduction by Stanley Morison*, (Cambridge Mass.-Chicago, 1947) and the reproduction of the 1527 ed. with an introduction by E. Casamassima, (Firenze, 1967), and by Geoffroi Tory, see G. Tory, *Champ Fleury*, (Paris, 1529).

[6] Hill, *A Corpus of Italian Medals of the Renaissance before Cellini*, I, 205–10, II, pl. 130–33.

[7] B. L. Ullman, *The Origin and Development of Humanistic Script*, (Roma, 1960) 54–56 and passim.   [8] Supra, 141.   [9] Weiss, *Un umanista veneziano*: *Papa Paolo II*, 45.

[10] R. Weiss, 'La lapide delle otto foglie di San Michele in Isola', *Archivio Veneto*, LXVIII (1961) 11–16.

[11] Cf. G. Lumbroso, 'Gli Accademici nelle Catacombe', *Archivio della R. Società Romana di storia patria*, XII (1889) 34–41, C. Stornaiolo, 'Il Giovanni Battista ed il Pantagato compagni di Pomponio Leto nella visita delle catacombe romane', *Nuovo Bullettino di archeologia cristiana*, XII (1906) 67–68.

extravagant inventions of Francesco Colonna.[1] Classical forms of dating were not overlooked. The monumental inscription which Lorenzo Manili placed in 1467 on the front of his newly built house in Rome,[2] has the dating 'ab urbe condita', while that placed by Cardinal Giuliano della Rovere, the future Pope Julius II, on the main tower of the fortress at Ostia in 1483 in order to record its foundation, is dated 'ab Ostia condita'.[3] Inscribed cippuses were also occasionally erected, as for instance that in memory of Domizio Calderini at Torri on Lake Garda,[4] or that at Padua commemorating the restoration of a bridge by Zaccaria Barbaro.[5] Occasionally humanist inscriptions would draw extensively from classical ones. Thus Francesco Barbaro's epitaph of Gattamelata,[6] the general immortalized by Donatello's equestrian statue at Padua, and that of Sir John Hawkwood in Paolo Uccello's fresco in Santa Maria del Fiore, Florence, are but echoes of the epigraphic eulogy of Fabius Maximus.[7]

Humanist inscriptions were not exclusively in Latin. The humanist Basinio Basini, for instance, composed one in Greek, which can still be seen in the Tempio Malatestiano at Rimini.[8] Other inscriptions, partly in Greek and partly in Latin, occur on the small monument of the humanist Platina in Santa Maria Maggiore, Rome,[9] on the epitaph of Vincenzo de Monfort of 1486, now on an outer wall of the cathedral at Trento,[10] and on that of the humanist Giovanni Calfurnio.[11] As for the appeal of inscriptions, this was also felt by artists. Already Jacopo Bellini, who derived his antiquarian interests from Pisanello, felt such an appeal, this being witnessed by a couple of sheets in one of his books of drawings.[12] The inscriptions given on these sheets had been found in the neighbourhood of Este and they figure here

[1] (F. Colonna) *Hypnerotomachia Poliphili*, (Venetiis, 1499) passim.

[2] Weiss, *Un umanista veneziano*: *Papa Paolo II*, 44.

[3] Weiss, *The Medals of Pope Sixtus IV* (1471–1484), 31–36.

[4] Pl. XIV, R. Weiss 'In Memoriam Domitii Calderini', *Italia Medioevale e Umanistica*, III (1960) 315–20.

[5] *Ibid.* 321.

[6] Saxl, *op. cit.* 25, n. 2.

[7] *C.I.L.* XI. 1828.

[8] A. Campana, 'Basinio da Parma', *Dizionario biografico degli Italiani*, VII, (Roma, 1965) 93.

[9] On which see A. Campana, 'Bartolomeo Platina e Antonio Blado', *Miscellanea bibliografica in memoria di don Tommaso Accurti*, (Roma, 1947) 45–50.

[10] R. Weiss, 'Due note Trentino Alto-Atesine: I. Una testimonianza per la conoscenza del Greco a Trento nel tardo Quattrocento', *Il Cristallo*, IV (1962) 45–51.

[11] V. Cian, 'Un umanista del Rinascimento—Giovanni Calfurnio', *Archivio Storico Lombardo*, XXXVII (1910) 231.

[12] M. Rothlisberger, 'Studi su Iacopo Bellini', *Saggi e Memorie di storia dell'arte*, II (1958–59) 70–71.

on partly or wholly invented monuments. Mantegna too included some partly re-elaborated inscriptions, one from Este (also figuring in Jacopo Bellini's Paris book of drawings) and one from the Arco dei Gavi at Verona, in two of his (now destroyed) frescoes in the Eremitani at Padua.[1] Another artist, Domenico Ghirlandaio, invented, or more exactly had invented for him by Bartolomeo Fonzio, the inscriptions in his *Adoration of the Magi* in the Sassetti chapel in Santa Trinita, Florence.[2]

The popularity of inscriptions brought a spate of forgeries in its wake. As a rule such forgeries were made either for one's amusement, or as a rhetorical exercise, or in order to prove a historical connexion, or for political purposes. Some of them were actually carved on stone, others, on the other hand, never went beyond circulating in manuscript or print. A typical rhetorical exercise was the inscription of Heliodorus the Carthaginian which Ciriaco gave as existing near Gades.[3] Attempts at establishing a historical connexion were the so called 'Sanctio' on the bridge near Cesena, the aim of which was to prove that the river flowing under it was Caesar's Rubicon,[4] and the stone at Rimini, later replaced by a sixteenth century one, indicating the spot where Caesar was supposed to have harangued his troops after crossing from Cisalpine Gaul into Italy.[5] They could also be political prophecies, like the one sent in 1505 by Valentinus Moravus to Hieronymus Münzer, which was clearly fabricated in support of Portuguese imperialism;[6] or the very clumsy one printed in 'translation' in Rome about 1510, dealing with the forthcoming conversion of the Turks to Christianity.[7] And there were of course the absurd fabrications of Annio da Viterbo,[8]

---

[1] A. Moschetti, 'Le iscrizioni lapidarie romane negli affreschi del Mantegna, *Atti del Reale Istituto Veneto di scienze, lettere ed arti*, LXXXIX. 2 (1929–30) 227–39. Mantegna himself placed a Latin inscription some time between 1482 and 1502 on his house near the church of San Sebastiano at Mantua, in order to record Ludovico Gonzaga's gift of the plot of land on which the house was built. The inscription is reproduced in *L'opera completa del Mantegna–Presentazione di Maria Bellonci*, (Milano, 1967) 85.

[2] Saxl, *op. cit.* 28–29. On inscriptions in Florentine paintings of the Quattrocento see D. Covi, 'Lettering in the Inscriptions of 15th Century Florentine Painters', *Renaissance News*, VII (1954) 46–50.

[3] *Supra*, 141.

[4] *Ibid.* 112.

[5] Campana, *Il cippo riminese di Giulio Cesare*.

[6] A. Momigliano, 'Enrico Caiado e la falsificazione di *C.I.L.* II, 30*', *Athenaeum*, N.S. XLII (1964) 3–10.

[7] *Prophetia trouata in Roma. Intagliata in marmoro in versi latini. Tratta in vulgar sentimento*, (Roma, S.A.).

[8] On which see Weiss, *An Unknown Epigraphic Tract by Annius of Viterbo*, passim.

which aimed at showing that his native town was the cradle of western civilization, one of which, the forged decree of Desiderius, King of the Lombards, which backed the claims of Viterbo to adjacent territories, was accepted by many as genuine as late as the eighteenth century.[1]

As everyone knows, inscriptions included as a rule a number of abbreviations, the interpretation of which was not always clear. Here an invaluable aid was provided by the handbook of Valerius Probus, which Poggio had discovered about 1417,[2] and the later one by Peter the Deacon of Montecassino, nor were humanists slow in appreciating their value. The tract by Probus was included several times in humanist sylloges; it figures for instance in that of Fra Giocondo.[3] It was therefore scarcely surprising that the first printed text of it, issued at Brescia in 1486, was edited by the well known epigraphist Michele Ferrarini, while the subsequent editions of it, Venice 1499, 1502, 1525, Rome, 1509, Paris, c. 1510, etc., as well as that by Mariangelo Accursio included in Mazzocchi's *Epigrammata antiquae Urbis* of 1521,[4] speak clearly for its popularity. Less popular was the one by Peter the Deacon, which seldom appears in sylloges[5] and was only printed for the first time in 1525. Of another work of the kind, the *De notis publica auctoritate approbatis* by the Roman curial official Andrea Santacroce, composed not long after 1464 and dealing with abbreviations and numbers on coins as well as inscriptions,[6] not so much is known, and it has not reached us.[7] One may, however assume, that it was very probably modelled upon Probus's tract.

The interpretation of inscriptions was not always easy. It was therefore not uncommon for a humanist to send a text to a friend or friends asking for their opinion of it, as for instance

---

[1] See especially *Ibid.* 119, n. 46.

[2] *Supra*, 147. For the use of Probus' *Notae* during the Renaissance see D. Maffei, *Gli inizi dell'umanesimo giuridico*, (Milano 1956) 94, n. 43.

[3] See for example Vatican Library, Ms. Vat. lat. 5236, ff. 1r–4r.

[4] *Supra*, 159.

[5] It occurs in both recensions of the sylloges of Marcanova, for which see *supra*, 148, see also Vatican Library, Ms. Vat. lat. 9152, ff. 1r–25v. The texts of both Probus and Peter the Deacon were corrected by Gian Pietro Ferretti before 1511, cf. Vatican Library, Ms. Vat. lat. 5835, f. 61r.

[6] G. Tiraboschi, *Storia della letteratura italiana*, VI. 2, (Milano, 1824) 971, n.*, G. B. Picotti, *Ricerche umanistiche*, (Firenze, 1955) 234. For Santacroce, who also prepared a sylloge, see *Inscriptiones Christianae Urbis Romae*, II. 1, 463.

[7] According to Tiraboschi, *Storia della letteratura italiana*, VI. 2, 971, n. *, a copy of Santacroce's tract was at Venice in the Library of San Francesco della Vigna. A discussion on epigraphic abbreviations, probably reflecting the views of Guarino da Verona, is in A. Decembrius, *Politia literaria libri septem*, (Basileae, 1562) 413–19.

we find Giacomo Gherardi of Volterra doing when, between 1478 and 1485 he sent an inscription of Trajan to Giovanni Battista Capranica, the 'Pantagatus' of Leto's Roman Academy.[1] It was also not unusual for a humanist to send an inscription to a friend. Feliciano did so;[2] Bartolomeo Partenio sent inscriptions from Rome to Girolamo Bologni[3] and Agostino Almadiani sent at least one from Viterbo to Mariangelo Accursio.[4] Sometime an epigraphic text could lead to an argument, as may be found in some letters exchanged between Ciriaco and Poggio. For on receiving from Ciriaco an inscription from Aquileia with IVNONIBVS SACRVM, Poggio had replied expressing disbelief, whereupon Ciriaco had answered by forwarding to him the text of an inscription at Parma where IVNONIBVS also occurred.[5] Needless to say, humanists only too often secured valuable evidence from inscriptions when trying to establish an archaeological or philological point. Tortelli's *De orthographia*, Politian's *Miscellanea*, Pontano's *De aspiratione* show their value in philological scholarship, while antiquarians like Flavio Biondo, Bernardo Rucellai, Francesco Albertini, and Andrea Fulvio, to name a few of them, also drew much valuable information from epigraphic sources. Humanist historians also greatly profited from epigraphic sources, the use of inscriptions in the historical writings of Giorgio Merula, Tristano Calchi, Elia Caprioli, Pellegrino Prisciani, Andrea Alciati, Benedetto Giovio, Pierio Valeriano, and many others, showing their reliance on them. Long before Rome was sacked in 1527 by the troops of the Emperor Charles V, epigraphic evidence had been recognized as an essential aspect of antiquarian science: the historian or philologist who presumed to dispense with it, did so at his own risk.

[1] *Il Diario Romano di Iacopo Gherardi da Volterra*, ed. E. Carusi, (Città di Castello, 1904) LXXXI.
[2] Pratilli, *op. cit.* 63.
[3] Museo Correr, Venice, Ms. Cicogna, 2393, f. 8[r-v], Biblioteca Marciana, Venice, Ms. Lat. XIV. 168 (4571) f. 2[v].
[4] Ambrosian Library, Milan, Ms. D. 420 inf., f. 237[r].
[5] Degli Abati Olivieri, *op. cit.* 28.

CHAPTER TWELVE

THE STUDY OF ANCIENT NUMISMATICS

The age of the Renaissance felt the fascination of ancient Greek and Roman coins. This was in part because they were tangible and handy relics of an age so much admired by the humanists, but also because so many of them bore the effigies of those great rulers whose names filled the history books. Ancient coins had, of course, been collected, imitated, and used as historical evidence before the fifteenth century.[1] But during this century interest in them assumed hitherto unknown proportions. Needless to say, the greatest Renaissance collections of coins were assembled by princes. The Medici at Florence, the Aragonese at Naples,[2] the Este at Ferrara,[3] the Gonzaga at Mantua,[4] as well as other Italian rulers, assembled very impressive coin collections. Among the Medici, Piero, son of Cosimo the Elder, was the keenest collector of them. Thus in 1455 his brother Carlo and the head of the local branch of the Medici bank were searching on his behalf in Rome for one hundred ancient silver coins.[5] Already in 1456 Piero had assembled fifty-three gold, three hundred silver, and thirty-three bronze specimens.[6] By 1465 these figures had been raised to one hundred in gold and

---

[1] *Supra*, passim. A short account of numismatic studies during the Renaissance is in *Illustrium Imagines di Andrea Fulvio . . . Nota di Robert Weiss*, (Roma, 1967).

[2] Müntz, *Les arts à la cour des Papes*, II, 174–75, P. Collenuccio, *Compendio de le istorie del Regno di Napoli*, ed. A. Saviotti, (Bari, 1929) 292. A sonnet by Pietro Jacopo de Jennaro accompanying the gift of a coin of Augustus to King Ferrante I is in Pietro Jacopo de Jennaro, *Rime*, ed. M. Corti, (Bologna, 1956) 55. De Jennaro was also the author of an *Opera deli huomini illustri sopra de le medaglie*, which, despite its title, has nothing to do with numismatics. On it see R. Renier, 'Opere inesplorate del Di Gennaro', *Giornale storico della letteratura italiana*, XI (1888) 472–75.

[3] Müntz, *Les arts à la cour des Papes*, II, 174. Flavio Biondo tells us in a letter of 1446 that Leonello d'Este had ten thousand bronze coins imitating Roman pieces struck, cf. Nogara, *op. cit.* 159–60. These 'coins', which bore Leonello's effigy, were doubtless the medals of this ruler. In the same letter Biondo says that he is sending some Roman coins to Leonello, so that he can understand better some passages in Ovid and Pliny, cf. *ibid.* 160. In 1494 the Este coin collection possessed 437 gold coins 'poste suso desenove tavolete' and 3385 silver ones, cf. G. Campori, *Raccolta di cataloghi ed inventari inediti*, (Modena, 1870) 28–29.

[4] Ciriaco d'Ancona tells us that he saw at Pavia in 1442 a fine collection of ancient gold, silver, and bronze coins belonging to Gian Lucido Gonzaga, son of the Marquis of Mantua, cf. Müntz, *Les arts à la cour des Papes*, II, 173. For the collecting activity in this field of Isabella d'Este, wife of Francesco Gonzaga, see *infra*, 171, n.6.

[5] Müntz, *Les arts à la cour des Papes*, II, 131, n. 2.

[6] E. Müntz, *Les Collections des Médicis au XVe siècle*, (Paris-Londres, 1888) 16.

five hundred and three in silver,[1] this great increase being doubtless due in part to the pieces inherited by Piero in the meantime from his father Cosimo the Elder. The heyday of the Medici collections, and not solely the numismatic ones, was, however, under Lorenzo de' Medici (1449–1492), when the contents of the family palace in Florence included over two thousand and three hundred pieces.[2]

Such an extraordinary increase is understandable when one realizes that at the death of Pope Paul II in 1471, Lorenzo had been able to acquire most of his collections.[3] Now during his lifetime there is no doubt that Paul II had been the greatest collector of all in the field of numismatics and other small antiquities, with the result that in 1457, while still Cardinal Pietro Barbo, he had assembled not less than ninety-seven gold and about one thousand silver coins.[4] Paul II was certainly a highly competent numismatist, a fact which had not escaped some of his contemporaries. Enea Silvio Piccolomini, not yet Pope Pius II, recalled Cardinal Barbo's activity as coin collector,[5] while his numismatic learning was mentioned by his two contemporary biographers, Gaspare da Verona and Michele Canensi.[6] Indeed the latter informs us how Pope Paul could tell at once to which Roman emperor a particular piece belonged.[7]

It is clear that the future Paul II had no scruples when it came to enlarging his collections,[8] in the enrichment of which he also sought the aid of friends and correspondents. So, for example, between 1450 and 1460 Archbishop Maffeo Vallaresso was securing coins and small antiquities for him.[9] Nor did his numismatic interests desert him once he became Pope. It was therefore typical of him that, upon hearing in 1468 of the discovery of a hoard of some three hundred Roman coins at Pienza, he hastened to write to Cardinal Ammannati in order to secure it.[10]

The inventory of the collections of Cardinal Pietro Barbo drawn up in 1457 displays his high competence in the field of

[1] *Ibid.* 38.
[2] *Ibid.* 79.
[3] Müntz, *Les arts à la cour des Papes*, II, 154–58, III, 15, 239.
[4] Weiss, *Un umanista Veneziano: Papa Paolo II*, 28.
[5] *Ibid.* 27.
[6] *Ibid.* loc. cit.
[7] *Ibid.* loc. cit.
[8] *Infra*, 171.
[9] Weiss, *Un umanista Veneziano: Papa Paolo II*, 28.
[10] *Ibid.* loc. cit.

Roman numismatics. For it is clear from his autograph notes on its margins, that he was able to tell when a Roman coin was genuine or not and whether it was scarce, though it is evident also that Greek coins were not his strong point.[1] Other prelates are also known to have indulged in coin collecting. Cardinals Domenico Grimani[2] and Andrea della Valle,[3] Pietro Bembo,[4] the future cardinal, and Angelo Colocci[5] were among them, and it was Bembo who presented the great printer Aldus with a gold coin of the Emperor Titus bearing a dolphin entwined around an anchor on its reverse, which Aldus adopted as his own printer's mark.[6]

Coin collecting was by no means the monopoly of princes and great prelates. Many humanists proved equally enthusiastic collectors. Here pride of place must be given to Niccolò Niccoli, whose antiquarian collections included a very impressive number of ancient coins.[7] Among the many who secured ancient coins for Niccoli, there was Ambrogio Traversari, whose interest appears to have been mainly in Greek numismatics and who is known to have obtained lead casts of pieces when unable to obtain the originals.[8] Traversari was always happy to inspect numismatic and antiquarian collections, as he did, for instance, in Venice in 1432–33,[9] and he appears to have been a very expert numismatist.[10] During this stay in Venice Traversari also met Ciriaco d'Ancona, who showed him some gold and silver coins, among which there were some with the effigies of Lysimachus,

[1] *Ibid.* 29.

[2] P. Paschini, 'Le collezioni archeologiche dei prelati Grimani nel Cinquecento', *Atti della Pontificia Accademia Romana di archeologia*, ser. 3, V (1926–27) 152, R. Gallo, 'Le donazioni alla Serenissima di Domenico e Giovanni Grimani', *Archivio Veneto*, ser. 5, L–LI (1952) 37.

[3] Fulvius, *Antiquitates Urbis*, f. R5ʳ.

[4] V. Cian, *Un decennio della vita di M. Pietro Bembo*, (Torino, 1885) 105–06.

[5] For Colocci's interest in ancient numismatics, see for instance the notes collected by him in Vatican Library, Ms. Vat. lat. 3436, Ms. Vat. lat. 5395, and Ms. Vat. lat. 6845. For his interests in ancient metrology see also P. De Nolhac, 'Les Correspondants d'Alde Manuce', *Studi e documenti di storia e diritto*, VIII (1887) 290, V. Fanelli, 'Le lettere di Mons. Angelo Colocci nel Museo Britannico di Londra', *Rinascimento*, X (1959) 117–19.

[6] L. Dorez, 'Études Aldines I: La marque typographique d'Alde Manuce', *Revue des Bibliothèques*, VI (1896) 143–60.

[7] Müntz, *Les arts à la cour des Papes*, II, 168, n. 3, 169, n. 2.

[8] *Ambrosii Traversarii . . . Latinae Epistolae*, ed. P. Cannetus, (Florentiae, 1759) 417–18. On such lead casts see R. Weiss, 'Nota sugli esemplari plumbei di medaglie Rinascimentali', *Italia Numismatica*, XV (1964) 71–72.

[9] *Ambrosii Traversarii . . . Latinae Epistolae*, 412, 417.

[10] His interests in metrology are also shown by his turning into Latin a Greek tract on weights and measures. This version is in Biblioteca Laurenziana, Florence, Ms. Ashburnham 259, ff. 67ʳ–69ʳ.

Philip of Macedonia, and Alexander the Great, which Traversari doubted to be genuine Macedonian issues.[1]

Also Ciriaco d'Ancona was a keen coin collector, though he is known to have occasionally parted with some of his pieces. This happened for instance in 1432 when, on meeting the Emperor Sigismund in Siena, he gave him a gold coin of Trajan as showing the features of a rightful prince and an example to follow,[2] or again in 1445, when he sent a Rhodian coin to his friend Bandino in Rhodes.[3] He was always glad to inspect or secure antique coins, as we find him doing in Florence and Fiesole in the Autumn of 1442,[4] and it is possible that drawings of coins figured in his *Collectanea*, as they did a couple of generations later in the sylloge of inscriptions of Giano Fantaguzzi.[5]

We know that among other humanist collectors was Poggio, who received at least one ancient gold coin from Andreolo Giustiniani,[6] and Giovanni Marcanova, whose collection is known to have been increased by the gift of two ancient silver pieces from the humanist churchman Matteo Bossi,[7] so that at his death in 1467 it numbered twenty-one gold and gilded pieces, one hundred and eighty silver ones, as well as others in bronze and lead.[8] Marcanova's assistant Felice Feliciano was also an enthusiastic collector,[9] and so was Giovanni Battista Egnazio.[10] All these collections were almost entirely of ancient Roman coins. But Sigismondo Tizio is also known to have collected Etruscan coins, while those of Greece aroused the interest of Ciriaco d'Ancona[11] and Ambrogio Traversari.[12] The somewhat satirical description of an imaginary coin collection

[1] *Ambrosii Traversarii . . . Latinae Epistolae*, 412, *Hodoeporicon B. Ambrosii Traversarii* in A. Dini-Traversari, *Ambrogio Traversari e i suoi tempi*, (Firenze, 1912) but with separate pagination, 65–66.

[2] C. Mitchell, 'Archaeology and Romance', *Italian Renaissance Studies—A tribute to the late Cecilia M. Ady edited by E. F. Jacob*, (London, 1960) 470–71.

[3] C. Mitchell, 'Ex libris Ciriaci Anconitani', *Italia Medioevale e Umanistica*, V (1962) 289.

[4] Degli Abati Olivieri, *op. cit.* 17–18.

[5] Biblioteca Classense, Ravenna, Ms. 468, f. 1ʳ.

[6] Müntz, *Precursori e propugnatori del Rinascimento*, 94–95.

[7] *Matthaei Bossi Veronensis . . . diversarum rerum epistolae*, (Bononiae, 1494) f. c6ᵛ. Bossi's letter to Marcanova accompanying the gift is assigned to 1466–67 in G. Soranzo, *L'Umanista canonico regolare lateranense Matteo Bosso di Verona (1427–1502)*, (Padova, 1965) 229.

[8] Sighinolfi, *La biblioteca di Giovanni Marcanova*, 198.

[9] Mitchell, *Felice Feliciano Antiquarius*, 199.

[10] G. Degli Agostini, 'Notizie istoriche spettanti alla vita e agli scritti di Batista Egnazio sacerdote viniziano', *Raccolta d'opuscoli scientifici e filologici*, XXXIII (Venezia, 1745) 115.

[11] *Supra*, n.3

[12] *Ibid.* 169.

in one of the letters[1] of Giovanni Filoteo Achillini was aimed at such enthusiasts as these.

It is scarcely surprising in view of the prevailing enthusiasm, that the discovery of a hoard of ancient coins aroused considerable interest. We have already seen the reactions of Pope Paul II in 1468 when he heard that one had been unearthed at Pienza.[2] It was therefore only natural that having learnt in 1494 that a peasant had unearthed some Roman coins near Reggio Emilia, Matteo Maria Boiardo should have hastened to inform his master, the Duke of Ferrara.[3] Nor is it surprising to find Caprioli recording in his history of Brescia the finding of an exceptionally large hoard of Roman imperial coins and of other minor hoards in the Brescia countryside about the very end of the fifteenth century.[4]

During the year 1455 the collecting mania had reached such proportions in Rome that it had created a veritable famine of such pieces. Carlo de' Medici complained of this to his brother Giovanni, and attributed the scarcity to the collecting activity of Cardinal Pietro Barbo, who had just tricked him out of some silver coins found in Pisanello's studio at the artist's death, which Carlo had just purchased from one of the assistants of the deceased.[5] Such a scarcity still prevailed in Rome half a century later. This we learn from a letter of Giorgio da Negroponte sent from Rome on 19 May 1507 to Isabella d'Este, the wife of Francesco Gonzaga, Marquis of Mantua, in which he emphasized the difficulty in securing ancient Roman coins owing to the great demand for them.[6]

The coins left in Pisanello's study at his death bring home to

[1] *Epistole di Gioanne Philotheo Achillino*, (S.L.N.A.) f. Bi.v Several coins, doubtless ancient, were also collected by Fra Franceschino da Cesena, cf. A. Domeniconi, 'Un inventario relativo a un custode della Biblioteca Malatestiana: Frate Franceschino da Cesena (1489)', *Studi Romagnoli*, XVI (1965) 179–81.

[2] *Supra*, 168.

[3] Matteo Maria Boiardo, *Opere volgari*, ed. P. V. Mengaldo, (Bari, 1962) 275.

[4] Capreolus, *op. cit.* f. A6r. The discovery of a pot full of silver denarii of the Republican period near Cesenatico in 1505 and of another pot full of silver coins at Verrucchio in 1507 are recorded in '*Caos' Cronache Cesenati del Sec. XV di Giuliano Fantaguzzi*, 226, 274. It is interesting to note about finds of ancient coins, that Girolamo Bologni pointed out that 'illud idem dicemus de numismatis quorum copia in Italia maxima est, et quotidie ab agriculis ... de Roma ipsa taceo ubi perenni vena scaturiunt', Biblioteca Marciana, Venice, Ms. Lat. XIV. 168 (4571) ff. 2v–3r.

[5] Weiss, *Un umanista Veneziano: Papa Paolo II*, 27–28. This scarcity is also emphasized in another letter of Carlo to Giovanni written from Rome on 13 March 1455, cf. Archivio di Stato, Firenze, M.A.P., fil. 9, 135.

[6] Archivio di Stato, Mantova, Archivio Gonzaga, serie E. XXV. 3, busta 857. For the collections of Isabella d'Este see A. Magnaguti, 'La più illustre collezionista del Rinascimento', *Rivista Italiana di Numismatica*, XXVI (1913) 388–94.

us the use of them by this great artist. In fact his image of Caesar, which he presented to Leonello d'Este, Marquis of Ferrara, and which is now lost,[1] doubtless had a coin as its iconographical source. On the other hand, the main inspiration of his medals came from the late medieval medallions of Constantine and Heraclius, and only to a lesser extent from the classical coinage.[2] Another painter who was also not without interest in such pieces was Jacopo Bellini, the father of Giovanni and Gentile as well as Mantegna's father in law, whose book of drawings now at the Louvre shows the recto and verso of a coin of the Emperor Domitian. [3] It would be too long to record here the various painters of the fifteenth and sixteenth century who sought the aid of ancient coins.[4] The same applies to sculptors, starting with Lorenzo Ghiberti, who not only copied but, if Vasari is to be believed, even counterfeited Greek and Roman coins.[5]

Another sculptor who sought their aid was Filarete, while he was engaged on the bronze doors of St. Peter's, Rome. Here in the panels with the martyrdoms of Saints Peter and Paul, the iconography of Nero derives from a coin, just as it does in the scene showing Saint Peter before this Emperor in the tabernacle of Sixtus IV now in the Grotte Vaticane.[6] The very borders of Filarete's bronze doors show several small medallions with heads in profile, some of which are clearly derived from Roman imperial coins.

Such an employment of coins as sources of decoration proved very popular, particularly in north Italy during the second half of the fifteenth and the first quarter of the sixteenth century. Enlarged versions of Roman coins were often carved on doorways or the fronts of churches or palaces during this period. The marble medallions on the front of the Cappella Colleoni at Bergamo and the Certosa of Pavia, those executed in 1502 on the doorway of Palazzo Thiene (now occupied by the Banca Popolare) at Vicenza, are typical examples of this fashion, to which belong too the three marble medallions of Quattrocento Lombard art

[1] M. Salmi, 'La "divi Julii effigies" del Pisanello', *Commentari*, VIII (1957) 91–95.

[2] Weiss, *Pisanello's Medallion of the Emperor John VIII Palaeologus*, 12.

[3] C. Ricci, *Jacopo Bellini e i suoi libri di disegni—I. Il Libro del Louvre*, (Firenze, 1908) pl. 50.

[4] One may just mention in this connexion the 'adlocutio' frescoed by Ghirlandaio on one side of the tomb of Francesco Sassetti in Santa Trinita at Florence, which is taken from the reverse of a coin of the Emperor Gordian, cf. A. Warburg, *La rinascita del paganesimo antico*, (Firenze, 1966) fig. 71 a–b.

[5] See Vasari, *op. cit.* II, 223.

[6] P. Giordani, 'Studii sulla scultura Romana del Quattrocento—I bassorilievi del tabernacolo di Sisto IV', *L'Arte*, X (1907) 271.

with Galba, Vespasian, and Alexander Severus, now at Milan[1] and originally on buildings.

The use of ancient coins as a decorative motive was also taken over by illuminators, especially at Florence during the second half of the fifteenth century. Roman imperial coins often appear on the borders of Florentine manuscripts de luxe, even when the text happened to be Philostratus[2] or a book of hours[3] and had therefore nothing to do with them. In many cases they were, however, connected with the text. That the obverse and reverse of a coin of Ptolemy III Euergetes[4] was illuminated on a copy of Ptolemy's Geography executed in 1490 now at Paris,[5] speaks for itself. And similarly obvious is the presence of 'reproductions' of Roman imperial coins on copies of the *Historia Augusta*,[6] Politian's Latin translation of Herodian,[7] or Suetonius,[8] their scope here being to show the effigies of personages mentioned in the text. On the other hand the medallists often copied and even oftener 'paraphrased' in their own reverses those of antique coins, which had particularly appealed to them.[9] Suffice it

---

[1] Museo del Castello Sforzesco, nn. 948–49, 1214. One may also recall here that the marble medallions of Roman Emperors by Agostino di Duccio in the Malatesta Temple at Rimini were based on Roman coins.

[2] See A. De Hevesy, *La Bibliothèque du Roi Matthias Corvin*, (Paris, 1923) pl. XXXI.

[3] See for instance the page of the Giraldi-Guicciardini Book of Hours reproduced on the frontispiece of catalogue no. 90 of Martin Breslauer, (London, 1958).

[4] *A Catalogue of the Greek coins in the British Museum. The Ptolemies Kings of Egypt*, (London, 1883) 55, no. 89, pl. XII. 1.

[5] T. De Marinis, *Un manoscritto di Tolomeo fatto per Andrea Matteo Acquaviva e Isabella Piccolomini*, (Verona, 1956) pl. III. It is interesting to note that the medallion on the child's neck in the *Virgin and Child* by Agostino di Duccio in the Victoria and Albert Museum reproduces the reverse of a Greek coin, cf. J. Pope-Hennessy, *The Virgin and Child by Agostino di Duccio*, (London, 1952) 10, pl. 2–3.

[6] Cf. for instance Biblioteca Vittorio Emanuele II, Rome, Ms 1004, on which see M. Salmi, 'Aspetti della cultura figurativa di Padova e di Firenze', *Arte Veneta*, VIII (1954) fig. 144, *Mostra Storica Nazionale della Miniatura . . . Catalogo*, (Firenze, 1953) 427–28, pl. LXXXIV, and Biblioteca Nazionale, Turin, Ms. E. III. 19, on which see Meroni, *op. cit.* 28, pl. 84–87. It is interesting to see Cardinal Francesco Gonzaga writing to his father from Rome on 15 October 1466 in order to borrow this Ms, so that an illuminator could copy the portraits of the emperors in it, cf. Luzio and Renier, *I Filelfo e l'umanesimo alla corte dei Gonzaga*, 137, n.

[7] See for instance the presentation copy to Pope Innocent VIII, now in the Biblioteca Vittorio Emanuele II, Rome, Ms. 1005, Pl. XV, for which see A. Perosa, *Mostra del Poliziano nella Biblioteca Medicea Laurenziana . . . Catalogo*, (Firenze, 1955) 89–90, pl. V, A. Campana, 'Osservazioni sui manoscritti della versione di Erodiano', *Il Poliziano e il suo tempo. Atti del IV Convegno Internazionale di studi sul Rinascimento*, (Firenze, 1957) 333. It seems fairly certain that Politian selected the coins illuminated on the title page.

[8] See the copy of the 1471 Venetian edition of Suetonius in the Biblioteca Trivulziana, Milan, inc. 13.87, on which cf. M. Bonicatti, 'Contributi marginali alla pittura veneta della Rinascita', *Rivista dell'Istituto Nazionale d'archeologia e storia dell'arte*, N.S. VII (1948) 254, figg. 8–9.

[9] See G. F. Hill, 'Classical Influence on the Italian Medal', *Burlington Magazine*, XVIII (1911) 259–69.

to remember in this connexion a couple of medals of Pope Paul II[1], Cristoforo Geremia's medallion of Constantine made in 1469,[2] and Bertoldo's medalet of Lorenzo de' Medici executed in 1478 immediately after the Pazzi conspiracy, the reverse of which was taken from that of a coin of Trajan.[3]

Petrarch's use of coins as pieces of historical evidence[4] was continued by fifteenth century humanists. Niccolò Niccoli is known to have relied on coins as well as inscriptions, in his now lost tract on Latin orthography.[5] As for the origins of Roman coinage, these were investigated by some humanists. Here the source was of course Pliny's *Natural History*,[6] which is clearly behind the short account of it in Poggio's *De avaritia*[7] (1427–28), as well as the longer one in Biondo's *Roma instaurata*,[8] and that included in the *De Orthographia* of Giovanni Tortelli under the entry 'Nummus'.[9] Also of some numismatic interest is the entry 'Talentum' in the same work,[10] where besides following Priscian in showing the relationship between the Greek and Roman talent and stating that a denarius was one third of a drachma, Tortelli tried to equate Greek and Roman coins and give the value of the latter, though not in terms of modern money. Tortelli is also known to have used Roman coins as evidence. Thus, for instance, we find him identifying a great bronze head near the Lateran as that of the Emperor Commodus because of its resemblance to the effigy on the coins of this ruler.[11] Other humanists too, such as for instance Antonio Costanzi,[12] Bernardo Rucellai,[13] and Andrea Fulvio,[14] are known to have relied on the evidence of coins. It was left to Politian, whose interest in ancient coins is also indicated by his notes on some seen while in Bologna in 1491,[15] to show in the *Miscellanea*

---

[1] Hill, *A Corpus of Italian Medals of the Renaissance before Cellini*, nn. 778, 785.
[2] *Ibid.* no. 755.   [3] *Ibid.* no. 916.
[4] *Supra*, 37-38.
[5] Zippel, *op. cit.* 47.
[6] *C. Plinii Naturalis Historiae*, XXXIII. xiii.
[7] The passage is given in Müntz, *Precursori e propugnatori del Rinascimento*, 90, n. 4. On the *De avaritia* see E. Walser, *Poggius Florentinus*, (Leipzig-Berlin, 1914) 126–34.
[8] *Supra*, 70. Another account of Roman monetation was given by Biondo in his *De Roma triumphante*, where he also emphasized the impossibility of assessing the true value of the Roman coinage, cf. Blondus, *Opera, De Roma triumphante*, 111.
[9] Tortellius, *op. cit.* f. i6ʳ.
[10] *Ibid.* f.s.4ʳ-ᵛ.   [11] *Supra*, 72.
[12] Weiss, *L'Arco di Augusto a Fano nel Rinascimento*, 353.
[13] *Supra*, 80.
[14] Fulvius, *Antiquitates Urbis*, passim.
[15] A. Campana, 'Contributi alla biblioteca del Poliziano', *Il Poliziano e il suo tempo. Atti del IV Congresso Internazionale di studi sul Rinascimento*, (Firenze, 1957) 215.

what a coin could reveal to a humanist of his calibre.[1] Nor should one omit to mention that Andrea Alciati's interpretation of a sum of sesterces in the inscription on the 'Monumentum Plinianum'[2] led to a correspondence with Benedetto Giovio, where the value of several Roman monetary units was also discussed.[3]

In view of the interest taken in Roman coins during the Renaissance, it is not surprising that treatises dealing with some aspects of classical numismatics were not long in making their appearance. This is a field in which a distinction is necessary between what were works on monetary theory, and therefore not on numismatics, and what really were studies of the ancient coinage. To the first class can be relegated such works as the *Tractatus de origine et jure necnon et de mutationibus monetarum* by Nicolas Oresme,[4] the *De potestate et utilitate monetarum* by Gabriel Biel,[5] or the *De Numismate Tractatus* by Alfonso of Portugal, Bishop of Evora (d. 1522).[6] To the other class belong various works, the authors of which were naturally humanists.

Sums of money were frequently mentioned in ancient writers, particularly historians. It was therefore but natural that humanists soon became anxious to have some idea what such sums meant in terms of modern money. Here was a subject fraught with difficulties, so that even as accomplished a humanist as Ermolao Barbaro had been unable to go into it very deeply, when dealing with the values of the sesterce and talent.[7] Similarly Politian's incursion into ancient metrology in one of his letters[8] was not a particularly happy one, and, inaccuracies apart, it suggests that he was not fully aware of the difficulties involved. The earliest known attempt to determine the relation between

[1] *Opera omnia Angeli Politiani*, (Venetiis, 1498) f. G6ᵛ. Also Politian's pupil Pietro Crinito discussed some aspects of numismatics, cf. P. Crinitus, *De honesta disciplina*, XVII. VII, XXI. IV.

[2] Ambrosian Library, Milan, Ms. D. 425 inf., pp. 18–19.

[3] *Lettere di Benedetto Giovio pubblicate dal sac. Santo Monti*, (Como, 1891) 139–41.

[4] N. Oresme, *Traktat über Geldabwertungen. (De Mutatione Monetarum Tractatus.)* Herausgegeben und eingeleitet von Edgar Schorer, (Jena, 1937).

[5] G. Biel, *Tractatus de potestate et utilitate monetarum*, (Oppenheim, 1516).

[6] See P. Batalha Reis, 'O primeiro tratado de Numismatica impresso en Portugal', *Numisma*, III (1953) 103–11.

[7] H. Barbarus, *Castigationes Plinianae Secundae*, (Romae, 1493) ff. f6ᵛ, g3ᵛ.

[8] *Opera omnia Angeli Politiani*, ff. Oiᶠ-O2ᶠ. The various kinds of Greek and Roman coins were also considered by Polidoro Vergilio, Raffaele Volaterrano, Celio Rodigino, and Alessandro d'Alessandro, see P. Vergilius, *De inventoribus rerum libri tres*, (Venetiis, 1499) ff. h2ᶠ–h3ᵛ, Volaterranus, *op. cit.* ff. MM3ᵛ–MM4ᵛ, L. Caelius Rhodiginus, *Lectionum Antiquarum libri*, (Venetiis, 1516) 254–55, *Alexandri de Alexandro Dies Geniales*, (Romae, 1522) ff. ii2ᵛ–ii4ᵛ.

coins and weights and their value in modern money was a Latin
tract by Giovanni Antonio Pandoni, the humanist better known
as Porcellio, who prepared it in 1459 for Cicco Simonetta, the
all powerful secretary of Francesco Sforza, Duke of Milan.[1]
Porcellio's tract shows him distinguishing, with the assistance of
classical texts, between the various kinds of talents and sesterces
and giving their approximate worth in ducats, without, however,
going too deeply into the matter. The small treatise, now lost, by
Andrea Santacroce, in which abbreviations and numerals on
Roman coins and inscriptions were considered, belongs to a
date after 1464, but of course dealt with a different aspect of
numismatics,[2] while it is not possible to say what were the
actual contents of another lost work, the *Commentariolus de
priscis nummis*, which Filippo Redditi was reporting as completed
in a letter to Bernardo Rucellai written not after 1492.[3] We must
therefore reach the year 1499 in order to find a work dealing
with the same aspects of ancient numismatics dealt with by
Porcellio, though far more extensively and thoroughly, when the
German curial official Jacobus Aurelius Questenberg completed
in Rome his *De sestertio, talento, nummis et id genus*, in which he
explained at much greater length than Porcellio and with the
help of classical sources, both Greek and Latin, the value of the
talent and the sesterce in terms of modern money.[4] Questenberg's little treatise was not meant for publication but for the
use of his patron Johann von Dalberg, Bishop of Worms, who
was then engaged on a work on ancient Roman coins in three
books, which has not reached us.[5] And to Dalberg, for whom he
also collected antique coins,[6] Questenberg also sent a tract in
Italian unknown but for his mention of it, on weights and their
relation to modern coinage.[7]

Much ampler than that of Questenberg is the treatise by
Leonardo da Porto of Vicenza edited by the Venetian humanist

[1] U. Frittelli, *Giannantonio de' Pandoni detto il 'Porcellio'*, (Firenze, 1900) 67. Porcellio's
work was printed, probably in Rome by Eucharius Silber, during the last quarter of the
fifteenth century: *Opusculum aureum de talento a Porcelio poeta ... elucubratum ...* (S.L.N.A.).

[2] *Supra*, 165.

[3] A. M. Bandini, *Collectio veterum aliquot monumentorum ad historiam praecipue litterariam
pertinentium*, (Arretii, 1752) 99.

[4] Questenberg's treatise is in the Vatican Library, Ms Vat. lat. 3906, ff. 1v–23v, Ms Vat.
lat. 5395, ff. 1r–16v; part of it is in Ms. Vat. lat. 3436, ff. 243r–52v.

[5] Mercati, *Opere minori*, IV, 443. On Dalberg's treatise see K. Morneweg, *Johann von
Dalberg, ein deutscher Humanist und Bischof*, (Heidelberg, 1887) 148, 155, n. 255, 280, 304.

[6] Mercati, *Opere minori*, IV, 440.

[7] *Ibid*. IV, 444, n. 22.

Giovanni Battista Egnazio and printed in Venice some years after 1516, and in all probability about 1520.[1] The *De sestertio* of Leonardo da Porto is an investigation into the Greek and Roman coinage, together with what he took to be the equivalent value of ancient coins in modern money and their relationship to weights. It also includes an attempt to establish the true value of stipends and expenditure in ancient times, as well as the system of measures then in use. As the same matters happened to be treated in Budé's *De asse et partibus eius*, published in Paris in 1515,[2] it might well be asked whether Leonardo had not perhaps plagiarized this work.

The precedence of Da Porto's work was vigorously upheld by Egnazio in his annotations on Suetonius printed in Venice in 1516,[3] where he asserted that the work of Da Porto had been written five years before, and later in his editorial preface to the *De sestertio*[4] without, however, convincing Erasmus.[5] What seems to have been the truth is this: that Leonardo's work was completed before that by Budé, while the latter's was the first to appear in print.

Whichever of the two was the first, it is undeniable that Budé's *De asse et partibus eius* was the greatest study of the kind produced by the Renaissance. In this work, which it is not exaggerated to call the philological masterpiece of the early Cinquecento, Budé succeeded better than any of his humanist predecessors in establishing the exact meanings of the monetary terminology of Greek and Roman antiquity, as well as the actual value not only of Roman, but also of Greek coins in relation to those of his own time. The first book of the *De asse* deals with the various parts of the 'aes' and their respective values, together with an investigation into the various meanings of 'sestertius'. The determination of the value of both Greek and Roman coins is carried out in Book Two, and here Budé broke new ground in his field of studies, by relying not only on literary sources, but also by actually weighing various antique coins. The gold coinage of Antiquity is particularly studied in Book Three, the

[1] *Leonardi de Portis iurisconsulti Vicentini de sextertio pecuniis ponderibus et mensuris antiquis libri duo*, (S.L.N.A.).

[2] For the actual date of Budé's treatise see L. Delaruelle, *Guillaume Budé*, (Paris, 1907) XXIII.

[3] *C. Suetonii Tranquilli XII Caesares* . . . (Venetiis, 1516) f. 17^r-^{v}.

[4] *Leonardi de Portis . . . de sextertio pecuniis . . .* , f. Aii^r.

[5] *C. Suetonii Tranquilli XII Caesares* . . . (Venetiis, 1521), ff. Ei^v-E2^r, *Opus Epistolarum Des. Erasmi Roterodami*, ed. P. S. Allen, VII, (Oxonii, 1928) 93.

ratio between gold and silver being also scrutinized and established here. Book Four consists mostly of digressions on various subjects connected with classical scholarship, while the fifth and last book deals with the ancient system of measures.

The tremendous scholarly powers of Budé appear at their highest in the *De Asse*. Besides displaying his immense learning in Greek and Latin literature, Budé showed here a most uncommon ingenuity in employing all the means at his disposal in order to prove his points, with an acumen and an imagination unseen in philological studies since the death of Politian in 1494. Of course he may occasionally have been wrong, as he was for instance in Book One, where he believed there was some correspondence between the Greek and Roman monetary systems. On the other hand, there are few aspects of classical philology which are not given some new light here—suffice it to say that more than one problem in the text of Pliny's *Natural History* is here supplied with a solution. After Budé's, no great contribution to the problems of ancient numismatics appeared for some time, the *De re nummaria antiquorum ad recentia tempora redacta compendiosa ratiocinatio* by Andrea Alciati being a brief essay showing the modern value of ancient coins.[1] Their equivalent value in Nuremberg money was instead shown in an equally short tract by the humanist Willibald Pirckheimer,[2] now chiefly remembered as Dürer's great friend.

Despite the interest taken in numismatics by the humanists, it was only in 1517 that a collection of reproductions of ancient coins appeared in print for the first time. This was the *Illustrium imagines* commonly attributed to Andrea Fulvio.[3] 'Reproductions' is perhaps not the exact word; for although the effigies on coins were exactly reproduced, the same cannot be said of their inscriptions. A problem connected with this work is: who was the real author of it? The probable answer is that although various humanists contributed to its compilation, Fulvio was doubtless responsible for the gathering and editing of the assembled materials.

[1] Printed in F. Argelati, *De monetis Italiae*, III, (Mediolani, 1750) Appendix, 23–8. Alciati also composed in Milan during the period 1522–27 a *Libellus de ponderibus et mensuris* printed at Hagenau in 1530, and in which coins were also discussed.

[2] *Bilibaldi Pirckheimeri Opera*, (Francoforti, 1610) 223–28. Some information on students of ancient numismatics in Germany during the early sixteenth century may be gathered from a letter of Johann Huttich written in July 1517, cf *Collectanea Antiquitatum in Urbe ac agro Moguntino repertarum*, f. Ai^v.

[3] *Illustrium imagines*, (Romae, 1517). A reproduction of this edition was published in Rome in 1967.

The real aim of the *Illustrium imagines* was to provide an iconographic repertory of the famous Romans. Here was a field in which this volume was the first of its kind. But not entirely so, for it had been preceded in some way by the *Priscorum heroum stemmata* by the Dominican Thomas Ochsenbrunner, published in Rome in 1494 and again in 1510, Fulvio being perhaps the 'Andreas Praenestinus' who contributed a Latin epigram in praise of it.[1] Perhaps it was the series of entirely fanciful portraits of some great Romans in Ochsenbrunner's work that suggested a work of the same type, but in accordance with the most up-to-date antiquarian science and with the iconography based on the coinage of ancient Rome.

In the *Illustrium imagines* each person has a medallion with his or her portrait taken whenever possible from a coin and a few biographical lines underneath, the series starting with the God Janus and ending with the medieval Emperor Conrad I. Needless to say most of the portraits in the republican and medieval sections are imaginary. Not so those of the imperial period, which were actually derived from contemporary coins. The *Illustrium imagines* naturally enjoyed a European success.[2] Reprinted at Lyons in 1524, they were imitated one year later in the *Imperatorum Romanorum Libellus una cum imaginibus ad vivam effigiem expressis*, by Johann Huttich, which was reprinted more than once. In a way the *Illustrium imagines* marks the end of the first stage of Renaissance numismatics, though it also marks the beginning of the long series of iconographic repertories based on coins. Altogether the new numismatics of the second half of the sixteenth century would scarcely have been possible without the earlier attempts. Here also the humanists were behind the new and more modern efforts.

[1] Weiss, *Andrea Fulvio Antiquario Romano*, 3, 16.
[2] *Ibid*. 40–41.

CHAPTER THIRTEEN

THE COLLECTIONS OF ANTIQUITIES

During the Renaissance the relics of classical antiquity were collected for a variety of reasons. Some people were attracted by their appearance; by some they were seen as the remains of a great age; some people liked to be surrounded by them in order to study them more thoroughly, or because they were needed as models and sources of aesthetic inspiration. And there was also the fact that the ownership of choice antique pieces, whether marbles, bronzes, pottery, or engraved gems, endowed one with a particular status and prestige and emphasized one's wealth, which was important in an age when ostentation was accepted and even praised as tangible evidence of magnificence and the power that went with it. Though not unknown during the fourteenth, it was only during the fifteenth century that the collecting of classical antiquities really began on a large scale. Here was a field where artists and humanists were probably the first and certainly among the first.

Artists were moved to gather pieces of ancient sculptures not in order to turn their 'botteghe' into museums, nor because they wanted to impress their patrons, friends and acquaintances. Their aim was actually more utilitarian. Admittedly they felt an aesthetic attraction for ancient statuary and carvings; but what was above all instrumental in making them secure all the pieces of ancient sculpture they could acquire, whether broken or intact, was a desire to have alongside with their pattern books[1] a selection of models which they could copy, adapt, or paraphrase whenever the necessity arose.

Already during the first quarter of the Quattrocento, the great sculptor Lorenzo Ghiberti had succeeded in assembling in his studio in Florence a very remarkable group of antique sculptures. These included a large marble vase allegedly brought from Greece,[2] a lifesize leg in bronze,[3] as well as many busts, vases,

---

[1] What is left of one such book put together by Pisanello, now at Milan in the Ambrosiana, includes several drawings from the antique, cf. A. Schmitt, *Disegni del Pisanello e di maestri del suo tempo,* (Venezia, 1966) passim. Cf. also M. Fossi Todorow, *I disegni del Pisanello e della sua cerchia,* (Firenze, 1966) passim.

[2] J. v. Schlosser, *Leben und Meinungen des florentinischen Bildners Lorenzo Ghiberti,* (Basel, 1941) 123, n. 50.

[3] *Ibid.* 123, n. 49.

and fragments of statues.[1] But the gem of his collection was the
so-called 'Letto di Policleto', this being a marble relief with a
male and a female figure on a bed, allegedly Venus and Vulcanus,
which was then believed to be the work of Polycletus and of
which several versions were known during the Renaissance.[2]

Just as fascinated by Antiquity as Ghiberti was Donatello,
who besides sedulously studying the ruins of Rome,[3] made a
thorough study of ancient sculpture. There is not much evidence
that he assembled a collection of his own, though it seems that
some pieces of ancient sculpture were actually to be seen in his
studio.[4] On the other hand, if the late witness of Vasari is to be
accepted, it was actually Donatello who aroused in Cosimo de'
Medici the Elder a desire to collect antiquities, and was responsible
for the restoration of some pieces in the Medici collection.[5]

Away from Florence the study of Antiquity was pursued by
Francesco Squarcione, an indifferent painter whose main title to
fame rests on his having been the teacher of Andrea Mantegna.
Squarcione's journey to Greece, to acquire ancient sculptures,
must now be dismissed as a groundless legend.[6] What is instead
certain is that although his museum never existed in reality,[7] he
nevertheless gathered some fragments of ancient statues and
carvings together with plaster casts of them, which he made or
caused his pupils to make for him.[8] Little wonder then, that
although Squarcione failed to show any of his antiquarian
interests in his own paintings, he was nonetheless able to transmit
them to the greatest of his pupils, Andrea Mantegna.

Of all Renaissance painters Mantegna was doubtless the one
who felt the impact of classical antiquity more than any other.
So strongly did he assimilate the spirit of the antique that his
paintings are really peopled by Roman statues, even when the
pictures have nothing to do with Antiquity. His portrait of
Cardinal Ludovico Trevisan at Berlin is really a Roman bust in

[1] *Ibid.* 123, n. 50.

[2] *Ibid.* 123–140. A handlist of antiques known to Ghiberti is in R. Krautheimer, *Lorenzo
Ghiberti*, (Princeton, 1956) 337–52.

[3] *Supra*, 62–63.

[4] Müntz, *Les collections des Médicis au XVe siècle*, 4. The sculptor Jacopo della Quercia
also appears to have owned some antique pieces. Such were in all probability 'una testa di
vecchio di metallo; due ignudi di metallo' belonging to him, cf. G. Milanesi, *Documenti
per la storia dell'arte senese*, II, (Siena, 1854) 189.

[5] A. Chastel, *Art et Humanisme à Florence au temps de Laurent le Magnifique*, (Paris, 1959) 31.

[6] G. Fiocco, 'Il museo imaginario di Francesco Squarcione', *Atti e memorie della
Accademia Patavina di scienze lettere ed arti*, LXXI, 3 (1958–59) 62–63.

[7] *Ibid.* 59–72.

[8] *Ibid.* 59–61.

the attire of a fifteenth century prelate, while the scenes painted
by him are very much more like ancient stone carvings than anything else. Mantegna's passion for classical antiquity is witnessed
by various sources,[1] and it is quite clear that ancient monuments
were seen by him as themes capable of any number of variations.
It is therefore scarcely surprising to learn that he sedulously
collected ancient pieces of sculpture. In his case, however,
there was not only the anxiety of the artist eager to gather useful
models, but also the enthusiasm of the humanist only happy
when surrounded by relics of classical antiquity. A marble head
of the Empress Faustina was the 'gem' of Mantegna's collection.
That he was very proud of such a possession is quite clear,[2] so
that the sale of it to Isabella d'Este shortly before his death in
1506,[3] was one of those very painful sacrifices which can only be
caused by economic necessity.

The artists so far mentioned were only a few of those who
collected antiquities. The influence of ancient art on so many of
them during the Renaissance makes it obvious that antique
pieces must have been constantly under their eyes. Of course
such pieces were even then by no means inexpensive. Still in
many cases fragments which would be despised by wealthy
collectors were appreciated and found useful. The fragments of
marble and terra cotta statues gathered by the painter Giovanni
Antonio Bazzi better known as 'Il Sodoma', were typical of such
'working collections'; but the bronze Apollo he owned was
certainly not.[4]

Even more enthusiastic as collectors of antiquities were the
humanists, which is scarcely surprising in view of their outlook.
Among them the greatest collector was undoubtedly Niccolò
Niccoli, whose anxiety to secure antiques was only matched by
the enthusiasm with which he gathered manuscripts for his
private library. Besides the ample means placed at his disposal
by Cosimo de' Medici,[5] Niccoli sought earnestly the assistance of
friends and acquaintances to provide him with choice antique

[1] *Supra.* 164. Also Mantegna's brother-in-law Gentile Bellini gathered some ancient
pieces. His will made in 1494 includes a torso of Venus and a bust of Plato, as well as some
drawings of Roman antiquities, cf. G. Gronau, *Die Künstlerfamilie Bellini*, (Bielefeld u.
Leipzig, 1909) 51.
[2] C. D'Arco, *Delle arti e degli artefici di Mantova. Notizie*, II, (Mantova, 1857) 61–62.
[3] *Ibid.* loc. cit. and 100. The bust of Faustina is still in the Ducal Palace at Mantua.
[4] G. F. Hill, 'Sodoma's Collection of Antiques', *Journal of Hellenic Studies*, XXVI (1906)
288–89.
[5] V. Da Bisticci, *Vite di uomini illustri del secolo XV*, ed. P. D'Ancona and E. Aeschlimann,
(Milano, 1951) 436.

pieces. Among these there was Ambrogio Traversari.[1] Others included Leonardo Bruni, who is known to have sent to him a jasper intaglio found at Ostia representing Narcissus,[2] and Andreolo Giustiniani.[3] As a collector he was certainly lucky, as is shown by his discovery of the famous intaglio, then believed to be by Polycletus, which he first saw hanging from the neck of a boy casually met in a street and which he purchased from the father for five florins and later ceded to Ludovico Trevisan, Patriarch of Aquileia, for two hundred ducats.[4] The collections of Niccoli included bronzes, cups, coins, cameos, and engraved gems, as well as statues. And such was his enthusiasm for Antiquity, that to him the objects so sedulously collected became an indispensable part of his own way of life. For besides having them constantly under his eyes, the precious vessels and cups on his dining table from which he ate and drank were genuine relics of the classical world.[5]

Among other humanists in Florence who collected antiquities in Niccoli's time, there was Carlo Marsuppini, whose ancient statues and coins were noticed with interest by Ciriaco d'Ancona.[6] But next to Niccoli the Florentine humanist who proved the most enthusiastic collector was Poggio Bracciolini, who appears to have been particularly interested in ancient statuary. It is quite clear from Poggio's correspondence that he tried everything in his power to secure antique marbles. We know, for instance, that he was very active in this direction during the years he spent at the Roman Curia, 1403–1418, 1423–1453,[7] one of the aims behind his collecting being to adorn the garden of his own country house in the Valdarno with statues[8] as the ancient Romans used to do.

In order to acquire statues, Poggio did not hesitate to beg them from other collectors, even when they happened to be complete strangers. We thus find him writing from Rome in 1431 or thereabouts to a resident of Rhodes called Suffretus, who was a collector of such objects, asking for the gift of some piece

[1] *Ambrosii Traversarii . . . Latinae Epistolae,* 412–22, etc.
[2] Müntz, *Les collections des Médicis au XVe siècle,* 6.
[3] *Infra,* 184.
[4] Da Bisticci, *op. cit.,* 438.
[5] *Ibid.* 442–43.
[6] Müntz, *Les collections des Médicis au XVe siècle,* 4.
[7] On Poggio at the Papal court see Walser, *op. cit.* 18–70, 83–281.
[8] Müntz, *Les collections des Médicis au XVe siècle,* 8.

from his collection,[1] an application which was not unsuccessful.[2] Upon learning about 1430 that the Franciscan Friar Francesco da Pistoia was to visit Greece, he commissioned him to secure what he could on his behalf.[3] One can therefore easily guess his delight when he was able to acquire during a visit to the Abbey of Montecassino in 1429 the marble bust of a woman unearthed during the digging of the foundations of a house.[4] Unfortunately Francesco da Pistoia did not prove as reliable as Poggio had hoped. It is true that he secured for him some marble heads of deities,[5] but neither these heads nor a complete statue for which Poggio had paid, ever reached him,[6] nor did some engraved gems which Andreolo Giustiniani had handed to Francesco for delivery to Poggio.[7] All the same Poggio achieved his desire to fill his garden with antiques, and the fact that he never succeeded in acquiring any really outstanding pieces is to be attributed mainly to his financial position, which made it impossible for him to disburse exceptionally high sums in order to enrich his collections.

Among those who helped Poggio in his quest of antiquities, Andreolo Giustiniani is certainly well worth remembering here. For this Genoese noble settled in Chios was an enthusiastic collector of statues, coins, and gems, and a very generous one at that. Besides Poggio, who also made use of him as an intermediary for the purchase of statues,[8] Niccolò Niccoli and Cosimo de' Medici the Elder were also among the beneficiaries of his generosity.[9] It is therefore not surprising in view of his reputation to find a fellow citizen of his, the humanist Giacomo Bracelli, writing to him from Genoa on July 2nd, 1440, asking him for a statue, by Pheidias or Praxiteles if possible.[10] Of another Genoese collector, Eliano Spinola, we know that he had imported several notable antiques from Greece and Asia Minor,[11] and also that he was in touch with that great collector Pope Paul

[1] *Poggii Epistolae*, I, 347–49.
[2] *Ibid.* II, 175.
[3] *Ibid.* I, 348.
[4] *Ibid.* I, 284.
[5] *Ibid.* I, 330.
[6] *Ibid.* II, 175.
[7] *Ibid.* loc. cit.
[8] *Ibid.* I, 323.
[9] *Ibid.* loc. cit.
[10] G. Mercati, 'Lettera inedita di Giovanni Argiropulo ad Andreolo Giustiniani', *Mélanges d'archéologie et d'histoire*, XXXIX (1921–22) 157.
[11] Müntz, *Les arts à la cour des Papes*, II, 132, n.

II.[1] Among the friends of Andreolo Giustiniani there was Ciriaco d'Ancona who, thanks to his long travels in Greece and Asia Minor, had also been able to assemble a remarkable collection of small antiquities. Apart from coins, Ciriaco seems to have specialized in engraved gems and small pieces of sculpture. Thus we hear of a head of Medusa owned by him.[2] And an outstanding item in his collection was an engraved gem with Scylla, which was so admired by his friends that in either 1442 or 1443 he gave lead casts of it to Theodor Gaza,[3] and in 1444 to Angelo Grassi, Bishop of Ariano, who has left us some lines in Latin verse about this gift.[4]

It would be hardly possible to mention all the humanists who gathered antique objects during the Renaissance. But among them one might perhaps mention Pandolfo Collenuccio, whose house at Pesaro was full of antiquities, including two exceptionally fine marble busts,[5] and one might also mention Fausto Andrelini on account of his painted Greek vase with mythological scenes which was broken by his lady love,[6] and Sigismondo Tizio, whose collection of pottery and other antiques mainly consisted of Etruscan objects, though it also included natural curiosities.[7] Nor perhaps should one omit Nicolò Tegrimi of Lucca (1447-1527), the humanist biographer of Castruccio Castracani, whom we know to have been the owner of a marble statue of a triton unearthed at Luni. Before belonging to him this statue had had a somewhat chequered history. For after being presented in 1510 by the Sarzana town council to the French governor of Genoa it was placed at a later date in the cathedral at Sarzana, from which it was stolen, only to reappear in Tegrimi's collection.[8]

A town where several collectors of classical antiquities were already to be found during the first half of the fifteenth century was Venice. During one of his journeys through Crete in 1415–18, Cristoforo Buondelmonti was particularly impressed by the ancient Greek statues in the garden of the country house of

[1] Ibid. loc. cit.
[2] Bertalot and Campana, op. cit. 368.
[3] Ibid. loc. cit.
[4] Ibid. loc. cit.
[5] Ziebarth, De antiquissimis inscriptionum syllogis, 231, n. 1.
[6] Saxl, op. cit. 39.
[7] Piccolomini, op. cit. 138.
[8] Supra, 114. Fragments of ancient statuary were also owned by Fra Franceschino da Cesena (d. 1489), cf. Domeniconi, op. cit. 185.

Nicolò Corner, a Venetian noble settled on the island.[1] Another
Venetian noble, Giovanni Dolfin, owned an impressive collection
which was much admired by Ciriaco d'Ancona, who inspected
it one night in November 1445 while at sea off Crete on Dolfin's
ship.[2] Of Dolfin's treasures one particularly aroused Ciriaco's
enthusiasm; it was a rock crystal carving with the head of
Athena, now in Berlin,[3] and then believed to represent Alexander
the Great.[4] Other Venetian collectors were Benedetto Dandolo,
who was well known to Niccoli and acquainted with Traversari,[5]
and Francesco Contarini, who died between 1460 and 1475; he
included inscriptions among the antiquities he gathered, and was
also a man of letters.[6] But the greatest Venetian collector of the
age was Pietro Barbo, the nephew of Pope Eugenius IV who
ruled the Church as Paul II from 1464 to 1471.

Even before Paul II some collecting of antiquities was not
altogether unknown in Rome. As a collector, all we know of
Stefano Porcari, the Roman noble hanged in 1453 for conspiring
against Pope Nicholas V, is that he owned at least one ancient
bronze statue[7] and that while in Bologna about 1433 he presented
a ring with an ancient cameo to Ambrogio Traversari, who gave
it to Pope Eugenius IV.[8] That Cardinal Prospero Colonna, the
patron of Biondo who died in 1463, felt the appeal of ancient
statues is confirmed by his ownership of a torso of Hercules[9] and
perhaps of the celebrated group of the three Graces now at
Siena.[10] On the other hand, Ludovico Trevisan's purchase
of the famous intaglio owned by Niccoli[11] does not mean that
this very wealthy prelate was a keen collector of antiquities,
for he definitely was not. It seems therefore not inaccurate to
say in the light of our present knowledge that it was only with
Cardinal Pietro Barbo that the collecting of antiquities on a large
scale did begin in Rome.

Pietro Barbo had already started collecting antiques in his

[1] Weiss, Un umanista antiquario, 114.
[2] Ashmole, Cyriac of Ancona, 39.
[3] Reproduced ibid. pl. XIVa.
[4] Ibid. 39. This was probably the 'chrystallinam Alexandri I imaginem' which Traversari
had been unable to see while in Venice in 1433, cf. Ambrosii Traversarii . . . Latinae Epistolae,
417.
[5] Ibid. loc. cit.
[6] Mercati, Ultimi contributi alla storia degli umanisti—Fascicolo II, 72*.
[7] Müntz, Les arts à la cour des Papes, II, 200.
[8] Lanciani, Storia degli scavi di Roma, I, 115.
[9] Ibid. I. 107.
[10] Ibid. loc. cit.
[11] Supra, 183.

youth[1] and subsequently he had done all he could to increase and improve his collections. As a result by 1457 he already owned forty-seven antique bronzes,[2] and two hundred and twenty-seven cameos,[3] as well as a very respectable number of ancient engraved gems and coins. He was also the owner of some late antique and early Christian ivories, among which was the famous 'dittico queriniano'[4] now at Brescia and still in the beautiful silver gilt frame he had made for it.[5] His cameos and intaglios, which included pieces with the portraits of Philip of Macedon and several Roman emperors, were as a rule set on silver gilt tablets with the cardinal's arms and some lines of Latin verse proclaiming his ownership.[6] But they were also mounted individually, as was the case with an amethyst 'Abundance', now at Paris, which he had set as a seal with his arms right under the stone.[7]

The collections of Pietro Barbo were sedulously studied by their owner. His fame as an antiquary was not inconsiderable.[8] A typical story about him as such is related by the humanist Giovanni Tortelli, who tells us that once while dining with the Cardinal the conversation had turned to whether 'ave' should be written with an initial *b*; whereupon the host had produced an engraved gem from his collection with 'have' engraved upon it.[9] Once Pope, Paul II continued to increase his collections. As a cardinal he had profited much from the assistance of his fellow citizen, Archbishop Maffeo Vallaresso, who in 1450–60 was busy supplying him with small antiquities, coins and engraved gems.[10] When he came to increase his collection he could occasionally be without many scruples.[11] Yet he was always firm in not accepting gifts, insisting instead on paying a fair price.[12] He was already Pope when, learning that the city of Toulouse owned an ancient

---

[1] Müntz, *Les arts à la cour des Papes*, II, 129.

[2] *Ibid.* II, 139.

[3] *Ibid.* II, 140.

[4] Which he probably acquired between 1451 and 1457, cf. Weiss, *Un umanista veneziano: Papa Paolo II*, 83. For the diptych see *ibid.* 83–87. One of the early ivories owned by Paul II appears in the inventory of Andrea Oddoni's collection made on June 23, 1555, cf. G. Gronau, 'Beiträge zum Anonymus Morellianus', *Italienische Forschungen*, IV (1911) 56.

[5] See G. Panazza, 'L'incorniciatura del dittico queriniano', *Miscellanea Queriniana in ricordo del II centenario della morte del cardinale Angelo Maria Querini*, (Brescia, 1961) 249–53.

[6] Müntz, *Les arts à la cour des Papes*, II, 223–226.

[7] Pl. XVI. 1., J. Pope-Hennessy, *Renaissance Bronzes from the Samuel H. Cress Collection*, (London, 1965) 77, no. 265, fig. 59. The stone is no longer in its fifteenth century setting.

[8] Weiss, *Un umanista veneziano—Papa Paolo II*, 24.

[9] *Ibid.* 29, n. 2.

[10] *Ibid.* 28.

[11] *Supra*, 171.

[12] Müntz, *Les arts à la cour des Papes*, II, 133.

cameo of outstanding beauty, he offered, beside a large sum and some privileges for their Basilica of St. Saturnin to build them a bridge, in exchange for it.[1]

After the death of Pope Paul II in 1471 his collections were quickly dispersed by his successor Sixtus IV. A considerable part of them was then acquired by Lorenzo de' Medici,[2] who was continuing with great keenness the collecting traditions of his father and grandfather. Whether or not it was Donatello who had first induced Cosimo de' Medici the Elder to collect antiquities,[3] it is certain that he very much felt their appeal. As a result ancient statues sent to him from Rome soon crowded the courtyard of his palace. Among these, if Vasari is to be believed,[4] there was the marble statue of Marsyas which was later restored by Verrocchio. Cameos, intaglios and gems were also sedulously gathered by him, among which there was a cameo with the head of Nero,[5] and the famous cornelian with Apollo and Marsyas which Ghiberti mounted in gold for him.[6]

Cosimo's tastes were inherited by his sons and especially his eldest son Piero, who was particularly interested in small antiquities, such as cameos, intaglios, and coins rather than in statuary.[7] Statues appear, on the other hand, to have particularly appealed to his brother Giovanni.[8] But the heyday of the Medici collections was under Piero's son, Lorenzo the Magnificent (1449–1492). As heir to the family collections Lorenzo strove to increase them by all possible means. His agents in Rome were busy sending to him what they could of the finds at Ostia and Grottaferrata, despite the difficulties placed against their export by Cardinal Giuliano della Rovere, the future Julius II.[9] The officials governing Florentine territories were also eager to please him by procuring antiquities for him. In fact those governing Sarzana were asked by him to buy pieces found at Luni, a task in which they were greatly assisted by the

---

[1] *Ibid.* 133, n. 4, Weiss, *Un umanista veneziano—Papa Paolo II*, 27, n. 2. This cameo can be identified with the 'Gemma Augustea', which remained at Toulouse until 1533 and is now at Vienna. On its history see *Filaretes Tractat über die Baukunst*, ed. W. von Oettingen, (Wien, 1890) 659 and F. Eichler und E. Kris, *Die Kameen im Kunsthistorischen Museum*, (Wien, 1927) 53.

[2] *Infra*, 189.

[3] *Supra*, 181.

[4] Müntz, *Les collections des Médicis au XVe siècle*, 5.

[5] *Ibid.* loc. cit.

[6] A. Morassi, *Il tesoro dei Medici*, (Milano, 1963) 9, n. 4, Schlosser, *op. cit.* 160–64.

[7] Müntz, *Les collections des Médicis au XVe siècle*, 16–17, 38–39.

[8] Gaye, *op. cit.* I, 164.

[9] *Ibid.* I, 285–86.

local humanist Antonio Ivani,[1] who also personally helped Lorenzo to increase his collections.[2] At the death of Cardinal Francesco Gonzaga in 1483 part of his treasures was bought by Lorenzo,[3] who thus enriched his already extraordinarily valuable collection of engraved gems.

Unlike Pope Paul II, Lorenzo de' Medici was only too willing to receive presents of antique objects. Thus he returned from his journey to Rome in 1471, where he had gone for the coronation of Pope Sixtus IV, with marble heads of Augustus and Agrippa which the Pope had presented to him,[4] as well as a choice selection of the treasures collected by Pope Paul II, which he had purchased,[5] these mainly being cameos, intaglios, and vases and cups in semi-precious stones. Nor was he uninterested in ancient pottery. We thus find him in 1490 acknowledging with pleasure the present of some 'vasi fictili', on which the donor had had engraved his own arms in order to be remembered.[6] During the following year he was the delighted recipient of a large Greek vase sent to him from Venice as a present by Zaccaria Barbaro, the father of the more famous Ermolao, the dispatching of it having been seen to by Politian, who then happened to be there.[7] We also hear how some other vases unearthed at Arezzo, doubtless Arretine ware, were given by the finder, Giorgio Vasari, the painter's grandfather, to Lorenzo during a visit to that town.[8] On his return to Florence from a visit to Naples, Baccio Valori, who later wrote the biography of Lorenzo, brought back as presents for him various antiquities, among which there were busts of Faustina and Scipio Africanus.[9] But doubtless few gifts can have given him greater pleasure than the bust of Plato, allegedly found in the very ruins of the Academy, presented to him by Girolamo Rossi of Pistoia.[10] At

[1] Sforza, *Gli studi archeologici sulla Lunigiana*, 85–86.
[2] *Ibid.* loc. cit.
[3] Müntz, *Les arts à la cour des Papes*, III, 45.
[4] *Ibid.* II, 156, n. 2.
[5] *Ibid.* loc. cit.
[6] Gaye, *op. cit.* I, 304–05.
[7] Müntz, *Les collections des Médicis au XVe siècle*, 57. Some Greek vases were introduced by Carpaccio in his painting of *St. Augustine in his study* in San Giorgio degli Schiavoni at Venice. The alleged influence of ancient vase painting on Antonio Pollaiuolo, cf. F. R. Shapley, 'A Student of Ancient Ceramics, Antonio Pollaiuolo', *Art Bulletin*, II (1919) 78–86, is not convincing.
[8] Morassi, op. cit. 244, Vasari, *op. cit.* II, 558. For some discoveries of Arretine pottery made in 1492 just outside Arezzo see Gorius, *op. cit.* II, 320, Fabroni, *op. cit.* 16–17.
[9] Müntz, *Les collections des Médicis au XVe siècle*, 57.
[10] *Ibid.* loc. cit.

the same time his gift of the well known bronze head of a horse to Diomede Carafa in 1471,[1] shows how he was also prepared to part with a choice masterpiece. The collections assembled by Lorenzo included all sort of treasures. There were bronze and marble statues, cups and vases in semi-precious stones, and count-less specimens of the glyptic art of the ancient world. According to the tastes of the time his vases and cups had been mounted for him in silver gilt,[2] Giusto da Firenze being one of the silver-smiths employed by him for such a task.[3] Moreover, though it may appear somewhat shocking to us, he had LAV. R. MED. engraved on these cups and vases[4] and even on his larger intaglios[5] so that there should be no mistake as to their owner-ship.

At the death of Lorenzo in 1492 his collection was the richest ever assembled in Renaissance Italy. His marble statuary was mostly placed in the gardens of his palace, where he was alleged to have struck a new note by opening them to young promising artists, so that they could study at first hand the masterpieces assembled there.[6] The end of Medici rule in 1494 was also the end of the Medici collections. Confiscated by the new govern-ment, the treasures of Lorenzo were quickly dispersed, the prices asked for them being so high that the goldsmith Caradosso, who had been sent by the Duke of Milan to purchase what he could, left Florence empty-handed.[7] Some of the statues ended in the Orti Oricellari.[8] On the other hand, Piero de' Medici was able to take away with him many of the cameos and intaglios, including those once belonging to Cardinal Francesco Gonzaga.[9] Other of the Medici treasures also remained in the hands of the family, while more were recovered when Florence came once more under Medici rule in 1512. Thus the palace of Cardinal Giovanni de' Medici (later Pope Leo X) in Rome, now Palazzo Madama, could display a considerable number of ancient statues, including one of a satyr which was singled out for special praise by Francesco Albertini.[10] But to return to Lorenzo, even if his

[1] Infra, 195.
[2] Morassi, op. cit. 12, pl. 3–18.
[3] Ibid. 12.
[4] Ibid. pl. 3–18.
[5] Pl. XVI. 2, Müntz, Precursori e propugnatori del Rinascimento, 144, n. 5.
[6] See, however, A. Chastel, 'Vasari et la légende Médicéenne: L'école du jardin de Saint Marc', Studi Vasariani, (Firenze, 1952) 159–67.
[7] Infra, 200.
[8] Müntz, Les collections des Médicis au XVe siècle, 107.
[9] Ibid. 105–06.   [10] Albertinus, op. cit. f. Z2v.

making the statuary in his gardens available to artists were true, this would have been only partly an innovation, for the idea of making ancient masterpieces available to the public had already occurred to Pope Sixtus IV. Thus the very pontiff who dispersed the collections gathered by his predecessor was also instrumental in the foundation of what might be called the first modern museum.

Sixtus IV had only been a few months on the papal throne, when he presented to the 'Conservatori', that is to say the municipal rulers of Rome, a collection of bronze statues. These statues, which were formerly at the Lateran, were placed in the palace of the Conservatori, a building erected on the Capitol in the time of Pope Nicholas V (1447–1455). They were that of the She-Wolf, which was placed at the entrance, the colossal head of the Emperor Constantius II, then believed to represent Commodus, and a hand holding a globe, from the same bronze colossus, both of which were placed under a porch, and the 'Spinarius' and the so-called 'Camillus', then believed to represent a gipsy, room for which was found in an upper chamber.[1] These statues were eventually joined by others. The bronze Hercules, found under Sixtus IV 'apud scholam Graecam sub Aventino', was placed in the courtyard,[2] Under Innocent VIII (1484–92) the head and some of the limbs of a marble colossus found near the so-called 'Templum Pacis',[3] were added to the collection, while in 1515 Leo X gave to the 'Museum' the three reliefs with episodes from the life of Marcus Aurelius, which had been up to then in the church of Santa Martina al Foro;[4] apart from these, several other pieces, a Pan tied to a tree trunk among them, could be seen there before 1527.[5] The purpose in gathering all these statues on the Capitol was not strictly artistic or archaeological. The aim was rather to assemble some tangible witnesses of Roman magnificence in the very seat of the city's municipal government, so that visitors could be impressed by such relics of what Rome had been, almost, one might say, by a museum of former Roman splendour.

[1] A. Michaelis, 'Storia della collezione capitolina di antichità fino all' inaugurazione del Museo (1738)', *Mittheilungen des Kaiserlich deutschen archaeologischen Instituts. Roemischer Abtheilung*, VI (1891) 12–15. On the gift of Sixtus IV see now W. S. Heckscher, *Sixtus IIII Aeneas Insignes Statuas Romano Populo Restituendas Censuit*, (S.-Gravenhage, s.a.). For the 'Commodus' head being really that of Constantius II cf. *ibid.* 46.

[2] Michaelis, *Storia della collezione capitolina di antichità*, 15–16.

[3] An inscription erected under Innocent VIII and still in the courtyard of the Palazzo dei Conservatori commemorates their being placed there.

[4] *Ibid.* 24–25.   [5] *Ibid.* 25.

Despite his rôle in the foundation of the Capitol 'Museum', Sixtus IV did not really have any antiquarian interests. The same cannot be said of some of his relatives. Cardinal Raffaele Riario, for instance, gathered several ancient statues in his Palazzo della Cancelleria, among which there was a Minerva.[1] And it may be worth recalling that this Cardinal was the purchaser of Michael Angelo's *Cupid*, which he bought in the belief that it was antique.[2] Just as fascinated by ancient sculpture was another relative of Sixtus IV, Cardinal Giuliano della Rovere who became Pope Julius II in 1503. As a cardinal, besides doing all he could to prevent the export of ancient masterpieces from Rome,[3] Giuliano della Rovere had striven to preserve them from ruin. It was he who was responsible for the rescue of the well known marble relief with an eagle, which he placed in the church of the Santi Apostoli not later than 1480,[4] where it can still be seen today. Moreover he was able to secure for himself and place in his gardens at San Pietro in Vincoli the *Apollo of Belvedere* shortly after its discovery.[5] It is not surprising then that as Pope he provided in the Vatican a building to house marble statues, just as the Capitol was used for those of bronze.

The first collection of sculptures in a place specially planned for that purpose, the statues court of the Vatican Belvedere, showed a new conception in the display of ancient masterpieces. Already nearing completion by March 1506, when the *Laocoon* was brought to it almost immediately after its discovery,[6] it was soon ready to be peopled by other important statues. By the end of 1509 the group of Hercules and Anteus, the *Venus Felix*, and the *Commodus* had been placed in it,[7] to be followed in 1511 by the installation of the famous *Apollo*.[8] The statue of the Tiber was placed there in 1512 immediately after its discovery,[9] the so-called *Cleopatra* also being probably installed then.[10]

[1] Lanciani, *Storia degli scavi di Roma*, I, 94.

[2] *Ibid.* loc. cit. Riario also encouraged artists to study the antiquities in his palace, cf. E. Wind, *Pagan Mysteries in the Renaissance*, (London, 1958) 147.

[3] Cf. for instance Gaye, *op. cit.* I, 285. Already in 1471 a brief of Sixtus IV commanded the governor of the castle at Ostia to forbid the export of statues and pillars, cf. Müntz, *Les arts à la cour des Papes*, III, 168.

[4] Weiss, *The Medals of Pope Sixtus IV*, 36, n.3.

[5] Michaelis, *Geschichte des Statuenhofes im vaticanischen Belvedere*, 10–11.

[6] J. S. Ackerman, *The Cortile del Belvedere*, (Città del Vaticano, 1954) 42.

[7] *Ibid.* 43.

[8] *Ibid.* 45.

[9] *Ibid.* 45, n. 3.

[10] *Ibid.* 46, n. 1.

Such an assembly of pagan characters in the abode of the head of the Christian Church could scarcely meet with universal approval. A puritan and devotee of Savonarola like Gianfrancesco Pico could only be shocked by it. But Pico was also a humanist. As might be expected he chose to air his views on the subject in a Latin poem completed in August 1512 and printed in Rome in 1513.[1] Needless to say, the poem did not make the slightest difference. On the contrary the collection was increased under Leo X, when the statue of the Nile and two of Antinous were added to it,[2] and under Clement VII, who had the famous Belvedere 'torso' placed there.[3]

By the time of Julius II collections of antiquities in Rome had become very numerous indeed, so numerous that it is no exaggeration to say that there was hardly a house or garden belonging to a wealthy person or a humanist which did not display statues, sarcophagi, reliefs, or at least some ancient inscriptions.[4] Needless to say, cardinals were in the forefront. Furthermore by May 1500 Cardinal Giuliano Cesarini struck a new note by throwing open his gardens full of antique statues to serious students.[5] Another cardinal, Francesco Piccolomini, who was Pope for a few weeks in 1503 as Pius III, was the owner of the famous group of the Three Graces now at Siena[6] and formerly almost certainly possessed by Cardinal Prospero Colonna.[7] Antique statues were also owned by other cardinals, such as Fazio Santoro, Livio Podocataro, and Andrea della Valle. But the greatest collector in the college of cardinals was the Venetian Domenico Grimani (1461–1523).[8] The interest in antiques of this prelate, who was equally enthusiastic about contemporary paintings,[9] and who is mainly remembered as the owner of the famous breviary now in the Marciana Library at Venice,[10] had probably been initiated by the consider-

---

[1] On it see E. H. Gombrich, 'Hypnerotomachiana', *Journal of the Warburg and Courtauld Institutes*, XIV (1951) 122–24.

[2] Ackerman, *op. cit.* 54, n. 1, Lanciani, *Storia degli scavi di Roma*, I, 155.

[3] *Ibid.* loc. cit.

[4] See *ibid.* I, passim. Some of the art monuments in Roman houses and churches were described in 1514 by Claude de Bellièvre of Lyons, cf. *C.I.L.* VI.1, XLV–VI.

[5] Lanciani, *Storia degli scavi di Roma*, I, 133, L. Schraderus, *Monumentorum Italiae . . . Libri Quatuor*, (Helmaestadii, 1592) f. 217ᵛ.

[6] Lanciani, *Storia degli scavi di Roma*, I, 114.

[7] *Supra*, 186.

[8] A biographic study of him is P. Paschini, *Domenico Grimani, Cardinale di S. Marco* (+1523), (Roma, 1943).

[9] *Der Anonimo Morelliano*, ed. T. Frimmel, (Wien, 1888) 100–104.

[10] On which see especially G. Coggiola, *Il Breviario Grimani*, (Leiden, 1910), T. Gasparrini Leporace, *Il Breviario Grimani*, (Milano, 1957).

able number of statues and other antiquities come to light during
the digging of the foundations of the palace he was having built
in his 'vigna'.[1] This garden, situated near to what is now Piazza
Barberini, stood on the site of some ancient baths,[2] which
of course explains the numerous finds made there. These were
already important enough in 1505 to be shown by him to the
Pope and the Venetian ambassadors.[3] But what was being
discovered in his gardens was not enough for Grimani, who also
purchased extensively. Whether it was he or his nephews who
acquired the colossal statues of Augustus and Agrippa from the
Pantheon is now uncertain;[4] on the other hand it is certain that
the famous bust of Vitellius was owned by him.[5] Grimani's
collections also included bronzes, ancient coins, cameos, and
intaglios. These he left to his nephew Marino,[6] his marbles
being instead bequeathed by him to the Republic of Venice.[7]
Some outstanding collections were also owned outside the
cardinal circles. Already during the fifteenth century the curial
official Agostino Maffei (d. 1496) had assembled a considerable
number of coins, sculptures, and other antiques.[8] But his
collections were far surpassed by those assembled in Rome by
some private persons during the early sixteenth century; which
is not surprising, as such collectors included the enormously
wealthy banker Agostino Chigi, whose magnificent gardens, the
'Suburbanum' were exalted in Latin verse by Blosio Palladio.[9]
But it would be hardly possible to give an account of all the
collections of antiquities in Rome during the period 1500–1527,
so numerous were they. The statues of Caesar, Brutus, and
Seneca in the palace of the Massimi,[10] the many statues dug up in
the garden of the curial official Ulisse Lanciarini da Fano and
placed by him in his magnificent mansion;[11] the busts, intaglios,

---

[1] Gallo, op. cit. 36.
[2] Ibid. 35–36.
[3] I Diarii di Marin Sanudo, VI, (Venezia, 1881) 172–73.
[4] Gallo, op. cit. 36.
[5] Ibid. loc. cit.
[6] I Diarii di Marin Sanudo, XXXIV, 401.
[7] A list of his bequest is printed in Levi, op. cit. II, 3–4. Grimani's bequest was commemorated by a Latin inscription by Pietro Bembo, cf. Paschini, Le collezioni archeologiche dei
prelati Grimani nel Cinquecento, 157. On the bequest see also B. Forlati Tamaro, L'origine
della raccolta Grimani, (Venezia, s.a.) 8.
[8] Maffei, op. cit. II, 142–43.
[9] Suburbanum Augustini Chisii per Blosium Palladium, (Romae, 1512). Another panegyrist of
this 'Villa' was Egidio Gallo, whose De viridario Augustini Chisii was printed in Rome in
1511.
[10] Lanciani, Storia degli scavi di Roma, I, 172.
[11] Ibid. I, 170.

and vases owned by Marcantonio Altieri,[1] are enough to give an idea of the enormous antiquarian wealth of these private collections; as for that of Angelo Colocci, it is now uncertain which of his antiques were kept in his house in Parione and which in his 'Villa' at the Acqua Vergine.[2] We know on the other hand that Colocci owned coins, cameos, and intaglios[3] as well as marbles. Among his statues there was one of Socrates embracing Alcibiades, one of Zeus Ammon, one of Proteus, one of Esculapius, etc.[4] But the most important pieces in his collection were the epigraphic monuments. Although among the three hundred or so inscriptions he owned[5] there were several forgeries,[6] there were also among them such supremely important pieces as the monument of Cossutius, commonly known as the 'piede Colotiano'[7] and the 'Fasti Consolari Colotiani'.[8]

Rome and Florence were the centres of Italian collecting. Other places in Italy were not, however, much behind them. At Naples King Alfonso V had owned statues, coins, and other antiques,[9] while the heir of King Ferrante I, Alfonso, Duke of Calabria, was the owner of an epigraphic calendar found 'in agro venusino'[10] and, if it ever reached him, of the famous intaglio with the effigy of Julius Caesar, formerly belonging to Cardinal Francesco Gonzaga, who had left it to him in his will.[11] Collecting in Naples was not, however, the monopoly of royalty. Although we can perhaps discount the statement of a seventeenth century writer, according to which Diomede Carafa, the trusted counsellor of Alfonso V and Ferrante I, had spent 17,000 scudi on his collections,[12] it is certain that his palace in Naples was filled with ancient statues,[13] among which there was the famous bronze head of a horse presented to him by Lorenzo de' Medici in 1471 and now in the Naples Museum.[14] Moreover, the houses of such

---

[1] *Ibid.* I, 101.

[2] V. Fanelli, 'Aspetti della Roma cinquecentesca—Le case e le raccolte archeologiche del Colocci', *Studi Romani*, X (1962) 394.

[3] *Ibid.* 399.

[4] Lanciani, *Storia degli scavi di Roma*, I, 203.

[5] Fanelli, *Aspetti della Roma cinquecentesca*, 399.

[6] *Ibid.* 400.

[7] *C.I.L.* VI. 3, 16534.

[8] On which see Fanelli, *Aspetti della Roma cinquecentesca*, 399, n. 36, *C.I.L.* I, 466.

[9] B. Facius, *De viris illustribus liber*, ed. L. Mehus, (Florentiae 1745) 78.

[10] *C.I.L.* I, 467–71.   [11] *Infra*, 197.

[12] B. Aldimari, *Historia genealogica della famiglia Carafa*, II, (Napoli 1691) 74.

[13] G. Ceci, 'Il palazzo dei Carafa di Maddaloni poi di Colubrano', *Napoli Nobilissima*, II (1893) 150–51.

[14] On which see A. De Rinaldis, 'Di un' antica testa di cavallo in bronzo attribuita a Donatello', *Bollettino d'arte del Ministero della Pubblica Istruzione*, V (1911) 241–60.

leading humanists as Pontano and Sannazzaro could also display several antique pieces besides inscriptions.[1]

In north Italy, Leonello d'Este, Marquis of Ferrara, had assembled a collection of engraved gems.[2] But after Leonello the only really enthusiastic collector of antiquities in the Este family was Isabella, the daughter of Duke Ercole I of Ferrara, who became the wife of Francesco Gonzaga, Marquis of Mantua. Isabella d'Este was not the first collector of antiquities in her husband's family. Ciriaco d'Ancona mentioned with admiration the collection of Roman coins assembled by Gian Lucido Gonzaga.[3] Nor is it surprising to find that Mantegna's and Alberti's patron, the Marquis Ludovico, was not indifferent to antiquities. Thus we find him in 1462 receiving with evident pleasure from the goldsmith Cristoforo Geremia, who was then in Rome, four antique heads together with the offer to send more antiquities if the Marquis liked such things, an offer which was promptly accepted.[4] Ludovico must also have been interested in cameos. For one year earlier Cristoforo Geremia had warned him through Bartolomeo Bonatti to be careful if anyone tried to sell some to him, as there was someone in Rome who was very able at counterfeiting them.[5] Which reminds us that one of Ludovico's sons, the Cardinal Francesco Gonzaga who died in 1483, was an enthusiastic collector of such things.

Like Pope Paul II, this Cardinal, whose features have been transmitted to us by one of Mantegna's frescoes in the 'Camera degli Sposi' at Mantua and a medal by Sperandio,[6] was a very enthusiastic collector of bronzes, vases, cameos, and intaglios. Perhaps it was this Pope's example that had set him on the path of collecting, just as it seems probable that it was from him that he derived the idea of having his gems and cameos set on silver tablets bearing his own arms.[7] That he liked to show and discuss his treasures there is no doubt. Thus in 1472 just before going from Rome to Bologna for a few days, he wrote to his father asking him to send Mantegna the painter to meet him in Bologna,

---

[1] See G. Pércopo, *Vita di Giovanni Pontano*, (Napoli, 1938) 301–02; Nicolini, *op. cit.* 41, 60.

[2] Decembrius, *op. cit.* 500–01, 504. Cameos and engraved gems appear in the 1494 inventory of the Este 'guardaroba', cf. Campori, *op. cit.* 25–27. On the other hand about 1517 Alfonso I, Duke of Ferrara, was trying to secure a piece of ancient sculpture not dissimilar from the 'Letto di Policleto' owned by Ghiberti, cf. Schlosser, *op. cit.* 124, n. 53.

[3] *Supra*, 168, n.4.

[4] U. Rossi, 'Cristoforo Geremia', *Archivio storico dell'arte*, I (1888) 409.

[5] *Ibid.* 411.

[6] Hill, *A Corpus of Italian Medals of the Renaissance before Cellini*, no. 390.

[7] Müntz, *Les collections des Médicis au XVe siècle*, 105–06.

as he was anxious to show and discuss with him his cameos, bronzes, and other objects from his own collection, which he was going to bring with him for the occasion.[1] That some cameos and engraved gems, which the goldsmith Giuliano di Scipione had ceded to Pope Paul II, were in the hands of the Cardinal on November 30th, 1471,[2] suggests that he had possibly appropriated them at the death of this Pope a few months earlier. And in view of his taste for the antique there can be no doubt that he received with pleasure the gift of a marble head of Portia, the wife of Brutus, from the humanist Giovanni Antonio Pandoni, commonly known as Porcellio.[3] At his death in 1483 the Cardinal bequeathed his bronzes to his elder brother, the Marquis Federico. His cameos and intaglios as well as his vases of crystal and other jewels were, on the other hand, to be sold in order to satisfy his creditors, the only exception here being his large cornelian with the head of Caesar, which he left to the Duke of Calabria.[4]

As we already saw,[5] the Cardinal's gems and cameos were eventually bought by Lorenzo de' Medici. In later years this must have been a matter of regret to Isabella d'Este, who would doubtless very much have liked such objects for her collections. Her husband Francesco Gonzaga was actually not indifferent to antiquities.[6] His interest in them was, however, practically non-existent compared with that of Isabella. For up to her death Isabella sedulously employed all the means at her disposal to secure as many antique pieces as she could. As a collector her interests ranged from marble statues to intaglios, from bronzes to coins and she never hesitated to ask the assistance of anyone she thought might prove useful to her. Already in 1492 she had received some pieces of Roman sculpture from the prothonotary Ludovico Agnelli, later Archbishop of Cosenza, and was asking him to let her have any antique intaglios which came his way.[7]

---

[1] E. Müntz, 'Essai sur l'histoire des collections italiennes d'antiquités', *Revue Archéologique*, XXXVII (1879) 91.

[2] Müntz, *Les arts à la cour des Papes*, II, 117–18.

[3] Vatican Library, Ms Vat. lat. 1670, f. 77ʳ⁻ᵛ.

[4] Müntz, *Les arts à la cour des Papes*, III, 298. This intaglio was still remembered in the early XVI century: 'El Cardinale de Mantoa ali nostri giorni ave uno Camoino antichissimo doue era scritta la immagine di Cesare belissimo Valea. 10. milia ducati', Biblioteca Classense, Ravenna, Ms. 468, f. 11ʳ.

[5] *Supra*, 189.

[6] A. Bertolotti, 'Artisti in relazione coi Gonzaga signori di Mantova', *Atti e memorie delle Deputazioni di storia patria per le Provincie Modenesi e Parmensi*, ser. 3, III, 1 (1885) 67–68.

[7] A. Luzio and R. Renier, 'Il lusso di Isabella d'Este', *Nuova Antologia*, ser. 4, LXIV (1896) 319.

Among those whom she asked to help her in securing ancient objects there was her brother, Cardinal Ippolito d'Este, Ariosto's unsatisfactory patron. To him Isabella was appealing in 1502 to send her some antiques from Rome as he had promised he would do,[1] and during the same year she was asking him to help her in getting from Caesar Borgia a small marble Venus and a Cupid once belonging to Guidobaldo, Duke of Urbino,[2] who had just been ousted from his duchy by the Borgia arms. One year later she was writing to her agent Lorenzo da Pavia to find her some antique statues. Intaglios to be used as seals were being asked for in 1505 from Girolamo Casio,[3] the poet who alternated the writing of indifferent verse with a flourishing trade in jewels, just as in 1506 we find her appealing to Pietro Bembo to help her with his authority to acquire an agate vase.[4] Needless to say, searches for definite objects were often made on her behalf. Already in 1492, for instance, Florimante Brugnoli was searching Rome for cameos and intaglios for Isabella[5] while during the years 1505-08 she was having the isles of Rhodes, Naxos, and Cos searched for antiques.[6] Nor, naturally enough, were offers of rare pieces to her quite uncommon occurrences. In 1503 she was being told from Rome that Piero de' Medici had pawned a very fine cameo ring for two hundred gold ducats and that she could have it at that price.[7] As we saw in 1506 the aged Mantegna just about to die was offering to her his cherished bust of the Empress Faustina,[8] which she eventually bought. Stazio Gadio was therefore sure to send welcome news when he wrote to her in 1511 in order to tell her about some antiquities then for sale in Rome.[9]

Throughout her life Isabella bought quite lavishly. Some bronzes, both heads and statuettes were bought by her in 1498 from the Venetian goldsmith Giovanni Andrea di Fiore.[10] Some

---

[1] *Ibid.* 321.

[2] Gaye, *op. cit.* II, 53-54. On it see also A. Luzio and R. Renier, *Mantova e Urbino*, (Torino-Roma, 1893) 170.

[3] Luzio-Renier, *Il lusso di Isabella d'Este*, 301.

[4] Cian, *Un decennio della vita di m. Pietro Bembo* (1521-1531), 108.

[5] Luzio-Renier, *Il lusso di Isabella d'Este*, 320.

[6] E. Müntz, 'Les collections d'antiquités formées par les Medici aux XVIe siècle', *Mémoires de l'Academie des Inscriptions et Belles-Lettres*, XXV. 2 (1895) 86, n.1.

[7] Luzio-Renier, *Il lusso di Isabella d'Este*, 321.

[8] *Supra*, 182.

[9] D'Arco, *op. cit.* 77-78.

[10] Luzio-Renier, *Il lusso di Isabella d'Este*, 321. When Fiore died in 1503 Isabella asked Lorenzo da Pavia to secure some busts owned by him for her collection, but he replied that they were not worth much, cf. *ibid.* 310-11.

stone statuettes, which later proved to be forgeries, were purchased by her in 1514 from Maestro Raffaello d'Urbino,[1] not to be confused with his famous namesake. And even in 1527 on her way back from Rome, where she had witnessed the horrors of the sack and lost many cherished possessions,[2] she yet found both the time and inclination to make some purchases.[3] Despite the ample means at her disposal, Isabella often refused to accept the price asked for an object which had particularly appealed to her. Cardinal Antoniotto Pallavicino was in fact bargaining on her behalf in Rome in 1504 for a statue of Cupid, which was eventually bought for her at the end of the following year by Ludovico Brugnoli.[4] Isabella bought right and left, but her collections were also increased by gifts. It was from Caesar Borgia that she received Michael Angelo's *Cupid* and an antique Venus as a present in 1502,[5] while a marble relief with the Rape of Proserpine was given to her by Hadrian VI in 1523[6]—the Pope whose attitude towards antiquities is summarized by his words on being shown the *Laocoon* and other statues in the Vatican Belvedere: 'sunt idola antiquorum'![7]

As a result of her ceaseless activity as a collector, Isabella d'Este assembled an imposing collection, which included statues, bronzes, and needless to say, small antiquities, ranging from engraved gems to coins. No wonder then that Giangiorgio Trissino wrote with rapture about her apartments filled with so many wonderful things.[8] Her taste as a collector was obviously catholic, her keenness to secure a painting or statue by a modern artist being by no means inferior to that with which she went after antique pieces. Her outlook was above all aesthetic and 'romantic'. For antiques appealed to her not only because they were ancient but also because, in many cases, of the splendour of the material of which they were made, their associations, and above all because they appealed to her eye. Her aim was not to create a museum, but to ennoble her apartments by filling them with beauty.

[1] Luzio-Renier, *Mantova e Urbino*, 284, Gaye, *op. cit.* II, 192–93, 195–96, 202–05, 207.
[2] *Ibid.* II, 178–79. A. Luzio, *Isabella d'Este e il sacco di Roma*, (Milano, 1908) 90.
[3] Magnaguti, *La più illustre collezionista del Rinascimento*, 392.
[4] Bertolotti, *op. cit.* 168–70.
[5] Luzio-Renier, *Mantova e Urbino*, 170–71.
[6] Gaye, *op. cit.* II, 155.
[7] E. A. Cicogna, 'Intorno la vita e le opere di Marcantonio Michiel', *Memorie dell' I. R. Istituto Veneto di scienze, lettere ed arti*, IX (1860) 381, n. 4.
[8] *I Ritratti del Trissino*, (Roma, 1524) f. Dii^r. The inventory of Isabella's 'Grotta' drawn up in 1542 is in Luzio, *Isabella d'Este e il sacco di Roma*, 162–73.

Of other Italian princes, the Sforza at Milan were not exceptionally interested in antiquities. True Galeazzo Maria Sforza was making enquiries in Rome in 1472 through the Bishop of Novara as to whether the Pope had 'Fiaschi, bochali e vasi de cristallo o de calcedonio o de simile materia' formerly belonging to his predecessor Paul II, and whether they would be expensive.[1] But what can be gathered from this is that he was looking for showy pieces with which to ennoble his tables and sideboards rather than antiques. As for Ludovico Maria Sforza, better known as Il Moro, he does not appear to have been indifferent to beautiful things. It may, on the other hand, be asked whether in his case collecting was not prompted by a desire to do what was expected from a person of his rank rather than by a genuine interest in antique objects. As soon as it was learnt in 1495 that the Medici treasures were up for sale in Florence, he hastened to send Caradosso there to acquire some of the Medici works of art.[2] The prices asked for them were, however, so high that in disgust he left for Rome, where he was able to secure some statues including a Leda for his employer, which he sent off by sea despite the prohibition to export antiquities.[3]

In the collecting of antiquities fifteenth century Venice had certainly been in the forefront. This applied also to Venice during the Cinquecento. Thanks to Marcantonio Michiel, the so-called 'Anonimo Morelliano', we know of many statues, vases, and other antiques in the houses of Francesco Zio,[4] Marco Antonio Foscarini,[5] of that Andrea Oddoni,[6] whose portrait by Lotto, who represented him surrounded by statuary, is now at Hampton Court, and others. And it should not be forgotten that in 1523–28 there arrived in Venice the statues and other marbles which Cardinal Domenico Grimani had bequeathed to the Republic in his will.[7] In neighbouring Padua the collection put together by the humanist Leonico Tomeo could boast when it was seen by Marcantonio Michiel a marble relief, ten marble busts, some bronze statuettes, pottery, coins and cameos.[8] But by far the most outstanding collection in the Venetian territory,

---

[1] Müntz, *Les arts à la cour des Papes*, III, 239, n. 1.
[2] Lanciani, *Storia degli scavi di Roma*, I, 127.
[3] *Ibid.* loc. cit.
[4] *Der Anonimo Morelliano*, 94–96.
[5] *Ibid.* 90–93.
[6] *Ibid.* 82–86.
[7] *Supra*, 194.
[8] *Der Anonimo Morelliano*, 16-18.

in fact the best private collection in Italy, was that which Pietro Bembo kept in his house in Padua.

Such was the passion of Pietro Bembo for anything connected with classical antiquity, that ancient sculpture and coins were topics which he delighted to discuss with visitors to his house in Padua.[1] His 'studio', which was kept there was famous throughout Italy. Here, according to a contemporary, all kinds of antiquities were to be seen, such as marble statues, bronzes, and of course countless coins.[2] Marcantonio Michiel noticed in it also some ancient glass and pottery, engraved gems set on rings, and several marble busts of Emperors as well as one of Brutus, a bronze head of Antoninus Pius, and a marble cupid asleep,[3] probably not dissimilar from that owned by Isabella d'Este.[4] But the gem of Bembo's collection was the famed 'Tabula Isiaca' (now at Turin), a magnificent imitation of Egyptian art made in the age of the Antonines,[5] which must have been acquired by him late in life as it was not in his 'Studio' when Michiel visited it.

Like his friend Isabella d'Este he thought any means were good for increasing his treasures. Besides purchase,[6] he therefore did not hesitate to beg for objects which had caught his fancy from friends and was displeased when they did not accede to his demands, as he was for instance with Giangiorgio Trissino, when he refused to let him have a coin with a head which looked like a woman he knew.[7] Encouraged in doing so by Raphael, we find him writing in 1515 to Cardinal Bibbiena, asking for the present of a small marble Venus, saying that he would have been very happy to place it in his study between Jupiter and Mercury.[8] A small bronze Diana belonging to Bibbiena had also caught his eye, and accordingly he did not hesitate to send a sonnet to the owner in which he begged for it as a gift.[9] In this case he had, however, to wait until the end of 1520, when the dying Bibbiena left it to him in his will.[10]

[1] Cian, *Un decennio della vita di m. Pietro Bembo* (1521–1531), 105.
[2] E. Zorzi, 'Un antiquario padovano del sec. XVI–Alessandro Maggi da Bassano', *Bollettino del Museo Civico di Padova*, LI (1962) 55.
[3] *Der Anonimo Morelliano*, 22–24.
[4] *Supra*, 199.
[5] E. Scamuzzi, *La 'Mensa Isiaca' del Regio Museo di Antichità a Torino*, (Roma, 1949).
[6] A. Ferrajoli, 'Il Ruolo della corte di Leone X', *Archivio della Società Romana di Storia Patria*, XXXVII (1914) 362–63.
[7] *Ibid.* 313.　　　　　　　　　　　[8] *Golzio, op. cit.* 44.
[9] Ferrajoli, *op. cit.* 312.
[10] *Ibid.* 313–14.

Pietro Bembo personified in a way the Renaissance collector at his best. Though physically separated from his collections during much of his life, he still saw to it all the time that they were safely looked after. A letter written by him in 1539 to his secretary Flaminio Tomarozzi,[1] in which he asked him to bring over to Rome some pieces which he particularly desired to see again and have near him, show how even in his old age his passion for the antique had not abated. In a way with Bembo ended that stage in the history of collecting which had had its beginnings in Florence and Venice during the early fifteenth century. And it was perhaps fitting that it should have ended with someone who had seen the Florence of Lorenzo de' Medici, been part of the Urbino of Castiglione's courtier, and lived long enough to see the Renaissance give way to the Counter-Reformation.

[1] *Lettere di M. Pietro Bembo cardinale*, III, (Milano, 1810) 333–35.

CHAPTER FOURTEEN

CONCLUSION

Archaeology was a creation of the Renaissance. Reverence for the antique has always, or nearly always, existed. But one would search the classical world or the Middle Ages in vain for a systematic study of Antiquity. Undeniably some antiquities were known and treasured during the medieval centuries. But, on the whole, they were generally appreciated for the wrong reasons. They were not cherished because of their associations or the information they could yield, but because of their pleasing appearance or the rarity of their materials, and only very seldom because of their link with a great man or a famous event. On the whole when they were valued, this was because they were precious or because they were useful, not because they were old. One is therefore left wondering whether the antique objects acquired by the Emperor Frederick II were collected by him only on account of their age.

Medieval men could hardly have been more indifferent to ancient ruins. To them such ruins were only useful stone quarries. Or, if they were exceptionally well preserved, they could be turned into churches, as happened to the Pantheon and the Parthenon, or into fortresses, as was the case with Hadrian's mausoleum. But they never struck anyone as worthy of preservation for their own sake, unless they happened to be outstanding monuments which had become part of the city's heritage, as was the case for instance with Trajan's column. An antique sarcophagus was seen as a potential tomb. As for statues, they were but pagan idols; and if they happened to be particularly pleasing they were seen as the images of particularly dangerous demons. The medieval legend about a statue of Venus,[1] which inspired Merimée's *Venus d'Ille* and D'Annunzio's *Pisanelle* is typical of the fascination and fear of medieval men when confronted with something which it was beyond their powers to create. The very fear which in 1357 made the Sienese authorities remove the statue of Venus which they had placed on the Fonte Gaia and which had aroused the admiration of the painter Ambrogio

[1] A. Graf, *Roma nella memoria e nelle leggende del medio evo*, II, (Torino, 1883) 388–402.

Lorenzetti,[1] was typical of the time. Not for nothing had Petrarch, for all his enlightened outlook, not hesitated to echo the Psalmist by writing in the margins of the Latin translation of the *Iliad* which he owned, 'omnes dei gentium demonia';[2] and when saying so he had the Middle Ages behind him! Similar views were being expressed some one hundred and sixty years later by Pope Hadrian VI when shown the court of statues in the Vatican Belvedere.[3] Yet during the interval of time between Petrarch and Hadrian VI the outlook had changed: the opinions of the Flemish puritan who succeeded Leo X may have been those of the schools of Louvain: they were not those of Italian humanism. For much had indeed occurred during those one hundred and sixty years.

During the thirteenth century the only ones who really understood the spirit of classical antiquity had been a few artists like Nicola Pisano and the sculptors who worked at Capua for Frederick II. But in general imitation of the antique had not gone beyond the letter. Even the early Paduan humanists saw classical antiquity through a Gothic mist. There were two main obstacles to be overcome before a clear picture could be secured: lack of criticism and lack of historical perspective. But there was to be no serious attempt at overcoming them—with the possible exception of Benzo d'Alessandria—before Petrarch. Petrarch when facing ancient monuments could, it is true, show unusual critical powers, but even he could also be extremely naive. All the same he was far ahead than his contemporary Cola di Rienzo, who could only view ancient Rome and its monuments with romantic eyes.

Modern archaeology really began when the *Mirabilia* ceased to be taken seriously. For their rejection was really the assertion of a new approach to history, a refusal to put up any longer with tales not backed by reliable evidence. More or less contemporary with this new attitude were the beginnings of a study of ancient remains on lines which were accurate as well as novel. Before Giovanni Dondi the scrutinizing of ancient ruins from a scholarly angle had been very exceptional. Even if some ancient Roman buildings had been very occasionally measured, this had simply been done from curiosity and without any ulterior motive. No

[1] *Supra*, 50.
[2] *Ibid*. loc. cit.
[3] *Supra*, 199.

one tried to see what they had originally looked like, and even during the first half of the Quattrocento Ciriaco's reconstruction of Hadrian's Mausoleum[1] shows more fancy than reality. Here was a field where Donatello and Brunelleschi on one side and Leon Battista Alberti on another proved to be pioneers. After Alberti this aspect of antiquarian study developed very quickly. It is present in the pages of Biondo and his followers, and also in the numerous sketches of Roman ruins, where these remains are not regarded as exceptional objects, but rather as pieces of evidence capable of revealing all kinds of valuable information to the intelligent seeker.

The new archaeology was founded during the first half of the Quattrocento, its greatest achievement being perhaps the mastery of the ancient building techniques. The second half of the century saw the consolidation of what the first half had achieved. The principles laid down by Alberti and Biondo were enthusiastically followed and a new methodology established. The critical approach introduced into philological studies by Lorenzo Valla had a counterpart in the methods used by Poggio and Biondo when considering what remained of Roman antiquity. With these two scholars a new sentiment can also be found. Petrarch may have bewailed the ruin of ancient Rome and dreamt of a return to the ancient glory, with himself as the new Virgil and the new Livy. Biondo and Poggio never entertained such illusions for one moment. Instead thanks to them a new need began to be felt, the imperious necessity of rescuing, or at any rate recording as much as possible of what was still left of ancient Rome before it should vanish for ever. In the work of rescue the worst enemies were not the ravages of time, but the contemporaries of Biondo. In fact, ironic as it may seem, the Renaissance brought more destruction on the Roman ruins than any other age: the new Rome of the Renaissance meant the annihilation of the old. Nor were the protests of humanists from Petrarch to Andrea Fulvio any more successful than the entreaties of preachers to love one's neighbour. But then it must be realized that even when the Renaissance was at its highest, its ideals were only intelligible to and cherished by a very small minority. The very fact that Sweynheim and Pannartz, the two Germans who brought printing to Italy in 1465 and to Rome two years later, went bankrupt in 1471 simply because there was no market for

[1] Ashmole, *Cyriac of Ancona*, pl. XII–XIII.

their editions of the Latin classics, the very fact that in 1487 Alessandro Farnese, the future Pope Paul III, had to move from Rome to Florence in order to find satisfactory tuition in Greek,[1] are indicative of the real situation. Even the Florence of Lorenzo de' Medici was hardly an exception; for the swiftness and depth of the reaction brought about by the preaching of Savonarola, suggest that even the foundations of the Medicean Renaissance cannot have been very solid.

During the fifteenth and the first quarter of the sixteenth century—what happened later is outside the terms of reference of our survey—wherever humanism flourished antiquarian studies flourished also. But despite the labours of Ciriaco d'Ancona, Renaissance archaeology was simply Roman archaeology. As for Etruscology and Egyptology, neither of them was approached really seriously, but they were mainly left to the charlatanry of Annio da Viterbo and the erudite phantasies of Pierio Valeriano. On the other hand, besides the actual antiquities of Rome, Roman remains in other parts of Italy were also studied and illustrated. After Biondo's *Italia illustrata* investigations into the early history and topography of a town and its countryside became a frequent pursuit among humanists. Sylloges of local Roman inscriptions began to be put together, playing the rôles of documentary corollaries to such dissertations. At the same time the new historiography as developed by Bruni and Biondo had broadened the range of materials essential to the historian. The testimony which could be extracted from ancient ruins, from statues and mosaics, but particularly from coins and inscriptions, was now fully appreciated, and any serious historian who dispensed with it, obviously did so at his personal risk.

The development of the study of classical epigraphy during the fifteenth century was also conditioned by the new requirements of historical writing. Without the help of epigraphy the history of Milan by Alciati or that of Ferrara by Pellegrino Prisciani—but two among the many examples—would have been quite different. The requirements of history were also at least partly responsible for the development of the study of ancient numismatics. For the evidence provided by coins was as valuable to the historian as it was to the philologist. If one was to interpret accurately the many passages in the ancient authors where sums of money were mentioned, a knowledge of the values of the

[1] *Carteggio umanistico di Alessandro Farnese*, ed. A. Frugoni, (Firenze, 1950) 32.

monetary denominations of classical antiquity was obviously essential. It was because of this that the metrological side of numismatics was approached before the actual classification and description of ancient coinages was ever attempted. Budé's *De Asse* was not only the philological masterpiece of his age, but also the culmination of the numismatic studies of the humanists.

The age stretching from 1300 to 1527 saw the beginnings and early development of archaeological science. Separated from and yet linked with philology (a word used here in its widest meaning and not as 'linguistics') archaeology became more and more an important part of the study of Antiquity, an aspect of it which no student could any longer overlook. Together with philology it was instrumental when still in its first stages in revealing a fairly accurate picture of Roman antiquity. Needless to say, today the handbooks of Biondo and Fulvio are no more essential reading to the archaeologist, than the historical works of Cluverius and Perizonius are to the beginner groping his way through Roman history. Yet much as scholarly standards have improved since 1527, these works are still important and their legacy remains as valuable as ever. The reason for this is that in countless instances, and this applies also to the works of Poggio, Leto, Albertini, and many others, they are the sole authority for a wealth of information about ancient remains which have now disappeared. Similarly the massive volumes of the *Corpus Inscriptionum Latinarum* would be certainly thinner without the many epigraphic texts transmitted to us solely by the sylloges of the humanists, just as the volumes of the Teubner collection of Greek and Roman writers would have been fewer without the discoveries and the rescue work which went on during the Renaissance.

The Renaissance antiquarians were the Descartes of archaeology. A new methodology was introduced by them into their field of study, which was really the new methodology pursued in the various provinces of humanist learning. They were the very methods which also led to the rise of modern science which, more than by its medieval heritage, was really brought about by the new understanding of classical science made possible by the humanists' knowledge of Greek and their rescue of many an essential text. Knowledge of Greek and the humanist ideals are ultimately responsible for the utilitarian squalors of our technological age.

ADDENDA

P. 1, n. 2: See also R. Chevallier, 'A propos du "Regisole" ', *Felix Ravenna*, ser. 3, fasc. 46 (1968) 21–25.

P. 15, n. 1: Late medieval representations of ancient monuments gave them a Gothic appearance. Thus in the (Giotto?) Assisi fresco showing the young St. Francis receiving the simpleton's homage in the main square of Assisi, the local temple of Minerva is made to look like a building in the style of Arnolfo di Cambio. It also has only five instead of six columns.

P. 16, n. 2: According to Guido da Pisa's commentary on the *Inferno of Dante* (completed c. 1330), the statue of Mars on the Ponte Vecchio was annually festooned with wreaths on the last day of March, cf. L. Jenaro-McLennan, 'The Dating of Guido da Pisa's Commentary on the *Inferno*', *Italian Studies*, XXIII (1968) 42.

P. 24, n. 7: What seems more probable is that Benzo copied, or had copied for him, some sections of the Ausonius manuscript which he found at Verona. This problem is being discussed by me in a paper I am preparing on the knowledge of Ausonius during the fourteenth century.

P. 37, n. 2: Petrarch actually composed two inscriptions for his grandson. On these and the original stones see A. Petrucci, *La scrittura di Francesco Petrarca*, (Città del Vaticano, 1967) 68–69, pl. XX. 1–2.

P. 82, n. 5: See also C. Dionisotti, *Gli umanisti e il volgare fra Quattro e Cinquecento*, (Firenze, 1968) 39–41, 47–52.

P. 96, n. 3: Molza's canzone is entitled 'in Morte Raph. Vrbin. pict. et archit. ad Le. X. P.M.', starts 'O beato et dal Cel diletto Padre', ends 'Haurebber nel primer stato rimessa', and occupies ff. 46ᵛ–49ʳ of the manuscript.

P. 103, n. 2: On the discovery of the 'Domus Aurea' and the graffiti written on its walls by Renaissance visitors, these including the painters Ghirlandaio and Pinturicchio, see especially N. Dacos, 'Graffiti de la Domus Aurea', *Bulletin de l'Institut Belge de Rome*, fasc. XXXVIII (1967) 145–74, pl. I–XXXVI, and N. Dacos, *La découverte de la Domus Aurea et la formation des grotesques à la Renaissance*, (London-Leiden, 1969), which the author's courtesy enabled me to see in proof.

P. 107, n. 2:   On early visitors of Hadrian's Villa, these including Raphael and Pietro Bembo, see N. Dacos, 'Visitatori di Villa Adriana', *Palatino*, IX (1965) 9–12.

P. 123, n. 7:   Some of the Roman remains of Florence of course found mention in early historians and humanists, cf. N. Rubinstein, 'Bartolomeo Scala's *Historia Florentinorum*', *Studi di bibliografia e di storia in onore di Tammaro de Marinis*, IV, (Verona, 1964) 54–59.

P. 146, n. 1:   A short account of epigraphic studies during the Renaissance is available in I. Calabi Limentani, *Epigrafia Latina*, (Milano-Varese, 1968) 42–51.

P. 150, n. 4:   A Latin epigram of Francesco Patrizi addressed to Fra Giocondo is printed in L. F. Smith, 'A Notice of the *Epigrammatica* of Francesco Patrizi, Bishop of Gaeta', *Studies in the Renaissance*, XV (1968) 120. It is interesting to know that Fra Giocondo's edition of Caesar, printed by Aldus in Venice in 1513, includes a map of Gaul, the plans of several towns, and pictures of the famous bridge on the Rhine.

P. 152, n. 4:   A second edition of Peutinger's sylloge of Augsburg inscriptions appeared in Mainz in 1520.

P. 153, n. 4:   An account of Benedetto Giovio is in L. Rovelli, *Gli storici locali comaschi*, (Como, 1955).

P. 156, n. 6:   No copies of the 1519 edition or of the edition of the Italian version, issued in Parma in 1523, are now known. A transcript of the 1523 edition made by V. Armanni is in Archivio di Stato, Gubbio, Ms. II.C.4. See also P. Cenci, 'La *Vita Beati Ubaldi* scritta da Giordano di Città di Castello', *Archivio storico per la storia ecclesiastica dell'Umbria*, IV (1917–19) 70–136.

P. 158, 2:   Also in that of Felice Feliciano, cf. Biblioteca Marciana, Venice, Ms. Lat. XI. 96 (3766), ff. 50^v, 53^r, 63^v.

P. 160, n. 5:   For the inscriptions composed by Pontano and set up in his 'tempietto' and Egidio da Viterbo see V. Cilento, 'Glosse di Egidio da Viterbo alla traduzione ficiniana delle Enneadi in un incunabulo del 1492', *Studi di bibliografia e di storia in onore di Tammaro de Marinis*, I (Verona, 1964) 282.

P. 161, n. 2:   A lapidary alphabet already occurs at f. 11^v of the ninth century Ms. 250 of the Bürgherbibliothek, Bern. The page is reproduced in *Karl der Grosse-Werk und Wirkung*, (Aachen, 1965) pl. 36.

P. 162, n. 5: See also on the subject E. Casamassima, *Trattati di scrittura del Cinquecento italiano*, (Milano, 1966). In his last will Aldus left instructions for a new capital alphabet to be made by Giulio Campagnola, cf. A. Firmin Didot, *Alde Manuce et l'Hellenisme à Venise*, (Paris, 1875) 490.

P. 163, n. 10: Also in Greek and Latin is the epitaph of the humanist Uberto Decembrio, printed in V. Forcella, *Iscrizioni delle chiese ed altri edifici di Milano*, III, (Milano, 1890) 231.

P. 167, n. 1: Another account is in R. Weiss, 'The Study of Ancient Numismatics during the Renaissance (1313–1517)', *Numismatic Chronicle*, ser. 7, VIII (1968) 177–87.

P. 169, n. 6: See also F. Colonna, *Hypnerotomachia Poliphili*, ed. G. Pozzi & L. A. Ciapponi, II, (Padova, 1964) 91–93.

P. 175, n. 8: Ancient coinage was also considered, though solely from literary sources, in the commentary on Suetonius by Filippo Beroaldo the Elder, cf. Suetonius, *Vitae*, (Mediolani, 1494) ff. a3[r], b7[r], d5[r], m4[v].

P. 195, n. 2: See also V. Fanelli, 'Le raccolte archeologiche dei Colocci', *Studi di bibliografia e di storia in onore di Tammaro de Marinis*, II, (Verona, 1964) 281–88.

P. 197, n. 3: Porcellio's poem is printed in A. Cinquini, *Il codice Vaticano-Urbinate* 1193....*Fasciolo secondo*, (Aosta, 1909) 46–47.

BIBLIOGRAPHY

The bibliography includes only those works published since the first edition of this book in 1969.

INTRODUCTION

Bober, P. P. and Rubinstein, R. O. *Renaissance Artists and Antique Sculpture: A Handbook of Sources*, London and Oxford, 1986, pp.23–4.

Nesselrath, A. 'The census of antique art and architecture known in the Renaissance' in L. Corti (ed.), *Census. Computerization in the History of Art*, I, Pisa and Los Angeles, 1984, pp. 86, 1–5.

Nesselrath, A. 'I libri di disegni di antichità. Tentativo di una tipologia', in S. Settis (ed.), *Memoria dell'antico nell'arte italiana*, 3 vols, Turin, 1986, vol. 3: *Dalla tradizione all'archeologia*, pp. 87–147.

Roma nel Rinascimento, bibliografia e note, [I, II], 1985, 1986, in progress.

Settis, S. (ed.) *Memoria dell'antico nell'arte italiana*. 3 vols, Turin, 1984–6.

Spring, P. W. H. 'The topographical and archaeological study of the antiquities of the city of Rome, 1420–1447', unpublished Ph.D. thesis, University of Edinburgh, 1973.

CHAPTER I

Agosti, G., Farinella, V., Gallo, D. and Tedeschi Grisanti, G. 'Visibilità e reimpiego: "A Roma anche i morti e le loro urne camminano"', in *Colloquio sul reimpiego dei sarcofagi romani nel medioevo* (Pisa, September 5–12, 1982), in B. Andreae and S. Settis, *Marburger Winckelmann – Programm*, Marburg, Lain, 1984, pp. 155–70.

Gramaccini, N. *Das Nachleben des antiken Monumentalplastik in der Öffentlichkeit des Mittelalters in Italien*, Habilitationsschrift, University of Trier, forthcoming (1988).

Master Gregorius. *The Marvels of Rome*, translated with an introduction and commentary by J. Osborne, Toronto, 1987.

Greenhalgh, M. 'Iconografia antica e sue trasformazioni durante il medioevo', in S. Settis (ed.) *Memoria dell'antico nell'arte italiana*, 3 vols, Turin, 1985, vol. 2: *I generi e i temi ritrovati*, pp. 155–97.

Schweikhart, G. 'Von Priapus zu Coridon. Benennungen des Dornausziegers in Mittelalter und Neuzeit', *Würzburger Jahrbücher für die Altertumswissenschaft*, NF. 3, 1977, pp. 243–52.

Seidel, M. 'Studien zur Antikenrezeption Nicola Pisanos', *Mitteilungen des Kunsthistorischen Institutes in Florenz*, XIX, 3, 1975, pp. 307–92.

Die Zeit der Staufer. Geschichte-Kunst-Kultur (exhibition catalogue), R. Haussherr et al. (eds), 4 vols, Stuttgart, 1977, vols 1 and 2.

CHAPTER II

Adami, C. 'Per la biografia di Giovanni Mansionario', *Italia medioevale e umanistica*, XXV, 1982, pp. 347–63.

Billanovich, M. P. 'Una miniera di epigrafi e di antichità. IL chiostro maggiore di S. Giustina a Padova', *Italia medioevale e umanistica*, XII, 1969, pp. 197–313.

Gargan, L. *Cultura e arte nel Veneto al tempo di Petrarca*, Padua, 1978, pp. 38, 42–4. [On Forzetto and the 'quattuor pueris'.]

CHAPTER III

Schmitt, A. 'Zur Wiederbelebung der Antike im Trecento: Petrarcas Rom-Idee in ihrer Wirkung auf die Paduaner Malerei. Die methodische Einbeziehung des römischen Münzbildnisses in die Ikonographie "Berühmter Männer"', *Mitteilungen des Kunsthistorischen Institutes in Florenz*, XVIII, 2, 1974, pp. 167–218.

CHAPTER IV

Blume, D. 'Vergessene Geschichte oder L'esperienza dei Trinci. Ein Kongress der Deputazione di Storia Patria per l'Umbria, Foligno, 10–13. Dezember 1986', *Kunstchronik*, 40, 1987, pp. 223–7.

Gilbert, N. W. 'A Letter of Giovanni Dondi dall'Orologio to Fra Guglielmo Centueri: A fourteenth-century episode in the quarrel of the ancients and the moderns', *Viator*, 8, 1977, pp. 299–346.

CHAPTER V

Bracciolini, Poggio, *Lettere*, H. Harth (ed.), 3 vols, Florence 1984, 1987, in progress.

Castelli, P. (ed.) *Poggio Bracciolini, un toscano del '400* (exhibition catalogue, Terranuova Bracciolini), Arezzo, 1980.

Gordan, Ph. W. G. *Two Renaissance Book Hunters. The Letters of Poggius Bracciolini to Nicolaus de Niccolis*, New York and London, 1974.

Martindale, A. *The Triumphs of Caesar by Andrea Mantegna in the Collection of H.M. the Queen at Hampton Court*, London, 1979.

Mazzocco, A. 'Some philological aspects of Biondo Flavio's *Roma Triumphans*', *Humanistica Lovaniensia. Journal of Neo-Latin Studies*, XXVIII, 1979, pp. 1–26.

Rinaldi, M. D. 'Fortuna e diffusione del "De Orthographia" di Giovanni Tortelli', *Italia medioevale e umanistica*, XVI, 1973, pp. 227–61.

CHAPTER VI

Amadio, A. A. *I mosaici di S. Costanza. Disegni, incisioni e documenti dal XV al XIX secolo* (*Xenia, quaderni* 7), Rome, 1986.

Bober, P. P. and Rubinstein, R. O. *Renaissance Artists and Antique Sculpture: A Handbook of Sources*, London and Oxford, 1986, pp. 215–16. [Raphael's observations on the Arch of Constantine.]

Buchner, E. 'L'orologio solare di Augusto', *Rendiconti della Pontificia Accademia Romana di Archeologia*, 53–4, 1980–2, pp. 331–45.

D'Amico, J. F. *Renaissance Humanism in Papal Rome. Humanists and Churchmen on the Eve of the Reformation*, Baltimore and London, 1983.

Fienga, D. 'The *Antiquarie prospettiche romane composte per Prospectivo Melanese Depictore'*, Ph.D. thesis, University of California, 1970, Ann Arbor, 1980.

Shearman, J. 'Raphael, Rome, and the Codex Escurialensis', *Master Drawings*, XV, 2, 1977, pp. 107–46.

CHAPTER VII

Bober, P. P. and Rubinstein, R. O. *Renaissance Artists and Antique Sculpture: A Handbook of Sources*, London and Oxford, 1986 nos 28, 70, 122, 125, 131, 143, 148–52. [Discoveries of Statues.]

Borsi, F. *Leon Battista Alberti*, Florence, 1975 chapter III: 'La Roma di Nicolò V'.

Brown, D. 'The *Apollo Belvedere* and the garden of Giuliano della Rovere at SS. Apostoli', *Journal of the Warburg and Courtauld Institutes*, XLIX, 1986, pp. 235–38.

Burns, H. 'A Drawing by L. B. Alberti' in J. Rykwert (ed.) 'Leon Battista Alberti', *Architectural Design*, XLIX, 5–6, 1979, pp. 45–56.

Fontana, V. and Morachiello, P. (eds), *Vitruvio e Raffaello. Il 'De Architectura' di Vitruvio nella traduzione inedita di Fabio Calvo Ravennate'*, Rome, 1975.

Müntz, E. *Les Arts à la cour des papes pendant le XVe et le XVIe siècle*, Paris, 1878–82, reprint, 3 vols in 1 vol., Hildesheim, Zürich, New York, 1983.

Nesselrath, A. 'Antico and Monte Cavallo', *The Burlington Magazine*, CXXIV, 1982, pp. 353–7.

Nesselrath, A. 'Raphael's archeological method' in *Raffaello a Roma*, Rome, 1986, pp. 357–71.

Pagliara, P. N. 'La Roma antica di Fabio Calvo: tipi e stereotipi', *Psicon: Rivista internazionale di architettura*, 8–9, 1976, pp. 65–87.

Vagnetti, L. and Orlandi, G. 'La "Descriptio Urbis Romae" di L. B. Alberti', in *Quaderno*, 1, Faculty of Architecture, University of Genova, 1968, pp. 25–88.

CHAPTER VIII

Pius II [Aeneas Sylvius Piccolomini] *Enea Silvio Piccolomini Papa Pio II, Commentarii . . .*, A. van Heck (ed.), 2 vols (*Studi e Testi*, 312–13), Vatican City, 1984.

Pius II *Enea Silvio Piccolomini Papa Pio II, I Commentarii*, L. Totaro (ed.) 2 vols, Milan, 1984.

Tizio, S. *Historia Senensis*, forthcoming edition by M. D. Garfagnini and G. Tomasi in the series *Rerum italicorum scriptores recentiores*.

CHAPTER IX

Annio da Viterbo, *Documenti e ricerche*, I, ed. G. Baffioni et al., Rome, 1981.

Bober, P. P. and Rubinstein, R. O. *Renaissance Artists and Antique Sculpture: A Handbook of Sources*, London and Oxford, 1986 no. 52A. [On Spreti: and the Ravenna Thrones.]

Chambers, D. and Martineau, J. (eds) *Splendours of the Gonzaga* (exhibition catalogue, Victoria and Albert Museum, London), London, 1981, no. 92. [On the monument to Virgil.]

Cipriani, G. *Il Mito etrusco nel Rinascimento fiorentino*, Florence, 1980.

Fortuna degli etruschi (exhibition catalogue, Spedale degli Innocenti, Florence), F. Borsi (ed.), Milan, 1985 pp. 37–43: 'Gli etruschi nei disegni degli architetti del Rinascimento'.

Franzoni, C. 'Il sarcofago di Biagio Pelicani e Macrobio a Parma', in *Colloquio sul reimpiego dei sarcofagi romani nel medioevo* (Pisa September 5–12, 1982), B. Andreae and S. Settis (eds) *Marburger Winckelmann – Programm*, 1983, Marburg, 1984 pp. 59–62.

Gallo, D. 'Itineraria archeologica italica, I: Fra Leandro Alberti, *Descrittione di tutta l'Italia . . . Nuovamente ristampata . . . revista et correta*, Venetia, 1596, I–II', *Annali della Scuola Normale Superiore di Pisa, classe di lettere e filosofia*, ser. 3, XI, 3, 1981, pp. 678–798.

Postel, G. *De Etruriae regionis originibus religione et moribus* [Florence 1557], G. Cipriani (ed.), Rome, 1986, introduction and commentary.

Schweikhart, G. *Le antichità di Verona di Giovanni Caroto con la riproduzione in facsimile della edizione del 1560 di Paolo Ravagnan*, Verona, 1977.

Trapp, J. B. 'The poet and the monumental impulse', *Society for Renaissance Studies, Occasional Papers*, 6, 1980.

CHAPTER X

Beschi, L. 'La Scoperta dell'arte greca', in S. Settis (ed.), *Memoria dell'antico nell'arte italiana*, 3 vols, Turin, 1986, vol. 3: *Dalla tradizione all'archeologia*, pp. 293–372.

Cyriacus de Ancona, [*Itinerarium*]. *Journeys in the Propontis and the Northern Aegean, 1444–1445*, E. W. Bodnar and C. Mitchell (eds) in *Memoirs of the American Philosophical Society*, 112, Philadelphia, 1976, pp. 138–42.

Dei, Benedetto. *La Cronica dall'anno 1400 all'anno 1500*, R. Barducci (ed.), Florence, 1984.

Lehmann, P. W. *Samothracian Reflections. Aspects of the Revival of the Antique*, Princeton University Press, Princeton, 1973.

Perry, M. 'Trophies of S. Marco: Legend, superstition, and archaeology in Renaissance Venice', *Journal of the Warburg and Courtauld Institutes*, XL, 1977, pp. 27–49.

Potts, A. D. 'Greek sculpture and Roman copies. I: Anton Raphael Mengs and the eighteenth century', *Journal of the Warburg and Courtauld Institutes*, XLIII, 1980, pp. 150–73.

Raby, J. 'Cyriacus of Ancona and the Ottoman Sultan Mehmed II', *Journal of the Warburg and Courtauld Institutes*, XLIII, 1980, pp. 242–6.

The Horses of San Marco (exhibition catalogue, The Royal Academy of Arts, London), London, 1979.

CHAPTER XI

Campana, A. 'Ciriaco d'Ancona e Lorenzo Valla sull'iscrizione greca del tempio dei Dioscuri a Napoli', *Archeologia Classica*, XXV-XXVI, 1973–4, pp. 84–102.

Chiarlo, C. R. '"Gli fragmenti dilla sancta antiquitate": studi antiquari e produzione delle immagini da Ciriaco d'Ancona a Francesco Colonna', in S. Settis (ed.), *Memoria dell'antico nell'arte italiana*, 3 vols, Turin, 1984, vol. 2: *L'uso dei classici*, pp. 269–97.

Degenhart, B. and Schmitt, A. (eds) *Jacopo Bellini, The Louvre Album of Drawings*, translated from the German by F. Mecklenburg, New York, 1984.

Giuliano, A. 'La Roma di Battista Brunelleschi', *Rendiconti dell'Accademia di archeologia lettere e belle arti di Napoli*, XLVI, 1971, pp. 43–50.

Kajonto, I. *Papal Epigraphy in Renaissance Rome*, Annales Academiae Scientiarum Fennicae, ser. B., vol. 222, Helsinki, 1982.

Kajonto, I. 'Poggio Bracciolini and classical epigraphy', *Arctos. Acta philologica Fennica*, 19, 1985.

Lightbown, R. *Mantegna, with a Complete Catalogue of the Paintings, Drawings and Prints*, Oxford, 1986.

Rhodes, D. E. 'Further notes on the publisher Giacomo Mazzocchi', *Papers of the British School at Rome*, XL, 1972, pp. 239–42.

Rubinstein, R. O. ' "Tempus edax rerum": a newly discovered painting by Hermannus Posthumus', *The Burlington Magazine*, CXXI, 1985, pp. 425–33, esp. p. 426, cat. no. 1.

Schmitt, A., forthcoming paper on inscriptions in Jacopo Bellini's drawings in the Acts, H. Wrede and R. Harprath (eds), of the colloquium on 'Antikenzeichnungen und Antikenstudium in Renaissance und Frühbarock', Veste Coburg, 1986.

Spanò Martinelli, S. 'Note intorno a Felice Feliciano', *Rinascimento*, XXV, 1985, pp. 221–38.

Wittkower, R. 'Hieroglyphics in the early Renaissance', in *Developments in the Early Renaissance*, Binghamton, New York, 1972; reprinted in R. Wittkower, *Allegory and the Migration of Symbols*, London, 1977, pp. 113–28.

CHAPTER XII

Seymour, C. 'Some reflections on Filarete's use of antique visual sources', *Arte Lombarda*, 38/39, 1973, pp. 36–7.

CHAPTER XIII

Beschi, L. 'Le antichità di Lorenzo il Magnifico: caratteri e vicende', in P. Barocchi and G. Ragionieri (eds), *Gli Uffizi, Quattro secoli di una galleria* (Florence, September 20–4, 1982), Florence, 1983, pp. 161–76.

Bober, P. P. and Rubinstein, R. O. *Renaissance Artists and Antique Sculpture: A Handbook of Sources*, London and Oxford, 1986, p.480. [Capitoline and Lateran collections.]

Brown, C. M. ' "Lo insaciabile desiderio nostro de cose antique": new documents on Isabella d'Este's collection of antiquities', in C. H. Clough (ed.) *Cultural Aspects of the Italian Renaissance. Essays in Honour of Paul Oskar Kristeller*, Manchester and New York, 1976, pp. 324–53.

Buddensieg, T. 'Die Statuenstiftung Sixtus' IV. im Jahre 1471', *Römisches Jahrbuch für Kunstgeschichte*, XX, 1983, pp. 33–73.

Chambers, D. and Martineau, J. (eds), *Splendours of the Gonzaga* (exhibition catalogue, Victoria and Albert Museum London) London, 1981, cat. nos 117 and 122. [Bust of Faustina; Proserpina Sarcophagus.]

Chambers, D. An inventory of Francesco Gonzaga's books, coins, gems etc. in a forthcoming volume of *Surveys and Texts*, Warburg Institute, University of London.

Cristofani, M. (ed.) *Siena: Le Origini. Testimonianze e miti archeologici* (exhibition catalogue, Siena), Florence, 1979, pp. 126–34.

Eiche, S. 'On the dispersal of Cardinal Bembo's Collections', *Mitteilungen des Kunsthistorischen Institutes in Florenz*, XXVII, 3, 1983, pp. 353–59.

Favaretto, I. 'Appunti sulla collezione rinascimentale di Niccolò Leonico Tomei', *Bollettino del Museo Civico di Padova*, 68, 1979, pp. 15–29.

Favaretto, I. '"Una tribuna ricca di marmi . . .": Appunti per una storia delle collezioni dei Grimani di Santa Maria Formosa', *Aquileia Nostra*, LXV, 1984, pp. 206–39.

Fletcher, J. M. 'Isabella d'Este, patron and collector', in D. Chambers and J. Martineau (eds), *Splendours of the Gonzaga* (exhibition catalogue, Victoria and Albert Museum London), London, 1981, pp. 51–63.

Fryde, E. B. *Humanism and Renaissance Historiography*, London, 1983 pp. 143–57. [On Lorenzo dei Medici's Patronage; financial background.]

Il tesoro di Lorenzo il Magnifico (catalogue Florence, 1972), 2 vols, vol. 1: *Le gemme*, N. Dacos, A. Giuliano, and U. Pannuti (eds), vol. 2: *I Vasi*, D. Heikamp and A. Grote (eds), Florence, 1973, 1974.

Perry, M. 'Cardinal Domenico Grimani's legacy of ancient art to Venice', *Journal of the Warburg and Courtauld Institutes*, XLI, 1978, pp. 215–44.

Perry, M. 'The statuario pubblico of the Venetian Republic', *Saggi e Memorie di storia dell'arte*, 8, Florence, 1972, pp. 75–150; plates 221–53.

Schmitt, A. 'Römische Antikensammlungen im Spiegel eines Musterbuchs der Renaissance', *Münchner Jahrbuch der bildenden Kunst*, ser. 3, XXI, 1970, pp. 99–128.

Schweikhart, G. 'Roma quanto fuit ipsa ruina docet. Kolloquium in der Bibliotheca Hertziana, Rom, 15–17 April 1986', *Kunstchronik*, 40, 1987, pp. 41–7.

INDEX OF MANUSCRIPTS

INDEX TO TEXT

Note: individual buildings, monuments and some statues are indexed under the places where they are found, e.g. the Parthenon is indexed under Athens.

Index by Justyn Balinski